VIETNAM DOCUMENTS: AMERICAN AND VIETNAMESE VIEWS OF THE WAR

VIETNAM DOCUMENTS: AMERICAN AND VIETNAMESE VIEWS OF THE WAR

EDITED BY

GEORGE KATSIAFICAS

M.E. Sharpe Inc. • Armonk, New York • London, England

Library of Congress Cataloging-in-Publication Data

Vietnam documents : American and Vietnamese views of the war / edited by George Katsiaficas.
p. cm.
Includes index.
ISBN 0-87332-896-5 — ISBN 0-87332-897-3 (pbk.)
1. Vietnamese Conflict, 1961–1975—Sources.
I. Katsiaficas, George, 1949– .
DS557.4.V55 1992
959.704′3—dc20
91-22957
CIP

Printed in the United States of America

The paper used in this publication meets the minimum requirements of American National Standard for Information Sciences— Permanence of Paper for Printed Library Materials, ANSI Z39.48–1984.

∞

MV(c) 10 9 8 7 6 5 4 3 2 1
MV(p) 10 9 8 7 6 5 4 3

Contents

Editor's General Introduction

As the title of this volume implies, the documents collected here illustrate the differing perceptions and beliefs that led the United States and Vietnam to fight a war that claimed more than two million lives. In selecting the contents of each chapter, I have provided a balance so the reader can experience directly these conflicting points of view. Contained here are the words of American presidents and Communist theoreticians, antiwar activists and Vietnamese allies of the United States. By juxtaposing these contradictory views, I hope to develop a "sociology of knowledge" perspective—to create a prism that clarifies our perception of the reality of the conflict. After all has been said and done, wars are themselves irrational, and a sociology of knowledge perspective is perhaps the only hope of explaining their origins and histories. This is particularly so for the Vietnam War, since it remains controversial nearly two decades after the peace treaty formally ending it was signed.

At the same time that a diversity of views is maintained, the topics of the chapters are ones that nearly all observers would agree are essential. The French defeat at Dien Bien Phu and the Geneva Conference of 1954 provide the context for the American entry into the Vietnamese quagmire. For us, that is an adequate starting point, although from the Vietnamese point of view, the origins of their quest for national independence can be traced back nearly two thousand years. Similarly, many issues between the United States and Vietnam have arisen since the end of the war in 1975. The fact that this volume does not address them says nothing about my judgment concerning their importance. Rather, I provide a selection of documents about the war itself, a topic of continuing interest and unresolved debate in the United States.

Some notes about the documents are necessary. To give the reader a feeling for the types of discourse in which the original authors or speakers were engaged, most documents have not been abridged. Moreover, somewhat in the manner of cinéma vérité, editorial commentary has been kept to a minimum, thereby allowing the documents to speak for themselves. Since I have no desire to inflate the events in question, I have consistently used conservative numbers in the chapter introductions. Finally, the reader will notice that in the documents several spellings are used for proper nouns like Vietnam (Viet Nam). The specific form of these words sometimes carries an ideological content, and the original spellings have been retained. By preserving these contradictions rather than seeking to resolve them, the reader is provided with a sense of the different styles characterizing the various authors.

For their help in the preparation of this manuscript, I wish to thank Joe Bangert, David Entin, Rosie Lynn, Jeff Potter, Ngo Vinh Long, Huu Ngoc, and Paul Joseph. Leon Cort has helped me better understand politics from the perspective of the Third World. Michael Weber, my editor at M.E. Sharpe, has been both sympathetic and critical, qualities whose combination greatly assisted me. My students at Tufts University and Wentworth Institute of Technology provided me with invaluable feedback used to structure the documents contained in this anthology.

My interest in Vietnam began over twenty years ago when I became active in the movement to end the war. I felt then, and continue to believe today, that Vietnam poses no threat to the United States except insofar as our own fear compels us to harm a people whose national pride is their most unifying value. During the 1960s, the American public's perception of Vietnam was polarized to the point of bitter confrontation. Only recently has dispassionate discourse about the war become possible. Simultaneously, there is considerable interest about the Vietnam War among scholars and students. This anthology has been designed to satisfy their needs.

George Katsiaficas

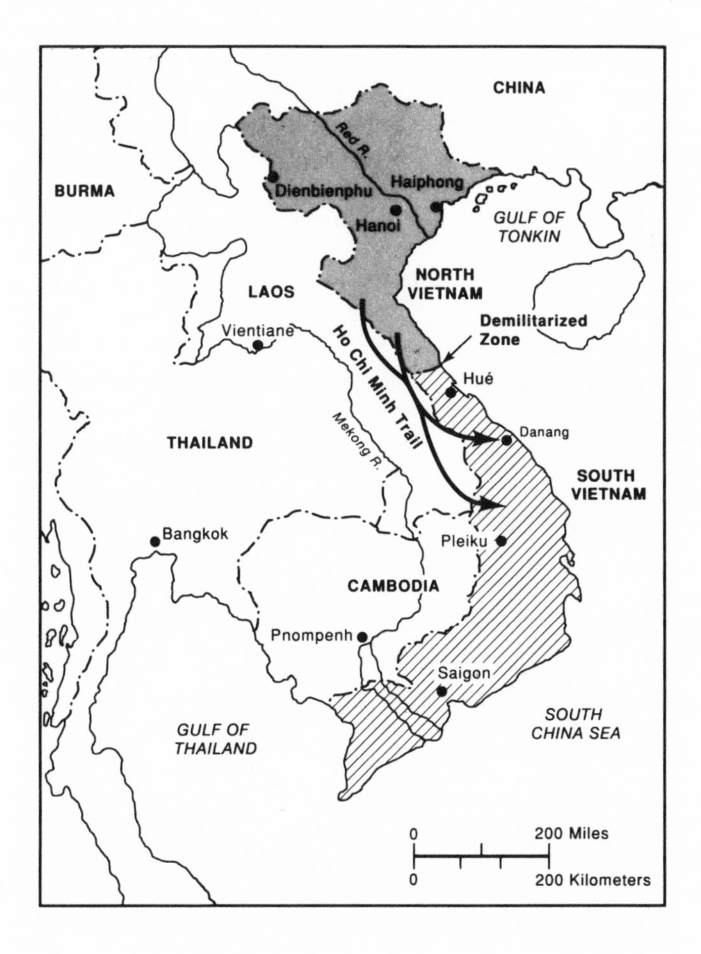
CHINA
Red R.
BURMA
Dienbienphu
Haiphong
Hanoi
GULF OF
TONKIN
NORTH
VIETNAM
LAOS
Demilitarized
Zone
Vientiane
Ho Chi Minh Trail
Hué
Mekong R.
THAILAND
Danang
SOUTH
VIETNAM
Bangkok
Pleiku
CAMBODIA
Pnompenh
Saigon
SOUTH
CHINA SEA
GULF OF
THAILAND
0
200 Miles
0
200 Kilometers

VIETNAM DOCUMENTS: AMERICAN AND VIETNAMESE VIEWS OF THE WAR

Chapter I

The First Indochina War—France

September 2, 1945, was a beautiful day in Hanoi, and a festive crowd of hundreds of thousands of people assembled outdoors to hear Ho Chi Minh declare Vietnam's independence. During this auspicious event an airplane flew overhead, causing some people to panic out of fear the plane might bomb them. When the plane flew lower and people could see that it was from the United States of America, the crowd cheered spontaneously. They believed its presence meant that the United States would help protect their country's new independence from French, Japanese, and Chinese threats.

In his speech that day (Document 1), Ho Chi Minh quoted from the American Declaration of Independence. Although he was a dedicated Communist, according to nearly everyone who knew him, Ho was a Vietnamese patriot first and a Communist second, and he knew the value of the American idea of national independence. He had lived briefly in the United States, studied our history, and when the time came for his own country to attain sovereign status, the American example was a powerful inspiration.

On August 30, a few days before his speech, Ho had met with the head of the U.S. Office of Strategic Services (the forerunner of the Central Intelligence Agency) in Vietnam. While they were having tea, Ho reported that he was preparing a speech that he would like the American "to have a look at." The typewritten document had many words crossed out and replaced in ink and numerous marginal notes in Vietnamese, and the text contained the following sentence: "This immortal statement was made in the declaration of independence of the United States of America in 1776." What happened next was described by Archimedes Patti, the American OSS chief: "I stopped and turned to Ho Chi Minh in amazement and asked if he really intended to use it in his own declaration. I do not know why it nettled me—perhaps a feeling of proprietary right or something equally inane. Nonetheless, I asked. Ho sat back in his chair, his palms together with fingertips touching his lips ever so lightly, as though meditating. Then with a gentle smile, he asked softly, 'should I not use it?' I felt sheepish and embarrassed. Of course, I answered, Why should he not?"

Recovering from his initial shock, Patti asked the translator to continue. He read, "All men are created equal. They are endowed by their creator with certain unalienable rights; among these are liberty, life and the pursuit of happiness." Although Patti was not certain, he thought he detected the transposition of the words liberty and life. When he pointed it out, Ho replied: "Why, of course, there is no liberty without life and no happiness without liberty." Ho entered the correction himself.

This was not the first time that U.S. officials had helped Ho and the Vietminh (Vietnam Nationalists), although it would be one of the last. During the Second World War, the Vietminh had fought on the side of the United States, rescuing downed American flyers and providing valuable intelligence on Japanese troop and naval deployments in Indochina, information that our French allies had been unable, or unwilling, to give us. On our side, an American doctor named Paul Hoagland was credited with saving Ho Chi Minh's life by giving him antimalaria medicine, and the United States provided the Vietminh with some arms.

Although the Vietminh were part of the Allied forces in Asia, less than a week after the Japanese formally surrendered to Gen. Douglas MacArthur aboard the battleship *Missouri*, British and Chinese troops arrived in Vietnam and began the process of reinstituting French colonial rule. The situation at the end of the World War II was complicated, particularly in Vietnam, where the Japanese were still in control even after they had surrendered. Furthermore, even though they had verbally admitted defeat on August 15, it was not until September 2 that Japan formally surrendered.

During this two-week interim period, a tremendous amount happened in Vietnam. On August 19, there was a general uprising led by the Vietminh. Throughout the country, people seized rice stores and called for a new government led by Ho Chi Minh. Insurrections in Hanoi, Saigon, and Hue, the country's three largest cities, created new Vietnamese administrations which ruled despite the presence of Japanese (and later British, French, and Chinese) troops.

The uprising that occurred was truly extraordinary. As one indication of its popularity, the Catholic Church, itself a product of French colonialism, endorsed the new government. Vietnam's Bishop Tang publicly asked the Pope to bless Vietnam's national independence and called on the country's two million Catholics to support the Vietminh government. On August 23, when the new government was finally announced, there were tremendous celebrations, and on August 30, Emperor Bao Dai abdicated, asserting that the new government was the only rightful one.

Not coincidentally, the day that Japan signed its surrender was also Vietnam's day of independence, but on that very day, renewed attacks by the

French were mounted against Vietnamese in Saigon. Many people were hurt, some were killed, and in the ensuing days and weeks, Vietnamese groups retaliated, thereby setting off an escalating spiral of attacks and counterattacks which would not end until nine years and over one million deaths later.

Faced with a deteriorating situation and with few available options only three weeks after declaring his country's independence, Ho Chi Minh sent a message to President Harry Truman asking for U.S. help. Although it may come as a surprise that Ho Chi Minh asked the United States to intervene, even earlier he had proposed making Vietnam an American protectorate, like Puerto Rico, in order to protect his country from foreigners.

It cannot be denied that French rule in Vietnam was highly unpopular. During their more than half a century of running Vietnam, the French had built 5,650 schools, but more than 20,850 jails. As one indication of the harshness of colonial rule, in 1944 a million and a half to two million peasants died of starvation in northern Vietnam (out of a population of fourteen million) at the same time as the French were exporting rice.

The French could not stage a comeback in Vietnam by themselves but needed help to drive the nationalist forces out of Saigon. Unbelievable as it may seem, it was the British Royal Air Force and the Japanese Air Force that together bombed and strafed Vietnamese positions on October 16, 1945. The next day, Gen. Douglas MacArthur commented, "If there is anything that makes my blood boil, it is to see our allies in Indochina deploy Japanese troops to reconquer those little people we promised to liberate."

That there was a betrayal of the Vietminh by their allies would be an understatement. During the war, Ho Chi Minh had been persuaded that the Allies would stand by their guarantee to all nations of the right to self-determination. Although Franklin Roosevelt had made Charles de Gaulle promise that no French colonies, especially those in Indochina, would be retained after the war, once Roosevelt died, de Gaulle was free to change his policy. By his own admission, Harry Truman knew next to nothing about Asia, but it was up to him to make a crucial decision about the future of Vietnam. At this time, U.S. foreign policy was concerned above all with strengthening the Western European nations against the perceived Communist threat from the Soviet Union. France did not want to allow Vietnam to become independent, and the United States did not want to pressure France. So Truman chose to give his ear to the Europeanists in the State Department, nearly all of whom maintained that the line against Communism must be drawn in Asia as well. Since Ho Chi Minh was a Communist, Truman simply refused to deal with him, and the United States assured France that Britain, China, and the rest of the Allies would have no part in stopping whatever France had to do to reinstate its control of Indochina. (Indeed, as time passed, the United States would go on to finance 80 percent of the French recolonization effort.) The British did not protest since they had their own hands full trying to maintain their colony in India, and the Chinese, for their part, before they withdrew received French assurances that all French concessions in China would be transferred to the Chinese government.

As the great powers sacrificed Vietnam's national independence on the altar of global geopolitical deal making, the Vietminh regrouped. Only after years of bloodshed, on May 7, 1954, did they finally defeat the French at the epic battle of Dien Bien Phu. As described by Bernard Fall in Document 2, Dien Bien Phu marked the end of French military influence in Asia. The Vietnamese version of what is today remembered as one of the great moments in their history is presented by General Hoang Van Thai (Document 3). The French completely underestimated the Vietnamese, mistakenly assuming, for example, that it would be impossible for them to bring artillery to such a rugged and isolated place as Dien Bien Phu. The Vietminh analyzed the campaign in meticulous detail. Thai's description of the battle, particularly his understanding of the French, is one facet of the superior effort mounted by the Vietminh.

1
Declaration of Independence of the Democratic Republic of Viet-Nam (September 2, 1945)

Ho Chi Minh

Source: Ho Chi Minh, *Selected Works* (Hanoi: Foreign Languages Publishing House, 1977).

"All men are created equal. They are endowed by their Creator with certain unalienable Rights; among these are Life, Liberty, and the pursuit of Happiness."

This immortal statement was made in the Declaration of Independence of the United States of America in 1776. In a broader sense, this means: All the peoples on the earth are equal from birth, all the peoples have a right to live, to be happy and free.

The Declaration of the French Revolution made in 1791 on the Rights of Man and the Citizen also states: "All men are born free and with equal rights, and must always remain free and have equal rights."

Those are undeniable truths.

Nevertheless, for more than eighty years, the French imperialists, abusing the standard of Liberty, Equality, and Fraternity, have violated our Fatherland and oppressed our fellow citizens. They have acted contrary to the ideals of humanity and justice.

In the field of politics, they have deprived our people of every democratic liberty.

They have enforced inhuman laws; they have set up three distinct political regimes in the North, the Center, and the South of Viet-Nam in order to wreck our national unity and prevent our people from being united.

They have built more prisons than schools. They have mercilessly slain our patriots; they have drowned our uprisings in rivers of blood.

They have fettered public opinion; they have practiced obscurantism against our people.

To weaken our race they have forced us to use opium and alcohol.

In the field of economics, they have fleeced us to the backbone, impoverished our people and devastated our land.

They have robbed us of our rice fields, our mines, our forests, and our raw materials. They have monopolized the issuing of bank notes and the export trade.

They have invented numerous unjustifiable taxes and reduced our people, especially our peasantry, to a state of extreme poverty.

They have hampered the prospering of our national bourgeoisie; they have mercilessly exploited our workers.

In the autumn of 1940, when the Japanese fascists violated Indochina's territory to establish new bases in their fight against the Allies, the French imperialists went down on their bended knees and handed over our country to them.

Thus, from that date, our people were subjected to the double yoke of the French and the Japanese. Their sufferings and miseries increased. The result was that, from the end of last year to the beginning of this year, from Quang Tri Province to the North of Viet-Nam, more than two million of our fellow citizens died from starvation. On March 9 [1945], the French troops were disarmed by the Japanese. The French colonialists either fled or surrendered, showing that not only were they incapable of "protecting" us, but that, in the span of five years, they had twice sold our country to the Japanese.

On several occasions before March 9, the Viet Minh League urged the French to ally themselves with it against the Japanese. Instead of agreeing to this proposal, the French colonialists so intensified their terrorist activities against the Viet Minh members that before fleeing they massacred a great number of our political prisoners detained at Yen Bay and Cao Bang.

Notwithstanding all this, our fellow citizens have always manifested toward the French a tolerant and humane attitude. Even after the Japanese *Putsch* of March, 1945, the Viet Minh League helped many Frenchmen to cross the frontier, rescued some of them from Japanese jails, and protected French lives and property.

From the autumn of 1940, our country had in fact ceased to be a French colony and had become a Japanese possession.

After the Japanese had surrendered to the Allies, our whole people rose to regain our national sovereignty and to found the Democratic Republic of Viet-Nam.

The truth is that we have wrested our independence from the Japanese and not from the French.

The French have fled, the Japanese have capitulated, Emperor Bao Dai has abdicated. Our people have broken the chains which for nearly a century have fettered them and have won independence for the Fatherland. Our people at the same time have overthrown the monarchic regime that has reigned supreme for dozens of centuries. In its place has been established the present Democratic Republic.

For these reasons, we, members of the Provisional Government, representing the whole Vietnamese people, declare that from now on we break off all relations of a colonial character with France; we repeal all the international obligation that France has so far subscribed to on behalf of Viet-Nam, and we abolish all the special rights the French have unlawfully acquired in our Fatherland.

The whole Vietnamese people, animated by a common purpose, are determined to fight to the bitter end against any attempt by the French colonialists to reconquer their country.

We are convinced that the Allied nations, which at Teheran and San Francisco have acknowledged the principles of self-determination and equality of nations, will not refuse to acknowledge the independence of Viet-Nam.

A people who have courageously opposed French domination for more than eighty years, a people who have fought side by side with the Allies against the fascists during these last years, such a people must be free and independent.

For these reasons, we, members of the Provisional Government of the Democratic Republic of Viet-Nam, solemnly declare to the world that Viet-Nam has the right to be a free and independent country—and in fact it is so already. The entire Vietnamese people are determined to mobilize all their physical and mental strength, to sacrifice their lives and property in order to safeguard their independence and liberty.

2
Dienbienphu: A Battle to Remember

Bernard B. Fall

Source: The New York Times Magazine (May 3, 1964).

On May 7, 1954, the end of the battle for the jungle fortress of Dienbienphu marked the end of French military influence in Asia, just as the sieges of Port Arthur, Corregidor, and Singapore had, to a certain extent, broken the spell of Russian, American, and British hegemony in Asia. The Asians, after centuries of subjugation, had beaten the white man at his own game. And today, ten years after Dienbienphu, Vietcong guerrillas in South Vietnam again challenge the West's ability to withstand a potent combination of political and military pressure in a totally alien environment.

On that day in May 1954 it had become apparent by 10 A.M. that Dienbienphu's position was hopeless. French artillery and mortars had been progressively silenced by murderously accurate Communist Vietminh artillery fire; and the monsoon rains had slowed down supply drops to a trickle and transformed the French trenches and dugouts into bottomless quagmires. The surviving officers and men, many of whom had lived for 54 days on a steady diet of instant coffee and cigarettes, were in a catatonic state of exhaustion.

As their commander, Brig. Gen. Christian de la Croix de Castries, reported the situation over the radiotelephone to General René Cogny, his theater commander 220 miles away in Hanoi in a high-pitched but curiously impersonal voice, the end obviously had come for the fortress. De Castries ticked off a long list of 800-man battalions which had been reduced to companies of eighty men and of companies that were reduced to the size of weak platoons. All he could hope for was to hold out until nightfall in order to give the surviving members of his command a chance to break out into the jungle under the cover of darkness, while he himself would stay with the more than 5,000 severely wounded (out of a total of 15,094 men inside the valley) and face the enemy.

By 3 P.M., however, it had become obvious that the fortress would not last until nightfall. Communist forces, in human-wave attacks, were swarming over the last remaining defenses. De Castries polled the surviving unit commanders within reach, and the consensus was that a breakout would only lead to a senseless piecemeal massacre in the jungle. The decision was made then to fight on to the end, as long as the ammunition lasted, and let individual units be overrun after destruction of their heavy weapons. That course of action was approved by the senior commander in Hanoi at about 5 P.M., but with the proviso that "Isabelle," the southernmost strongpoint closest to the jungle, and to friendly forces in Laos, should be given a chance to make a break for it.

Cogny's las conversation with de Castries dealt with the dramatic problem of what to do with the wounded piled up under the incredible conditions in the various strongpoints and in the fortress's central hospital—originally built to contain forty-two wounded. There had been suggestions that an orderly surrender should be arranged in order to save the wounded the added anguish of falling into enemy hands as isolated individuals. But Cogny was adamant on that point:

"*Mon vieux,* of course you have to finish the whole thing now. But what you have done until now surely is magnificent. Don't spoil it by hoisting the white flag. You are going to be submerged [by the enemy], but no surrender, no white flag."

"All right, *mon général,* I only wanted to preserve the wounded."

"Yes, I know. Well, do as best you can, leaving it to your [static: subordinate units?] to act for themselves. What you have done is too magnificent to do such a thing. You understand, *mon vieux.*"

There was a silence. Then de Castries said his final words:

"*Bien, mon général.*"

"Well, goodby, *mon vieux,* said Cogny. "I'll see you soon."

A few minutes later, de Castries' radio operator methodically smashed his set with the butt of his Colt .45, and thus the last word to come out of the main fortress, as it was being overrun, came at 5:50 P.M. from the radio operator of the 31st Combat Engineer Battalion, using his regulation code name:

"This is 'Yankee Metro.' We're blowing up everything around here. *Au revoir.*"

Strongpoint "Isabelle" never had a chance. While the main defenses of Dienbienphu were being mopped up, strong Vietminh forces already had tightened their grip around the thousand Legionnaires, Algerians, and Frenchmen preparing their breakout. At 9:40 P.M., a French surveillance aircraft reported to Hanoi that it saw the strongpoint's depots blowing up and that heavy artillery fire was visible close by. The breakout had been detected. At 1:50 A.M. on May 8, 1954, came the last message from the doomed garrison, relayed by the watchdog aircraft to Hanoi:

"Sortie failed—Stop—Can no longer communicate with you—Stop and end."

The great battle in the valley of Dienbienphu was over. Close to 10,000 captured troops were to begin the grim death march to the Vietminh prison camps 300 miles to the east. Few would survive. About 2,000 lay dead all over the battlefield in graves left unmarked to this day. Only seventy-three made good their escape from the various shattered strongpoints, to be rescued by the pro-French guerrilla units awaiting them in the Laotian jungle. Eight thousand miles away, in Geneva, the North Vietnamese and Red Chinese delegations attending the nine-power conference which was supposed to settle both the Korean and the Indochinese conflicts toasted the event in pink Chinese champagne.

What had happened at Dienbienphu was simply that a momentous gamble had been attempted by the French High Command and had backfired badly. The Indochina War, which had broken out in December 1946 after Ho Chi Minh's Vietminh forces felt that France would not agree to Vietnam's eventual independence, had slowly bogged down into a hopeless seesaw.

Until Red China's victorious forces arrived on Vietnam's borders in December 1949, there had been at least a small hope that the French-supported Vietnamese nationalist government, headed by ex-emperor Bao Dai, could wean away from the Communist-led Vietminh the allegiance of much of Vietnam's population. But with the existence of a Red Chinese "sanctuary" for the Vietminh forces, that became militarily impossible. By October 1950 twenty-three regular Vietminh battalions, equipped with excellent American artillery coming from Chinese Nationalist stocks left on the mainland, smashed the French defense lines along the Chinese border and inflicted on France its biggest colonial defeat since Montcalm died before Quebec. Within a few weeks, the French position in North Vietnam had shrunk to a fortified perimeter around the Red River delta; a continuous belt of Communist-held territory stretched from the Chinese border to within 100 miles of Saigon. For all practical purposes the Indochina Was was lost then and there.

What changed the aspect of the war for a time was the influx of American aid, which began with the onset of the Korean War. With Communism now a menace at both ends of the Far Eastern arc, the Indochina War, from a colonial war, became a "crusade"—but a crusade without a real cause. Independence, given too grudgingly to the Vietnamese nationalist regime, remained the catchword of the adversary.

But, militarily at least, disaster had temporarily been averted. The key Red River delta was more or less held by the French—at least during the daytime, for at night the enemy was everywhere—and the rice-rich Mekong delta in South Vietnam, where anti-Communist Buddhist sects were fighting on the French side, was held more solidly by Western forces in 1953–54 than in 1963–64.

In Laos the situation was just as grim then as it is now: the Laotian and French forces held the Mekong valley and the airfields of the Plain of Jars, and the enemy held the rest. Only Cambodia, then as now, was almost at peace: Prince Sihanouk (then King) had received independence from France in 1953 and galvanized his people into fighting against the guerrillas. They were so successful that, at the ensuing Geneva cease-fire conference, Cambodia did not have to surrender a province as a "regroupment area" for Communist forces.

This totally stalemated situation left the French with but one choice: to create a military situation of the kind that would permit cease-fire negotiations on a basis of equality with the enemy. To achieve this, the French commander-in-chief, General Henri Navarre, had to win a victory over the hard core of Communist regular divisions, whose continued existence posed a constant threat of invasion to the Laotian kingdom and to the vital Red River delta with its capital city of Hanoi and the thriving port of Haiphong. And to destroy those divisions and prevent their invasions into Laos, one had to, in American military parlance, "find 'em and fix 'em."

General Navarre felt that the way to achieve this was by offering the Communists a target sufficiently tempting for their regular divisions to pounce at, but sufficiently strong to resist the onslaught once it came. That was the rationale for the creation of Dienbienphu and for the battle that took place there.

There were other considerations also. Laos had signed a treaty with France in which the latter promised to defend it. Dienbienphu was to be the lock on the backdoor leading into Laos. Dienbienphu was also to be the test for a new theory of Navarre's. Rather than defend immobile lines, he wanted to create throughout Indochina "land-air bases" from which highly mobile units would sally forth and decimate the enemy in his own rear areas, just as the Vietminh guerrillas were doing in French rear areas. All that rode on Dienbienphu: the freedom of Laos, a senior commander's reputation, the survival of some of France's best troops and—above all—a last chance of coming out of the eight-year-long frustrating jungle war with something else than a total defeat.

But Navarre, an armor officer formed on the European battlefields, apparently (this was the judgment of the French Government committee that later investigated the disaster) had failed to realize that "there are no blocking positions in country lacking European-type roads." Since the Vietminh relied largely on human porters for their front-line units, they could easily bypass such bottlenecks as Dienbienphu or the Plain of Jars while bottling up the forces contained in those strongholds at little expense to themselves.

The results were evident: soon after French forces arrived at Dienbienphu on November 20, 1953, two of General Vo Nguyen Giap's regular 10,000-man divisions blocked the Dienbienphu garrison, while a third bypassed Dienbienphu and smashed deeply into Laos. On Christmas Day, 1953, Indochina, for the first time in the eight-year war, was literally cut in two. The offensive stabs for which Dienbienphu had been specifically planned became little else but desperate sorties against an invisible enemy. By the time the battle started for good on March 13, 1954, the garrison already had suffered 1,037 casualties without any tangible result.

Inside the fortress, the charming tribal village by the Nam Yum had soon disappeared along with all the bushes and trees in the valley, to be used either as firewood or as construction materials for the bunkers. Even the residence of the French governor was dismantled in order to make use of the bricks, for engineering materials were desperately short from the beginning.

Major André Sudrat, the chief engineer at Dienbienphu, was faced with a problem that he knew to be mathematically unsolvable: by normal military engineering standards, the materials necessary to protect a battalion against the fire of the 105-mm howitzers the Vietminh now possessed amounted to 2,550 tons, plus 500 tons of barbed wire. He estimated that to protect the 12 battalions there initially (five others were parachuted in during the battle) he would need 36,000 tons of engineering materials—which would mean using all available transport aircraft for a period of *five months.*

When he was told that he was allocated a total of about 3,300 tons of airlifted materials, Sudrat simply shrugged his shoulders. "In that case, I'll fortify the command post, the signal center, and the X-ray room in the hospital; and let's hope that the Viet has no artillery."

As it turned out, the Vietminh had more than 200 artillery pieces, reinforced during the last week of the siege by Russian "Katyusha" miltitube rocket launchers. Soon, the combination of monsoon rains, which set in around mid-April, and Vietminh artillery fire smashed to rubble the neatly arranged dugouts and trenches shown to eminent visitors and journalists during the early days of the siege. Essentially, the battle of Dienbienphu degenerated into a brutal artillery duel, which the enemy would have won sooner or later. The French gun crews and artillery pieces, working entirely *in the open* so as to allow the pieces all-around fields of fire, were destroyed one by one; replaced, they were destroyed once more, and at last fell silent.

The artillery duel became the great tragedy of the battle. Colonel Piroth, the jovial one-armed commander of the French artillery inside the fortress, had "guaranteed" that his twenty-four 105-mm howitzers could match anything the Communists had and that his battery of four 155-mm heavy field howitzers would definitely muzzle whatever would not be destroyed by the lighter pieces and the fighter-bombers. As it turned out, the Vietminh artillery was so superbly camouflaged that to this day it is doubtful whether French counterbattery fire silenced more than a handful of the enemy's fieldpieces.

When, on March 13, 1954, at 5:10 P.M., Communist artillery completely smothered strongpoint "Beatrice" without noticeable damage from French counterbattery fire, Piroth knew with deadly certitude that the fortress was doomed. And as deputy to General de Castries, he felt that he had contributed to the air of overconfidence and even cockiness—had not de Castries, in the manner of his ducal forebears, sent a written challenge to enemy commander Giap?—which had prevailed in the valley prior to the attack.

"I am responsible. I am responsible," he was heard to murmur as he went about his duties. During the night of March 14–15, he committed suicide by blowing himself up with a hand grenade, since he could not arm his pistol with one hand.

Originally, the fortress had been designed to protect its main airstrip against marauding Vietminh units, not to withstand the onslaught of four Communist divisions. There never was, as press maps of the time erroneously showed, a continuous battle line covering the whole valley. Four of the eight strongpoints were from one to three miles away from the center of the position. The interlocking fire of their artillery and mortars, supplemented by a squadron of ten tanks (flown in piecemeal and reassembled on the spot), was to prevent them from being picked off one by one.

This also proved to be an illusion. Gen. Vo Nguyen Giap decided to take Dienbienphu by an extremely efficient mixture of 18th-century siege techniques (sinking TNT-laden mineshafts under French bunkers, for example) and modern artillery patterns plus human-wave attacks. The outlying posts which protected the key airfield were captured within the first few days of the battle. French losses proved so great that the reinforcements parachuted in after the airfield was destroyed for good on March 27 never sufficed to mount the counterattacks necessary to reconquer them.

From then onward the struggle for Dienbienphu became a battle of attrition. The only hope of the garrison lay in the breakthrough of a relief column from Laos or Hanoi (a hopeless concept in view of the terrain and distances involved) or in the destruction of the siege force through aerial bombardment of the most massive kind. For a time a U.S. Air Force strike was under consideration, but the idea was dropped for about the same reasons that make a similar attack against North Vietnam today a rather risky affair.

Like Stalingrad, Dienbienphu slowly starved on its airlift tonnage. When the siege began, it had about eight days' worth of supplies on hand and required 200 tons a day to maintain minimum levels. The sheer magnitude of preparing that mass of supplies for parachuting was solved only by superhuman feats of the airborne supply units on the outside—efforts more than matched by the heroism of the soldiers inside the valley, who had to crawl into the open, under fire, to collect the containers.

But as the position shrunk every day (it finally was the size of a ball park), the bulk of the supplies fell into Communist hands. Even de Castries's general's stars, dropped to him by General Cogny with a bottle of champagne, landed in enemy territory.

The airdrops were a harrowing experience in that narrow valley which permitted only straight approaches. Communist antiaircraft artillery played havoc among the lumbering transport planes as they slowly disgorged their loads. A few figures tell how murderous the air war around Dienbienphu was: of a total of 420 aircraft available in all of Indochina then, sixty-two were lost in connection with Dienbienphu and 167 sustained hits. Some of the American civilian pilots who flew the run said that Vietminh flak was as dense as anything encountered during World War II over the Ruhr.

When the battle ended, the 82,926 parachutes expended in supplying the fortress covered the battlefield like freshly fallen snow. Or like a burial shroud.

The net effect of Dienbienphu on France's military posture in Indochina could not be measured in losses alone. It was to little avail to say that France had lost only 5 percent of its battle force; that the equipment losses had already been more than made good by American supplies funneled in while the battle was raging; and that even the manpower losses had been made up by reinforcements from France and new drafts of Vietnamese. Even the fact, which the unfortunate French commander-in-chief, Navarre, was to invoke later, that the attack on Dienbienphu cost the enemy close to 25,000 casualties and delayed his attack on the vital Red River delta by four months, held little water in the face of the wave of defeatism that swept not only French public opinion at home but also that of her allies.

Historically, Dienbienphu was, as one French senior officer masterfully understated it, never more than an "unfortunate accident." It proved little else but that an encircled force, no matter how valiant, will succumb if its support system fails. But as other revolutionary wars—from Algeria to the British defeats in Cyprus and Palestine—have conclusively shown, it does not take pitched "set-piece" battles to lose such wars. They can be lost just as conclusively through a series of very small engagements, such as those now fought in South Vietnam, if the local government and its population loses confidence in the eventual outcome of the contest—and that was the case of both the French and of their Vietnamese allies after Dienbienphu.

But as the French themselves demonstrated in Algeria, where they never again allowed themselves to be maneuvered into such desperate military straits, revolutionary wars are fought for *political* objectives, and big showdown battles are necessary neither for victory nor for defeat in that case. This now seems finally to have been understood in the South Vietnam war as well, and Secretary of Defense McNamara may well have thought of Dienbienphu when he stated in his major Vietnam policy speech of March 26 that "we have learned than in Vietnam, political and economic progress are the *sine qua non* of military success. . . ." One may only hope that the lesson has been learned in time.

But on May 7, 1954, the struggle for Indochina was almost over for France. As a French colonel looked out over the battlefield from a slit trench near his command post, a small white flag, probably a handkerchief, appeared on top of a rifle hardly fifty feet away from him, followed by the flat-helmeted head of a Vietminh soldier.

"You're not going to shoot anymore?" said the Vietminh in French.

"No, I'm not going to shoot anymore," said the colonel.

"*C'est fini?*" said the Vietminh.

"*Oui, c'est fini,*" said the colonel.

And all around them, as on some gruesome Judgment Day, soldiers, French and enemy alike, began to crawl out of their trenches and stand erect for the first time in 54 days, as firing ceased everywhere.

The sudden silence was deafening.

3
Dien Bien Phu: Why and How?

General Hoang Van Thai

Source: This article originally was serialized in the daily *Nhan Dan* in February and March on the occasion of the 30th anniversary of the victory of Dien Bien Phu. It is taken from a book by General Hoang Van Thai entitled *The Winter 1953–Spring 1954 Strategic Offensive and Its Apex—the Dien Bien Phu Campaign,* translated by *Vietnam Courier* in April 1984 (excerpts).

On the Eve of the Battle

On 8 May 1953, the French Government appointed General Navarre as Commander-in-Chief of the French Expeditionary Corps in Indochina. Immediately, the US granted France an aid of 285 million dollars, raising US aid from 650 million in 1953 to 1,284 million in 1954, which represented 75% of total French war expenditure in Indochina. Besides supplying the French with an additional 123 war planes and 213 naval craft the US also saw to the equipment of over 50 puppet battalions and many newly set up artillery, mechanized, and transport units.

Entrusted with the task of "finding an honourable way out" for France, after one month's investigation Navarre buckled down to the elaboration of a plan to implement that Franco-American strategic policy. His goal was to win a complete victory or at least to so weaken his opponent that the latter would be compelled to negotiate on terms advantageous to France.

Relying on the huge American aid and the numerical increase of his forces, he worked out a new strategic operational plan in which he conjectured that in the winter of 1953 and spring of 1954 our forces would essentially attack in the delta for there our regular forces were then mainly deployed, the people's war was very active, and supply was easy.

As the North Vietnam delta was the main battlefield, the "gateway to Southeast Asia," its loss would lead to a general debacle in Indochina. For this reason, Navarre was resolved to defend it at any cost and would concentrate the bulk of his crack mobile forces and his material means there to counter our attacks. He was sure he could do this for he had there most of his forces (47% of the total) and the most solid defences. In his plan, Navarre also guessed that our main forces could possibly attack Lai Chau and coordinate their action with the Pathet Lao forces to attack Upper Laos where French positions were vulnerable. But he held that in this hill-forest region, we would meet with great difficulties in supply and could not deploy large forces. Central and Lower Laos were important battlefields, French positions there showed many loopholes, and the military situation would turn in our favour if we reaped important successes there. However, difficulties in transport and supply would prevent us from fielding big forces. As this region was a most important battlefield, if it was attacked, Navarre would increase his forces there to prevent us from crossing the Plain of Jars—Dong Hoi line. On the basis of this calculation and in pursuance of his goal, he drew up a strategic plan to be carried out in 18 months. This plan was divided into two stages:

Stage 1: In winter 1953–spring 1954: he would engage in strategic defensive north of the 18th parallel and strategic offensive south of this parallel.

As he had resolved to defend the North Vietnam delta and the Plain of Jars—Dong Hoi line, Navarre mustered 44 mobile battalions in the delta to mop up our guerilla bases and constantly threaten our free zones in order to keep our regular forces off balance and the North Vietnam delta under his control in winter 1953. In the spring of 1954, as soon as he found our regular forces exhausted and incapable of making large-scale attacks, he would muster his forces to launch strategic offensives in the South, begin Operation Atlante against the liberated regions of the 5th Inter-zone, pacify South and Central Indochina, and build up large regular forces.

Stage 2: In autumn and winter 1954 once the mobile strategic forces built, he would launch a strategic offensive in North Vietnam, inflict heavy losses on our regular forces and win decisive victory, paving the way for the French Government to negotiate from a victor's position and to withdraw from Indochina in honour.

Navarre personally went back to France with the plan bearing his name. The French Commission of Chiefs-of-Staff and the National Defence Commission gave their approval. Concerning the reinforcement question, however, on account of the many difficulties being met with by France only 9 battalions and a squadron of transport planes were sent to Indochina by November. The French National Defence Commission also discussed the question of the defence of Laos but reached no decision and the matter was left to Navarre's discretion. On November 13, following the meeting of the National Defence Commission, the new French Government made clear to Navarre that the aim to be pursued in the execution of his plan was to convince the opponent that he could not win a decisive military victory.

After being informed of the Navarre plan, O'Daniel, Commander of the US Armed Forces in the Pacific, reported to the Pentagon that a French victory was at hand.

On our side, in its 4th plenum held in January 1953, the Party Central Committee had assessed the situation as follows: Since the Border Campaign in 1950, we had kept the initiative in the North Vietnam battlefield but the development of our forces had been uneven. The enemy was strong in the North and relatively weak in other regions. Our strategic direction was to strike at the enemy where he was the weakest and to force him to scatter his forces. We should strike hard blows and make sure advances. We should strike only when we were sure to win, and resolutely abstain when we were not. Our territory was not large; our manpower not numerous; we should win at every turn and could not afford a defeat.

While drafting our strategic plan for 1954–1955, we had anticipated the construction of roads for large-scale attacks in the south in the following years, but at that time we did not have the necessary conditions for doing so. There remained the uplands and the delta, where the people's war had greatly developed, and supply was easy. But there the enemy was strongest, and our regular forces could not as yet launch a large-scale campaign. Only a plan remained which consisted in hitting the enemy with only a part of our forces. These forces would take turns attacking him by way of training.

As soon as this operational plan was proposed, however, the Intelligence Department of our General Staff was able to learn important points of the Navarre plan: US aid had greatly increased, troop reinforcements had been sent from France and North Africa, the puppet troops had increased in number, mobile combat groups had been set up and more would be. We knew in particular that the enemy was fielding 44 mobile battalions in the North Vietnam delta and that the situation had greatly changed. In these circumstances, we could not send our regular forces to fight by rotation in the delta as an exercise. The problem was now to thwart the Navarre plan at all costs. Only then could our resistance end victoriously, otherwise, it would meet with great difficulties. To wreck the Navarre plan was an urgent task at this stage. The Party Political Bureau and President Ho Chi Minh instructed the Central Military Commission and the High Command to work out a program to this end.

On October 22, the French Government had signed an agreement recognizing the independence of Laos within the French Union and was thus pledged to protect Laos and its capital (Luang Prabang) though the pledge had not been explicitly stipulated. Luang Prabang was not located on vantage ground nor did it have a large airfield. It was not possible to set up there a base for the deployment of both ground and air forces. So, Navarre thought he would turn Dien Bien Phu, which had a fairly big airfield, into such a base to stop our advance into Upper Laos. He considered Dien Bien Phu to be the key to Upper Laos. On 2 November 1953, he had instructed Cogny, Commander of the French forces in North Vietnam, to make preparations for the occupation of Dien Bien Phu before 1 December 1953. A few months previously, both Cogny and Salan had approved a plan for this occupation, but they had not yet been able to execute it. The situation changed at the beginning of November. Now, wanting to keep troops to defend the North Vietnam delta, Cogny and his staff expressed disapproval of Navarre's scheme of occupation of Dien Bien Phu. But after being informed of our regular forces' advance on the Northwest, Navarre disregarded their views and gave Cogny the order to launch the operation he had planned. On 20, 21, and 22 November, 1953, six battalions of crack European and African troops (4,500 men) were dropped on Muong Thanh and seized Dien Bien Phu. Besides his intention to set up a base from which to check our advance on Upper Laos, Cogny wanted to turn Dien Bien Phu into a spring-board from which to liaise with Lai Chau and make thrusts into Tuan Giao and possibly Son La and Na San. That is why he merged the forces garrisoning Dien Bien Phu and Lai Chau into a single combat group called GONO (Groupe opérationnel du Nord-Ouest). Furthermore, on 25 November, Navarre ordered Crèvecœur, the commander of the French forces in Laos, to send up six battalions from Luang Prabang for an attack on the Lao free zone in the Nam Hu river basin with a view to establishing liaison with Dien Bien Phu. In Central Laos, to prevent our forces from crossing the Plain of Jars—Dong Hoi line, at the beginning of December 1953 Navarre moved his élite G.M. 2 (Groupement Mobile 2) and three independent battalions from North Vietnam to the Vietnam–Laos frontier.

That was, in a nutshell, the situation on the enemy's side in November

1953. Basically, our General Staff was informed of this situation although some points were to be clarified only later.

Thus, as soon as our forces were deployed a new situation arose. We had succeeded in attracting enemy forces to Dien Bien Phu and to Central Laos. The news of the enemy airdrops on Dien Bien Phu on the 20th came just at a time when our High Command was holding a conference to acquaint our division commanders with the operational plan for Winter 1953–Spring 1954 (the meeting lasted from 19 to 23 November). Informed of this occupation of Dien Bien Phu by French paratroops, our High Command considered several possible developments: the enemy could either hold Lai Chau and Dien Bien Phu or only one of these bases, probably Dien Bien Phu; he could also withdraw from both. However the situation may evolve, the enemy's parachuting troops into Dien Bien Phu was welcomed news: it meant that we had succeeded in moving six battalions of picked French troops to Dien Bien Phu; now we would keep them there and draw even more of them into this place. On the proposal of the General Staff, the High Command ordered the 316th Division to go and attack the enemy in Lai Chau while the 308th Division was to beleaguer him at Dien Bien Phu.

Our feints succeeded and our secrets were well kept. On 28 November, the enemy command in North Vietnam released the information that our 308th, 312th, and 351st divisions had moved to the Northwest. Cogny suggested that Navarre should order an attack on Phu Tho, Yen Bai or Thai Nguyen to pin down our regular forces there. But as he was contemplating a strategic attack in South Vietnam early in the spring of 1954 and had sent part of his regular forces to Dien Bien Phu and Central Laos, Navarre rejected Cogny's suggested operations: they would cost too much and stretch his forces too thin. The problem facing him was whether or not to dispatch more main-force troops to Dien Bien Phu to give battle to us. He reckoned that Dien Bien Phu was too far from our bases, that we would have great difficulties in supply, and could at most deploy one reinforced division there. For its part, the 2e Bureau (French army intelligence) held the view that we could not field more than two divisions and mobilize more than 20,000 civilian carriers; that we could not use mechanized artillery, but at most only 75-mm mountain guns. So, Navarre accepted battle with us at Dien Bien Phu. His idea was to dispatch more reinforcements and build Dien Bien Phu into an entrenched camp even more powerful than the one at Na San—an impregnable fortress. Accordingly, on 3 December, he sent to Dien Bien Phu three more battalions, raising its garrison from six to nine infantry battalions, plus about three artillery battalions. The units garrisoning Lai Chau could either be maintained there if conditions permitted, or they could be sent as reinforcements to Dien Bien Phu. Navarre held that this decision of his was quite judicious in that our regular forces would be immobilized at Dien Bien Phu and would take heavy casualties should they attack this stronghold. In this way, the French could at the same time stand firmly in the Northwest, defend Upper Laos and the North Vietnam delta, and particularly carry out their planned strategic offensive in the South. By strengthening the Dien Bien Phu garrison and accepting battle with us there, Navarre had unwittingly turned Dien Bien Phu into the centrepiece of his strategic plan though at that time he still considered his offensive in South Vietnam as its kingpin.

For our part, though the previous year our regular forces had not been able to capture Na San, this year they had learned the technique of striking at entrenched camps. They had been reorganized and strengthened and were now armed with 105-mm howitzers. So, we should be quite able to tackle Dien Bien Phu. We would run into great difficulties in supply, but with good organization and mobilization of our rear areas they could be overcome.

But another problem arose: would the enemy stay at Dien Bien Phu or would he withdraw from there? If he stayed and received reinforcements, we would fight him with our regular forces. This tallied with our plan. But if we sent in our regular forces and he withdrew—probably by air as he had done at Na San—we would be off balance. That is why though preparations had been made for this campaign, we still could not immediately send troops to Dien Bien Phu.

The Battle Begins

Dien Bien Phu lies in a vast valley in the western part of the Northwest highlands, 18km by 6–8km in size, surrounded with high mountains and dense forests. It is the largest, richest and most populous valley of the Northwest. Situated near the Vietnam–Laos border, Dien Bien Phu was the strongest entrenched camp in Indochina, an "impregnable fortress," a perfect "hedgehog" with sophisticated defences. Navarre, Cogny, and O'Daniel, the US Commander in the Pacific, had many times come to inspect Dien Bien Phu and were confident that the Vietnamese could not knock it out. Of course, this entrenched camp had some weak points, but at that time the French strategists were not aware, or not fully aware of them. Only after its collapse did they point to some of its weak points: its situation in a valley hemmed in by mountains exposed it to enemy artillery, its airfield could come under fire, the base could be encircled and isolated, etc.

For our part, we had some superiority over the enemy, but it was not very great: 27 infantry battalions pitted against 12 battalions and 7 companies, or twice the enemy forces; 62 heavy guns against 49, but we had much less ammunition. We had A.A. guns, but the enemy had planes and tanks. (To explain away the collapse of the French forces at Dien Bien Phu, French propaganda and many French and Western historians and correspondents said that we fielded a total of 100,000 troops—as many as 80,000 on the frontline. This was extravagant exaggeration as we used only half this figure.) As our superiority was not overwhelming our guideline was "steady attack and steady advance." The Command of the Campaign proposed to launch two waves of attack:

First wave: Knock out the enemy's outer defences; hamper then completely cut off his reinforcements and supplies.

These first victories would sap the enemy's morale in the whole of the entrenched camp.

Second wave: Knock out the Central Sector and launch a general assault to capture the whole of Dien Bien Phu.

As it turned out, the campaign comprised three waves of attack:

First wave: Our troops destroyed the enemy's forward positions in the north and the northeast, i.e., Him Lam and the whole Northern Sector.

Second wave: Our troops destroyed the key defensive area of the enemy's Central Sector, captured the eastern hills, the airfield, created a ring around the enemy and gradually tightened it, narrowing the enemy-occupied area and his air space and eventually cutting off all reinforcements and supplies.

Third wave: On the basis of the results scored in the first and second waves of attack, our troops kept on attacking the enemy's last position in the east, captured it, and launched a general assault on the whole of the entrenched camp.

The third wave of attack of the campaign began on the night of 1 May 1954.

At 12:00 hours on 1 May 1954, our artillery began pounding at the enemy gun emplacements, headquarters and various positions. Enemy guns at Hong Cum were paralyzed and the munitions depot there blasted.

At 20:30 hours the same day, the 98th Regiment of the 316th Division completely overran C1. Then it nibbled at C2 and got ready to storm it while consolidating the occupied ground and standing ready to break up enemy counter-attacks. At last, after 32 days and nights of fierce fighting our troops now occupied the hills. They tightened their encirclement and closed in.

Thus, in the first actions of the third wave of attack our troops had won resounding victories. East of Nam Rom the enemy now had only two positions left: A1 and C2. In the west, our encirclement tightened on De Castries' headquarters. Meanwhile, the garrison's food and ammunition were running out. In face of this critical situation, on 2 May, Navarre flew from Saigon to Hanoi and gave De Castries his last paratroop battalion held in reserve—the First Colonial Paratroop Battalion. However, as the dropping zone had shrunk, only two companies were dropped by 6 May. At his wits' end the Commander of the French Expeditionary Forces had to order the Dien Bien Phu garrison to leave the camp. De Castries planned to divide his troops into three columns which would flee west, south and southeast to Laos. Navarre also ordered Crèvecœur to turn his diversionary move into a relief operation in support of De Castries' troops. According to the enemy's order of operation this plan was to be carried out on the night of 7 May 1954.

At 18:00 hours on 6 May, we opened up with all our heavy guns. Besides the artillery of the front there was a newly-arrived 122-mm rocket company. Each volley from the 12 launchers comprised 72 rockets, which terrified the enemy.

At 18:45 hours, when the big explosive charge on Hill A1 exploded, the 174th Regiment stormed the position, taking the enemy by surprise. A thrust to the west stopped an enemy counter-attack with infantry and tanks. However, the enemy on Hill A1 recovered and stubbornly resisted, and the fight lasted until 4:00 hours on 7 May when Hill A1 was occupied.

Parallel with the attack on Hill A1, the 98th Regiment seized position C2. The 312th Division seized fort 506 north of Muong Thanh. In the west, the 308th Division took fort 310. Our encirclement ring was a mere 300 metres from De Castries' command post. The enemy resisted stubbornly to the last minute. To defeat him our troops had to overcome many difficulties and make great sacrifices. Our units fulfilled their tasks and readied themselves for the general assault planned for the night of 7 May.

While we were stepping up our preparations for the general assault, on the morning of 7 May, army intelligence noted that enemy planes carrying weapons and ammunition to Dien Bien Phu were ordered back; only those bringing food would go and drop their cargoes. The planes carrying the last paratroop company were also ordered to return to Gia Lam. On the ground, our troops discovered that enemy soldiers were throwing their weapons into the Nam Rom river while from Muong Thanh heavy explosions were heard.

At 14:00 hours on 7 May, one of our units attacked fort 507 near the Muong Thanh bridge. After a weak resistance the enemy surrendered. After that our troops knocked out forts 508 and 509 on the left bank of the Nam Rom river.

The Campaign Command believed that the enemy was now in a state of utter confusion with no fighting spirit left, and ordered our troops to stand ready for a general assault.

At 15:00 hours on 7 May, our troops were ordered not to wait for the night but to seize the opportunity and to launch the general assault.

Implementing this order our units rushed forward to strike at the enemy remaining positions. So irresistible was their onslaught that wherever they attacked enemy white flags would appear. Groups of enemy soldiers left their trenches and threw down their weapons. A squad of the 312th Division crossed the Muong Thanh bridge, dashed to the De Castries' command post and captured this General commander of the entrenched camp along with his entire staff. It was 17:30 hours on 7 May 1954. Our "Fight and Win" flag flew over Dien Bien Phu, now a historic site.

In Hong Cum Sector the 304th Division used loudspeakers to call on enemy soldiers to surrender, but they fled under cover of darkness. We pursued them and captured them all at 24:00 hours.

The historic Dien Bien Phu campaign had ended in total victory, crowning our army's and people's strategic offensive in winter 1953–spring 1954.

Chapter II

The Geneva Conference of 1954 and Its Aftermath

On the same day that the French garrison at Dien Bien Phu was overrun, the great powers were meeting in Geneva, Switzerland, to negotiate future political arrangements for Asia in the aftermath of the Korean War. Acutely aware that the schedule called for the assembled representatives in Geneva to turn their attention to Vietnam, the Vietminh expended tremendous energy to make sure that Dien Bien Phu fell before discussions about their country began. The 10,000 French prisoners of war they captured provided them with ample bargaining power to put forth a strong position for Vietnamese independence.

When all was said and done at Geneva, however, Vietnam's complete independence remained unaccomplished. Instead, the Soviet Union and China brokered an agreement with France in which Vietnam was temporarily divided at the seventeenth parallel. According to the conference's final agreement (Document 4), free national elections to reunify the country were to be held in two years, time during which the French would leave, taking with them any Vietnamese who wished to depart. Those members of the Vietminh who feared French reprisals would go to northern Vietnam, where Ho Chi Minh and the Vietminh established their government.

The Final Declaration of the Geneva Conference is quite straightforward. Point 7 is critical since it recognizes the unity of Vietnam, thereby explicitly noting the temporary nature of the division of Vietnam into northern and southern zones. Most significantly, a national election was scheduled for July 1956 to reunify the two zones.

Although the United States was not a signatory of the Final Declaration, Walter Bedell Smith, the American representative at the conference, "took note" of the agreements and declared on behalf of the U.S. government that the United States would "refrain from the threat or use of force to disturb them." Nonetheless, as Document 5 shows, the United States immediately began conducting covert actions in northern Vietnam designed to weaken the Vietminh. The Central Intelligence Agency's program of destabilization of northern Vietnam included psychological warfare aimed at creating a mass exodus of Catholics. Messages that the Virgin Mary was moving south appeared, and for non-Christians, astrologers were hired to make dire predictions of forthcoming disasters in the North. This program was quite successful when one considers that nearly one million northerners did leave to move to the South. Besides this psychological warfare, the CIA printed and distributed massive amounts of counterfeit money to undermine the economy of the North and sabotaged gasoline supply tanks and buses, scarce resources vitally important to peacetime reconstruction.

At the same time as the Vietminh areas were under American pressure, the administration in southern Vietnam was elevated into the status of a sovereign government. The French were supposed to remain in South Vietnam to guarantee the peace until the nationwide elections scheduled for July 1956 but they withdrew prematurely. The United States assisted the prime minister of South Vietnam, Ngo Dinh Diem, in conducting a plebiscite, not to reunify the country as agreed in Geneva, but to depose permanently Emperor Bao Dai, who in 1949 had been persuaded by the French to serve as figurehead of their Vietnamese government. With American help, the plebiscite went overwhelmingly against the emperor, leaving Diem in a position of uncontested power in the South.

Even before the Geneva agreement, President Eisenhower maintained that the United States could not afford to "lose" Indochina. At a press conference on April 7, 1954 (Document 6), Eisenhower was quite candid in saying that there were resources involved, specifically tin, tungsten, and rubber plantations. More importantly, Eisenhower argued that, like falling dominoes, if Indochina were to go Communist, Thailand and Burma might be next, then possibly Indonesia, Japan, Formosa, and even Australia and New Zealand. That is why the United States and Diem made sure the planned elections never happened. As shown in the next two documents in this chapter, one day before the date set in Geneva for consultations, the North Vietnamese sent a letter to the administration of South Vietnam to begin the process of setting up the elections, but Diem was unwilling to attend even preliminary consultative discussions, and no response was ever made to the North. At the time, President Eisenhower stated that if free elections had been held according to the timetable agreed upon in Geneva, Ho Chi Minh would have received 80 percent of the votes, an outcome that the United States would not allow.

The justification for Eisenhower's course of action was anticommunism. In the era after the Korean War, anticommunism claimed first place on both the American domestic and foreign agendas. In terms of foreign policy, the enemy in Vietnam (as everywhere else) was the same one that had been fought in Korea. There was little need for a public justification of the U.S. decisions to install Diem and forego elections, particularly since the fear of dominoes falling to communism was widespread.

As Dr. Benjamin Spock points out in Document 9, Diem was handpicked by American policymakers while he was living in New Jersey, and he was sent back to Vietnam to build a new nation—South Vietnam. Like the French, during the nine years in which Diem ruled South Vietnam, he built more jails than schools. Thousands of people were arrested. More than four million people (about a third of the population of South Vietnam) were relocated by the strategic hamlet program. As he consolidated power, a series of extraordinarily repressive laws were passed prohibiting freedom of speech and peaceful protest at the same time as vast tracks of land were being taken away from the peasantry and given to the Catholic immigrants from the North. Between 1954 and 1960, 80,000 people were killed by Diem's army and police, 23,000 were wounded, and 275,000 were detained.

Popular protests intensified as did the government's repression, until finally, in 1960, a new group was formed to lead the opposition—the National Liberation Front (NLF, or "Viet Cong" as it was called by Diem). Within two years, this group controlled 80 percent of the countryside and as much as 75 percent of the population of South Vietnam. Although it was set up by Communists, the NLF was not simply an organization of Communists. It included Buddhists, Catholics, businessmen, women's groups, liberals, peasants, students, and minority groups. A little-known fact is that the North Vietnamese had actively discouraged southerners from taking offensive action against the Diem government. While party cadre complied with Hanoi's instructions, a grassroots movement against the government's brutality spontaneously emerged, compelling Hanoi to provide leadership. In its manifesto (Document 10), the NLF's program is discussed.

4
Final Declaration of the Geneva Conference, July 21, 1954

Final declaration, dated July 21, 1954, of the Geneva Conference on the problem of restoring peace in Indochina, in which the representatives of Cambodia, the Democratic Republic of Viet-Nam, France, Laos, the People's Republic of China, the State of Viet-Nam, the Union of Soviet Socialist Republics, the United Kingdom, and the United States of America took part.

1. The Conference takes note of the agreements ending hostilities in Cambodia, Laos, and Viet-Nam, and organizing international control and the supervision of the execution of the provisions of these agreements.

2. The Conference expresses satisfaction at the ending of hostilities in Cambodia, Laos, and Viet-Nam; the Conference expresses its conviction that the execution of the provisions set out in the present declaration and in the agreements on the cessation of hostilities will permit Cambodia, Laos, and Viet-Nam henceforth to play their part, in full independence and sovereignty, in the peaceful community of nations.

3. The Conference takes note of the declarations made by the governments of Cambodia and of Laos of their intention to adopt measures permitting all citizens to take their place in the national community, in particular by participating in the next general elections, which, in conformity with the constitution of each of these countries, shall take place in the course of the year 1955, by secret ballot and in conditions of respect for fundamental freedoms.

4. The Conference takes note of the clauses in the agreement on the cessation of hostilities in Viet-Nam prohibiting the introduction into Viet-Nam of foreign troops and military personnel as well as of all kinds of arms and munitions. The Conference also takes note of the declarations made by the governments of Cambodia and Laos of their resolution not to reqest foreign aid, whether in war material, in personnel or in instructors except for the purpose of the effective defence of their territory and, in the case of Laos, to the extent defined by the agreements on the cessation of hostilities in Laos.

5. The Conference takes note of the clauses in the agreement on the cessation

of hostilities in Viet-Nam to the effect that no military base under the control of a foreign state may be established in the regrouping zones of the two parties, the latter having the obligation to see that the zones allotted to them shall not constitute part of any military alliance and shall not be utilized for the resumption of hostilities or in the service of an aggressive policy. The Conference also takes note of the declarations of the governments of Cambodia and Laos to the effect that they will not join in any agreement with other states if this agreement includes the obligation to participate in a military alliance not in conformity with the principles of the Charter of the United Nations or, in the case of Laos, with the principles of the agreement on the cessation of hostilities in Laos or, so long as their security is not threatened, the obligation to establish bases on Cambodian or Laotian territory for the military forces of foreign Powers.

6. The Conference recognizes that the essential purpose of the agreement relating to Viet-Nam is to settle military questions with a view to ending hostilities and that the military demarcation line is provisional and should not in any way be interpreted as constituting a political or territorial boundary. The Conference expresses its conviction that the execution of the provisions set out in the present declaration and in the agreement on the cessation of hostilities creates the necessary basis for the achievement in the near future of a political settlement in Viet-Nam.

7. The Conference declares that, so far as Viet-Nam is concerned, the settlement of political problems, effected on the basis of respect for the principles of independence, unity and territorial integrity, shall permit the Vietnamese people to enjoy the fundamental freedoms, guaranteed by democratic institutions established as a result of free general elections by secret ballot. In order to ensure that sufficient progress in the restoration of peace has been made, and that all the necessary conditions obtain for free expression of the national will, general elections shall be held in July, 1956, under the supervision of an international commission composed of representatives of the Member States of the International Supervisory Commission, referred to in the agreement on the cessation of hostilities. Consultations will be held on this subject between the competent representative authorities of the two zones from 20 July 1955 onwards.

8. The provisions of the agreements on the cessation of hostilities intended to ensure the protection of individuals and of property must be most strictly applied and must, in particular, allow everyone in Viet-Nam to decide freely in which zone he wishes to live.

9. The competent representative authorities of the Northern and Southern zones of Viet-Nam, as well as the authorities of Laos and Cambodia, must not permit any individual or collective reprisals against persons who have collaborated in any way with one of the parties during the war, or against members of such persons' families.

10. The Conference takes note of the declaration of the government of the

French Republic to the effect that it is ready to withdraw its troops from the territory of Cambodia, Laos, and Viet-Nam, at the request of the governments concerned and within periods which shall be fixed by agreement betwen the parties except in the cases where, by agreement betwen the two parties, a certain number of French troops shall remain at specified points and for a specified time.

11. The Conference takes note of the declaration of the French government to the effect that for the settlement of all the problems connected with the reestablishment and consolidation of peace in Cambodia, Laos, and Viet-Nam, the French government will proceed from the principle of respect for the independence and sovereignty, unity and territorial integrity of Cambodia, Laos, and Viet-Nam.

12. In their relations with Cambodia, Laos, and Viet-Nam, each member of the Geneva Conference undertakes to respect the sovereignty, the independence, the unity, and the territorial integrity of the above-mentioned states, and to refrain from any interference in their internal affairs.

13. The members of the Conference agree to consult one another on any question which may be referred to them by the International Supervisory Commission in order to study such measures as may prove necessary to ensure that the agreements on the cessation of hostilities in Cambodia, Laos, and Viet-Nam are respected.

5
Report of U.S. Central Intelligence Agency Covert Operations Team in Vietnam, 1955

Central Intelligence Agency

Source: The Pentagon Papers as Published by the New York Times (Bantam Books, 1971), pp. 53–66 (excerpts).

Towards the end of the month, it was learned that the largest printing establishment in the north intended to remain in Hanoi and do business with the Vietminh. An attempt was made by SMM [Saigon Military Mission] to destroy the modern presses, but Vietminh security agents already had moved into the plant and frustrated the attempt. This operation was under a Vietnamese patriot whom we shall call Trieu; his case officer was Capt. Arundel. Earlier in the month they had engineered a black psywar strike in Hanoi: leaflets signed by the Vietminh instructing Tonkinese on how to behave for the Vietminh takeover of the Hanoi region in early October, including items about property, money reform, and a three-day holiday of workers upon takeover. The day following the distribution of these leaflets, refugee registration tripled. Two days later Vietminh currency was worth half the value prior to the leaflets. The Vietminh took to the radio to denounce the leaflets; the leaflets were so authentic in appearance that even most of the rank and file Vietminh were sure that the radio denunciations were a French trick.

The Hanoi psywar strike had other consequences. Binh had enlisted a high police official of Hanoi as part of his team, to effect the release from jail of any team members if arrested. The official at the last moment decided to assist in the leaflet distribution personally. Police officers spotted him, chased his vehicle through the empty Hanoi streets of early morning, finally opened fire on him and caught him. He was the only member of the group caught. He was held in prison as a Vietminh agent.

* * *

Hanoi was evacuated on 9 October. The northern SMM team left with the last French troops, disturbed by what they had seen of the grim efficiency of the Vietminh in their takeover, the contrast between the silent march of the victorious Vietminh troops in their tennis shoes and the clanking armor of the well-equipped French whose Western tactics and equipment had failed against the Communist military-political-economic campaign.

The northern team had spent the last days of Hanoi in contaminating the oil supply of the bus company for a gradual wreckage of engines in the buses, in taking the first actions for delayed sabotage of the railroad (which required teamwork with a CIA special technical team in Japan who performed their part brilliantly), and in writing detailed notes of potential targets for future paramilitary operations (U.S. adherence to the Geneva Agreement prevented SMM from carrying out the active sabotage it desired to do against the power plant, water facilities, harbor, and bridge). The team had a bad moment when contaminating the oil. They had to work quickly at night, in an enclosed storage room. Fumes from the contaminant came close to knocking them out. Dizzy and weak-kneed, they masked their faces with handkerchiefs and completed the job.

Meanwhile, Polish and Russian ships had arrived in the south to transport southern Vietminh to Tonkin under the Geneva Agreement. This offered the opportunity for another black psywar strike. A leaflet was developed by Binh with the help of Capt. Arundel, attributed to the Vietminh Resistance Committee. Among other items, it reassured the Vietminh they would be kept safe below decks from imperialist air and submarine attacks, and requested that warm clothing be brought; the warm clothing item would be coupled with a verbal rumor campaign that Vietminh were being sent into China as railroad laborers.

SMM had been busily developing G-5 of the Vietnamese Army for such psywar efforts. Under Arundel's direction, the First Armed Propaganda Company printed the leaflets and distributed them, by soldiers in civilian clothes who penetrated into southern Vietminh zones on foot. (Distribution in Camau was made while columnist Joseph Alsop was on his visit there which led to his sensational, gloomy articles later; our soldier "Vietminh" failed in an attempt to get the leaflet into Alsop's hands in Camau; Alsop was never told this story). Intelligence reports and other later reports revealed that village and delegation committees complained about "deportation" to the north, after distribution of the leaflet. . . .

* * *

The patriot we've named Trieu Dinh had been working on an almanac for popular sale, particularly in the northern cities and towns we could still reach. Noted Vietnamese astrologers were hired to write predictions about coming disasters to certain Vietminh leaders and undertakings, and to predict unity in the south. The work was carried out under the direction of Lt. Phillips, based on our concept of the use of astrology for psywar in Southeast Asia. Copies of the almanac were shipped by air to Haiphong and then smuggled into Vietminh territory.

Dinh also had produced a Thomas Paine type series of essays on Vietnamese patriotism against the Communist Vietminh, under the guidance of Capt. Arundel. These essays were circulated among influential groups in Vietnam; earned front-page editorials in the leading daily newspaper in Saigon. Circulation increased with the publication of these essays; the publisher is known to SMM as The Dragon Lady and is a fine Vietnamese girl who has been the mistress of an anti-American French civilian. Despite anti-American remarks by her boy friend, we had helped her keep her paper from being closed by the government . . . and she found it profitable to heed our advice on the editorial content of her paper.

Arms and equipment for the Binh paramilitary team were being cached in the north in areas still free from the Vietminh. Personnel movements were covered by the flow of refugees. Haiphong was reminiscent of our own pioneer days as it was swamped with people whom it couldn't shelter. Living space and food were at a premium; nervous tension grew. It was a wild time for our northern team.

First supplies for the Hao paramilitary group started to arrive in Saigon. These shipments and the earlier ones for the Binh group were part of an efficient air smuggling effort by the 581st [word illegible] Wing, U.S. Air Force, to support SMM, with help by CIA and Air Force personnel in both Okinawa and the Philippines. SMM officers frequently did coolie labor in manhandling tons of cargo, at times working through the night . . . All . . . officers pitched in to help, as part of our "blood, sweat and tears." . . .

By 31 January, all operational equipment of the Binh paramilitary group had been trans-shipped to Haiphong from Saigon, mostly with the help of CAT [Civilian Air Transport], and the northern SMM team had it cached in operational sites. Security measures were tightened at the Haiphong airport and plans for bringing in the Hao equipment were changed from the air route to sea. Task Force 98, now 98.7 under command of Captain Frank, again was asked to give a helping hand and did so. . . .

. . . Major Conein had briefed the members of the Binh paramilitary team and started them infiltrating into the north as individuals. The infiltration was carried out in careful stages over a 30-day period, a successful operation. The Binhs became normal citizens, carrying out every day civil pursuits, on the surface.

We had smuggled into Vietnam about eight and a half tons of supplies for the Hao paramilitary group. They included fourteen agent radios, 300 carbines, 90,000 rounds of carbine ammunition, 50 pistols, 10,000 rounds of pistol ammunition, and 300 pounds of explosives. Two and a half tons were delivered to the Hao agents in Tonkin, while the remainder was cached along the Red River by SMM, with the help of the Navy. . . .

6
President Eisenhower Explains the Domino Theory, 1954

Source: Presidential Press Conference, April 7, 1954.

Q. Robert Richards, Copley Press: Mr. President, would you mind commenting on the strategic importance of Indochina to the free world? I think there has been, across the country, some lack of understanding on just what it means to us.

The President: You have, of course, both the specific and the general when you talk about such things.

First of all, you have the specific value of a locality in its production of materials that the world needs.

Then you have the possibility that many human beings pass under a dictatorship that is inimical to the free world.

Finally, you have broader considerations that might follow what you would call the "falling domino" principle. You have a row of dominoes set up, you knock over the first one, and what will happen to the last one is the certainty that it will go over very quickly. So you could have a beginning of a disintegration that would have the most profound influences.

Now, with respect to the first one, two of the items from this particular area that the world uses are tin and tungsten. They are very important. There are others, of course, the rubber plantations and so on.

Then with respect to more people passing under this domination. Asia, after all, has already lost some 450 million of its peoples to the Communist dictatorship, and we simply can't afford greater losses.

But when we come to the possible sequence of events, the loss of Indochina, of Burma, of Thailand, of the Peninsula, and Indonesia following, now you begin to talk about areas that not only multiply the disadvantages that you would suffer through loss of materials, sources of materials, but now you are talking about millions and millions and millions of people.

Finally, the geographical position achieved thereby does many things. It turns the so-called island defensive chain of Japan, Formosa, of the Philippines and to the southward; it moves in to threaten Australia and New Zealand.

It takes away, in its economic aspects, that region that Japan must have as a trading area or Japan, in turn, will have only one place in the world to go—that is, toward the Communist areas in order to live.

So, the possible consequences of the loss are just incalculable to the free world.

7
Message from Ho Chi Minh and Foreign Minister Pham Van Dong to RVN Chief of State Bao Dai and Prime Minister Ngo Dinh Diem, July 19, 1955

Source: Democratic Republic of Vietnam Ministry of Foreign Affairs, *Documents Related to the Implementation of the Geneva Agreements* (Hanoi, 1956), pp. 41–44 (excerpts).

The holding on schedule of the consultative conference by the competent authorities of the North and the South is of great importance, and has a bearing not only on the prospect of the unity of our country but also on the loyal implementation of the Geneva Agreements, and the consolidation of peace in Indo-China and in the world.

Following the June 6, 1955 declaration by the Government of the Democratic Republic of Viet-nam, Sai-gon Radio on July 16, 1955, made known the "position of the Government of the State of Viet-nam on the problem of general elections for the unification of the national territory." The statement mentioned general elections and reunification but did not touch upon a very important and most realistic issue, that of the meeting of the competent representative authorities of the two zones, of the holding of the consultative conference on the question of general elections and reunification, as provided for by the Geneva Agreements. Moreover there were in the statement things which are untrue and which would not help to create a favourable climate for the convening of the consultative conference.

Our compatriots from the South to the North, irrespective of classes, creeds, and political affiliations have deeply at heart the reunification of the country, and are looking forward to the early convening of the consultative conference and to its good outcome. All the countries responsible for the guarantee of the implementation of the Geneva Agreements and in general all the peace-loving countries in the world are anxious to see that the consultative conference will be held and yield good results and that the reunification of our country will be achieved.

The Government of the Democratic Republic of Viet-nam proposes that you appoint your representatives and that they and ours hold the consultative conference from July 20, 1955 onwards, as provided for by the Geneva Agreements, at a place agreeable to both sides, on the Vietnamese territory, in order to discuss the problem of reunification of our country by means of free general elections all over Viet-nam.

8
Ngo Dinh Diem's Rejection of a Consultative Conference

Source: Embassy of the Republic of Vietnam, Washington, D.C., Press and Information Service, July 22, 1955, and August 19, 1955.

The National Government has emphasized time and time again the price it has paid for the defense of the unity of the country and of true democracy. We did not sign the Geneva Agreements. We are not bound in any way by these Agreements, signed against the will of the Vietnamese people. Our policy is a policy of peace, but nothing will lead us astray from our goal: the unity of our country—a unity in freedom and not in slavery.

Serving the cause of our nation more than ever, we will struggle for the reunification of our homeland. We do not reject the principle of free elections as peaceful and democratic means to achieve that unity. Although elections constitute one of the bases of true democracy, they will be meaningful only on the condition that they are absolutely free.

Faced now with a regime of oppression as practiced by the Vietminh, we remain skeptical concerning the possibility of fulfilling the conditions of free elections in the North. We shall not miss any opportunity which would permit the unification of our homeland in freedom, but it is out of the question for us to consider any proposal from the Vietminh if proof is not given that they put the superior interests of the national community above those of Communism, if they do not cease violating their obligations as they have done by preventing our countrymen of the North from going South or by recently attacking, together with the Communist Pathet Lao, the friendly state of Laos.

The mission falls to us, the Nationalists, to accomplish the reunification of our country in conditions that are most democratic and most effective to guarantee our independence. The free world is with us. Of this we are certain. I am confident that I am a faithful interpreter of our state of mind when I affirm solemnly our will to resist Communism.

To those who live above the 17th Parallel, I ask them to have confidence. With the agreement and the backing of the free world, the National Government will bring you independence in freedom.

* * *

In a radio broadcast of last July 16, the Government of the State of Vietnam clearly defined its position regarding the problem of territorial reunification.

The Government does not consider itself bound in any way by the Geneva Agreements which it did not sign. It affirms once again that, placing the interests of the nation as its first consideration, it is determined, in any circumstances, to reach the obvious goal of its policy—the unity of the country in peace and freedom.

The Vietminh authorities sent a letter dated July 19 to the Government in which they asked for a pre-election consultation conference, thus, for propaganda purposes, seeking to give credence to the false idea that they would be defenders of territorial unity.

It is recalled that last year at Geneva, the Vietminh claimed a viable economic zone while recommending the partition. At the same time, the delegation of the State of Vietnam proposed an armistice, even though provisional, without partitioning Vietnam in order to safeguard the sacred right of the Vietnamese people to territorial unity, national independence, and freedom. Through the voice of its delegation, the Government affirmed that it hoped to fulfill the aspirations of the Vietnamese people by every means at its disposal resulting from the independence and sovereignty solemnly recognized by France toward the State of Vietnam which is the only legal State.

The policy of the Government remains unchanged toward the partitioning of the country accomplished against its will. Serving the cause of true democracy, the Government is anxious that all Vietnamese throughout the entire country may live without fear and that they be totally free from all dictatorship and oppression. The Government considers the principle of essentially free elections a democratic and peaceful institution, but believes that conditions of freedom of life and of voting must be assured beforehand. From this point of view, nothing constructive will be done as long as the Communist regime of the North does not permit each Vietnamese citizen to enjoy democratic freedoms and the basic fundamental rights of man.

9
How We Got Involved—The Vietnamese and the French

Benjamin Spock and M. Zimmerman

Source: From *Dr. Spock on Vietnam* by Dr. Benjamin Spock and Mitchell Zimmerman (Dell Publishing Co., Inc., 1968), pp. 15–26.

"I went to Vietnam a hard-charging Marine Second Lieutenant, sure I had answered the pleas of a victimized people," a soldier in Vietnam wrote to Senator Fulbright last year.

> That belief lasted about two weeks. Instead of fighting communist aggressors I found that 90 percent of the time our military actions were directed against the people of South Vietnam.
>
> Much has been written about the terror tactics used by the Viet Cong. From my own experience, the terror and havoc we spread makes the VC look like a Girl Scout picnic. We are engaged in a war in Vietnam to pound a people into submission to a government that has little or no popular support.

What is the war really about? Is it really, as the President says, a war against "communist aggression from the North"? Or is the Marine Second Lieutenant right? Perhaps if we can find out how we got into Vietnam in the first place, we can figure out the best way to get out. The place to start is with the struggle of the Vietnamese people for independence from France. At the end of World War II, the British, French, and Dutch empires were swept away.

The colonial peoples raised their voices, their fists, their guns—to insist that they did not want foreigners to rule over them—in British Burma, in India and Pakistan, in the Sudan, in French Morocco, in Dutch Indonesia.

In Vietnam, the people were determined to throw off the rule of the French. Since the 1880s the French had been reaping the profits from Vietnam's rubber and rice, and humiliating the Vietnamese people in order to do so.

"In France I like the French," a Vietnamese who had been to Europe told a visitor then. "They were chic and generous, and we had many friends among them. I have happy memories of Frenchmen in France. But Frenchmen here?" He leaned across the table. "I hate them. We all hate them with a hatred that must be inconceivable to you, for you have not known what it is to live as a slave under a foreign master."

In their 1945 Declaration of Independence, the Vietnamese nationalists cried out:

> They have built more prisons than schools.
>
> They have mercilessly slain our patriots; they have drowned our uprisings in rivers of blood. . . . To weaken our race they have forced us to use opium and alcohol.
>
> They have fleeced us to the backbone, impoverished our people, and devastated our land. They have robbed us of our rice fields, our mines, our forests, and our raw materials.

The Vietnamese people declared their independence from France, much as we declared our independence from England in 1776. Their war of independence was fought by a united front of various political groups and was led by the communist patriot Ho Chi Minh. To some Americans "communist patriot" may sound like a contradiction in terms. Not to the Vietnamese. Ho is simply the man who led their struggle to oust the French. Ho is sometimes called the George Washington of Vietnam. He is a communist, but this is not so important to his people as the fact that he is a Vietnamese.

The Vietnamese fought their French masters for eight years—from 1946 to 1954. It cost the Vietnamese people one million lives.

For the French, too, it was a long and cruel war. Year after year the French generals predicted that victory was just around the corner, and at the same time pleaded for more troops. The French had all the planes and tanks, and their soldiers were better trained and armed. Yet the ragged guerrillas of Ho's "Viet Minh" could not be beaten. ("Viet Minh" was the name of the alliance of various Vietnamese nationalist organizations led by Ho Chi Minh.) The Viet Minh fought harder and more effectively than the French, as men who fight in defense of their homes always do. They fought with the full support of the Vietnamese people. American columnist Joseph Alsop was in a Viet Minh–controlled area of South Vietnam in 1954, and reported:

> It was difficult for me, as it is for any Westerner, to conceive of a communist government's genuinely "serving the people." I could hardly imagine a communist government that was also a popular government and almost a democratic government. But this was just the sort of government the palm hut [Viet Minh] state actually was while the struggle with the French continued. The Viet Minh could not possibly have carried on the resistance for one year, let alone nine years, without the people's strong, united support.

America Supported the French

Though it was the French whom the Vietnamese were fighting, American officials from the Secretary of State down were denouncing the Vietnamese nationalists as aggressors.

Vietnamese soldiers were fighting for the independence of Vietnam in Vietnam against Frenchmen who were six thousand miles from home. The Vietnamese were aggressors only in the sense that the Americans were guilty of aggression in 1776 when they fought the Redcoats.

U.S. support for the French was not limited to moral support. Secretary of State Rusk in 1966 told the Senate Foreign Relations Committee that the United States had given France "approximately $2 billion" in support of the war. The exact figure, according to Senator Hartke of Indiana, was $2.6 billion—80 percent of the cost of the war from 1950 until 1954.

This sheds a new light on the current claim that the United States is committed to preserving the "independence" of the people of Vietnam. When we first got involved in support of the French, it was simply to keep the Vietnamese subjected to France.

President Eisenhower indicated what our real motives were in helping the French in Indochina. (Indochina is the name for the three Southeast Asian countries which were then French colonies—Vietnam, Laos, and Cambodia.) He told the 1953 U.S. Governors Conference:

> Now let us assume that we lost Indochina. . . . The tin and tungsten that we greatly value from that area would cease coming. . . . So when the United States votes 400 million dollars to help that war, we are not voting a give-away program. We are voting for the cheapest way . . . to prevent the occurrence of something that would be of the most terrible significance to the United States

> of America, . . . [the loss of] our power and ability to get certain things we need from the riches of the Indochinese territory and from Southeast Asia.

So we first got involved in Vietnam for the same reasons nations have always interfered in business of other peoples: they had something and we wanted it.

What mainly mattered to our leaders was that the Vietnamese people were led by communists, and we feared that, if they won, our businessmen might not be allowed to get what they wanted from that part of the world.

The Geneva Conference

In May 1954, the Vietnamese nationalists utterly defeated the 15,000-man French force at Dien Bien Phu in one of the major battles of modern history. But the Vietnamese were to lose at the conference table, and afterward, much of what they had won on the battlefield.

Even in 1954 there were men in the United States who wanted to send American boys in to stave off the impending French defeat. Admiral Arthur B. Radford, who was the Chairman of the Joint Chiefs of Staff, Secretary of State John Foster Dulles, and Vice-President Richard M. Nixon were among them. There was even talk of using atomic bombs.

General Matthew B. Ridgway, the Army Chief of Staff, was one of those who advised President Eisenhower against intervening. He wrote in his memoirs in 1956:

> . . . When the day comes for me to face my Maker and account for my actions, the thing I would be most humbly proud of was the fact that I fought against, and perhaps contributed to preventing, the carrying out of some hare-brained tactical schemes which would have cost the lives of thousands of men. To that list of tragic accidents that fortunately never happened I would add the Indochina intervention.

On May 30, 1954, the day after the fortress at Dien Bien Phu fell, a conference of the Great Powers—the United States, England, France, Russia and China—began in Geneva, Switzerland. This conference had been arranged some months before, mainly in hope of settling the Korean War. But the critical situation in Southeast Asia attracted their attention.

After the French defeat, the other Great Powers feared that the United States would intervene, that they, too, might be drawn into the war—and that eventually it might become a World War. So they used their combined influence at Geneva to try to bring about peace in Indochina.

At the time the Geneva Conference began, the Vietminh—Ho Chi Minh's nationalist coalition—controlled about three-quarters of Vietnam, North and South. Yet the Soviet Union and Communist China were so fearful of U.S.

intervention that they were able to persuade the Vietnamese temporarily to give up much of this advantage.

What did the Geneva Agreement provide? There were four main points:

1. Vietnam was to be temporarily divided into two zones (*not* into two countries) at the 17th parallel. (The Agreement emphasized that the line was temporary and "provisional and *should not in any way be interpreted as constituting a political boundary.*") The Vietnamese nationalists and their leader, Ho Chi Minh, were to be responsible for administering the northern zone, and the French, the southern zone, until the country was reunited. (The purpose of this temporary division was to allow the French and the Vietnamese aristocrats who fought on their side to settle their affairs and get out if they wished.)
2. There would be an internationally supervised election, by secret ballot, to reunify the country under whatever government was freely chosen by the Vietnamese people. This election would take place within two years—by the summer of 1956.
3. Until the country was reunited, neither zone would receive any military aid from outside, or make any alliances.
4. The military forces of the two sides were to be separated and be "regrouped." French forces north of the 17th parallel were to move south, and Viet Minh soldiers in the south were to move north. Civilians were to be free to move from one zone to the other.

(One hundred and fifty thousand Viet Minh soldiers and their families moved north, in accordance with this provision. They anticipated only a two-year delay before they could return to their homes in the south of a reunited Vietnam. When, more than five years later, their country was still divided and their fellow southerners had rebelled, many of them would return to their homes in the south—and often to families whom they had left behind. The United States would charge that their return proved that the war in the south was controlled by North Vietnam.)

(At the same time that the 150,000 moved north, nearly 900,000 moved south. Eighty-five percent of them were members of the small Catholic minority—less than ten percent of Vietnamese are Catholic—and they were responding to an intensive propaganda campaign conducted by the United States, whose themes were "Christ has gone to the South," and the "Virgin Mary has departed from the North." The non-Catholics who went with them were Vietnamese who had thrown their lot in with the French, and now feared the Vietnamese nationalists. In other words, very few average North Vietnamese peasants chose to move south.)

If the Geneva Agreement had been respected, we would not be at war today. Vietnam would be a single country at peace, united according to the will of its people as expressed in a free election in 1956.

The U.S. Installs a Puppet

General Walter Bedell Smith, the United States delegate to the final session of the General Conference, read an official American declaration on July 21, 1954, in which the United States promised "it will refrain from the threat or the use of force to disturb" the Agreement. The Declaration seemed to endorse the 1956 reunifying election: "In the case of nations now divided against their will, we shall continue to seek to achieve unity through free elections. . . ."

But in fact our leaders were not willing to risk a free election. President Eisenhower has made it clear in his book *Mandate for Change* that we know what the choice of the Vietnamese people would have been:

> I have never talked or corresponded with a person knowledgeable in Indochinese affairs who did not agree that had elections been held . . . possibly 80 percent of the population would have voted for the Communist Ho Chi Minh as their leader rather than [pro-Western Emperor] Bao Dai.

It was not difficult for our government to see to it that the election did not take place. We swiftly selected a new ruler for South Vietnam. Our choice: Ngo Dinh Diem, a Vietnamese aristocrat who had been living in Ossining, New York. Diem had no following in the land of his birth. His main support came from the United States.

"Secretary of State John Foster Dulles picked him," reported *Look* magazine (January 28, 1964). "Senator Mike Mansfield endorsed him, Francis Cardinal Spellman praised him, Vice-President Richard M. Nixon liked him, and President Dwight D. Eisenhower O.K.'d him."

The rights of the people of South Vietnam—and the promises made to them at Geneva—were ignored.

Our leaders made the decision without consulting us. Most Americans no more knew that we had installed Diem, and were supporting his government, than they knew we had underwritten the cost of the war for the French for the previous four years.

Once our government had decided to establish South Vietnam as an American bastion, it had to violate the key terms of the Geneva Agreement.

The free election promised for July 1956 for the purpose of reunifying Vietnam was canceled by Diem, with the backing of the United States.

Since Diem could only be sure of keeping the South Vietnamese under his control by force, the United States had to supply him with military assistance, again violating the Geneva Agreement.

An impartial International Control Commission, composed of Canadian, Indian, and Polish delegations, was entrusted by the Great Powers with supervising the Geneva Agreement. In 1957—before the civil war broke out—the Commission reported the first violations, the beginning of the illegal U.S.–Saigon military build-up:

> The violations of Articles 16 and 17 mentioned above concern introduction into South Vietnam of United States military aircraft, a few aircraft wheel tires, 1,000 revolvers and 610 cases of revolver ammunition.

We were not aiding an independent country with our guns and ammunition. We were equipping an American Foreign Legion, organized by our man Diem, to hold onto what we regarded as our territory. According to Joseph Buttinger, who was with the International Rescue Committee in Vietnam, Diem himself repeatedly remarked, "that the borders of the United States extend to the 17th parallel," the northern boundary of South Vietnam.

In fact, down to the present day most of the expenses of the South Vietnamese Army—weapons, uniforms, salaries—have been paid for by the United States of America.

That's not the whole story. "Two-thirds of the entire costs of South Vietnam's government is paid by the United States," reported the *New York Times* (November 4, 1957). This is still true. Over the last 14 years, the United States has paid the great majority of even the *non*military expenses of the "South Vietnamese" government.

Despite the scuttling of the Geneva Agreement by the United States and Diem, North Vietnam did not attack South Vietnam. The North Vietnamese were bitter over the U.S.–Diem denial of peaceful reunification, but they were also tired of war, and more interested in rebuilding their country in the North than in liberating the South.

But the South Vietnamese people had reasons of their own to rise up against the U.S.–Diem government.

10
Manifesto of the South Viet Nam National Front for Liberation

Source: South Viet Nam National Front for Liberation, *Documents* (Giai Phong Publishing House, December 1968), pp. 11–18.

Compatriots in the country and abroad!

Over the past hundred years the Vietnamese people repeatedly rose up to fight against foreign aggression for the independence and freedom of their fatherland. In 1945, the people throughout the country surged up in an armed uprising, overthrew the Japanese and French domination, and seized power. When the French colonialists invaded our country for the second time, our compatriots, determined not to be enslaved again, shed much blood and laid down many lives to defend their national sovereignty and independence. Their solidarity and heroic struggle during nine years led the resistance war to victory. The 1954 Geneva Agreements restored peace in our country and recognized "the sovereignty, independence, unity and territorial integrity of Viet Nam."

Our compatriots in South Viet Nam would have been able to live in peace, to earn their livelihood in security and to build a decent and happy life.

However, the American imperialists, who had in the past helped the French colonialists to massacre our people, have now replaced the French in enslaving the southern part of our country through a disguised colonial regime. They have been using their stooge—the Ngo Dinh Diem administration—in their downright repression and exploitation of our compatriots, in their manœuvres to permanently divide our country and to turn its southern part into a military base in preparation for war in Southeast Asia.

The aggressors and traitors, working hand in glove with each other, have set up an extremely cruel dictatorial rule. They persecute and massacre democratic and patriotic people, and abolish all human liberties. They ruthlessly exploit the workers, peasants and other labouring people, strangle the local industry and trade, poison the minds or our people with a depraved foreign culture, thus degrading our national culture, traditions and ethics. They feverishly increase their military forces, build military bases, use the army as an instrument for repressing the people and serving the U.S. imperialists' scheme to prepare an aggressive war.

Never, over the past six years, have gun shots massacring our compatriots ceased to resound throughout South Viet Nam. Tens of thousands of patriots here have been murdered and hundreds of thousands thrown into jail. All sections of the people have been living in a stifling atmosphere under the iron heel of the U.S.-Diem clique. Countless families have been torn away and scenes of mourning are seen everywhere as a result of unemployment, poverty, exacting taxes, terror, massacre, drafting of manpower and pressganging, usurpation of land, forcible house removal, and herding of the people into "prosperity zones," "resettlement centres," and other forms of concentration camps.

High anger with the present tyrannical regime is boiling among all strata of the people. Undaunted in the face of barbarous persecution, our compatriots are determined to unite and struggle unflaggingly against the U.S. imperialists' policy of aggression and the dictatorial and nepotic regime of the Ngo Dinh Diem clique. Among workers, peasants and other toiling people, among intellectuals, students and pupils, industrialists and traders, religious sects and national minorities, patriotic activities are gaining in scope and strength, seriously shaking the U.S.-Diem dictatorial regime.

The attempted coup d'état of November 11, 1960 in Saigon in some respects reflected the seething anger among the people and armymen, and the rottenness and decline of the U.S.-Diem regime. However, there were among the leaders of this coup political speculators who, misusing the patriotism of the armymen, preferred negotiation and compromise rather than to overthrow Ngo Dinh Diem. Like Ngo Dinh Diem, they persisted in following the pro-American and traitorous path, and also used the anti-communist signboard to oppose the people. That is why the coup was not supported by the people and large numbers of armymen and, consequently, ended in failure.

At present, our people are urgently demanding an end to the cruel dictatorial rule; they are demanding independence and democracy, enough food and clothing, and peaceful reunification of the country.

To meet the aspirations of our compatriots, the *South Viet Nam National Front for Liberation* came into being, pledging itself to shoulder the historic task of liberating our people from the present yoke of slavery.

The *South Viet Nam National Front for Liberation* undertakes to unite all sections of the people, all social classes, nationalities, political parties, organizations, religious communities and patriotic personalities, without distinction of their political tendencies, in order to struggle for the overthrow of the rule of the U.S. imperialists and their stooges—the Ngo Dinh Diem clique—and for the realization of independence, democracy, peace and neutrality pending the peaceful reunification of the fatherland.

The *South Viet Nam National Front for Liberation* calls on the entire people to unite and heroically rise up as one man to fight along the line of a program of action summarized as follows:

1. To overthrow the disguised colonial regime of the U.S. imperialists and the dictatorial Ngo Dinh Diem administration—lackey of the United States— and to form a national democratic coalition administration.
2. To bring into being a broad and progressive democracy, promulgate freedom of expression, of the press, of belief, of assembly, of association, of movement and other democratic freedoms. To grant general amnesty to all political detainees, dissolve all concentration camps dubbed "prosperity zones" and "resettlement centres," abolish the fascist 10–59 law and other anti-democratic laws.
3. To abolish the economic monopoly of the United States and its henchmen, to protect home-made products, encourage home industry and trade, expand agriculture and build an independent and sovereign economy. To provide jobs for the unemployed, increase wages for workers, armymen and office employees. To abolish arbitrary fines and apply an equitable and rational tax system. To help those who have gone South to return to their native places if they so desire, and to provide jobs for those among them who want to remain in the South.

4. To carry out land rent reduction, guarantee the peasants' right to till their present plots of land, redistribute communal land and advance toward land reform.
5. To do away with enslaving and depraved U.S.-style culture, build a national and progressive culture and education. To wipe out illiteracy, open more schools, carry out reforms in the educational and examination system.
6. To abolish the system of American military advisers, eliminate foreign military bases in Viet Nam and build a national army for the defense of the fatherland and the people.
7. To guarantee equality between men and women and among different nationalities, and the right to autonomy of the national minorities; to protect the legitimate interests of foreign residents in Viet Nam; to protect and take care of the interests of Vietnamese living abroad.
8. To carry out a foreign policy of peace and neutrality, to establish diplomatic relations with all countries which respect the independence and sovereignty of Viet Nam.
9. To re-establish normal relations between the two zones, pending the peaceful reunification of the fatherland.
10. To oppose aggressive war; to actively defend world peace.

Compatriots!

Ours are a heroic people with a tradition of unity and indomitable struggle. We cannot let our country be plunged into darkness and mourning. We are determined to shatter the fetters of slavery, and wrest back independence and freedom.

Let us all rise up and unite!

Let us close our ranks and fight under the banner of the *South Viet Nam National Front for Liberation* to overthrow the rule of the U.S. imperialists and Ngo Dinh Diem—their henchman.

Workers, peasants and other toiling people! The oppression and misery which are now heavily weighting on you must be ended. You have the strength of tens of millions of people. Stand up enthusiastically to save your families and our fatherland.

Intellectuals! The dictatorial rulers have stripped us of the most elementary human rights. You are living in humiliation and misery. For our great cause, stand up resolutely!

Industrialists and traders! A country under the sway of foreign sharks cannot have an independent and sovereign economy. You should join in the people's struggle.

Compatriots of all national minorities! Compatriots of all religious communities! Unity is life, disunity is death. Smash all U.S.-Diem schemes of division. Side with the entire people in the struggle for independence, freedom and equality among all nationalities.

Notables! The interests of the nation are above all else. Support actively the struggle for the overthrow of the cruel aggressors and traitors.

Patriotic officers and soldiers! You have arms in your hands. Listen to the sacred call of the fatherland. Be definitely on the side of the people. Your compatriots have faith in your patriotism.

Young men and women! You are the future of the nation. You should devote your youthful ardour to serving the fatherland.

Compatriots living abroad! Turn your thoughts toward the beloved fatherland, contribute actively to the sacred struggle for national liberation.

At present the movement for peace, democracy and national independence is surging up throughout the world. Colonialism is irretrievably disintegrating. The time when the imperialists could plunder and subjugate the people at will is over. This situation is extremely favourable for the struggle to free South Viet Nam from the yoke of the U.S. imperialists and their stooges. Peace-loving and progressive people in the world are supporting us. Justice is on our side, and we have the prodigious strength of the unity of our entire people. We will certainly win! The U.S. imperialist aggressors and the Ngo Dinh Diem traitorous clique will certainly be defeated. The cause of liberation of South Viet Nam will certainly triumph.

Compatriots around the country!

Let us unite and march forward confidently and valiantly to score brilliant victories for our people and our fatherland!

Chapter III

The Gulf of Tonkin Incident

The United States never declared war on Vietnam, but the Gulf of Tonkin Resolution (Document 11) was a functional equivalent. In response to reported attacks on American ships by North Vietnam in August 1964 in the Tonkin Gulf (off the coast of North Vietnam), Congress overwhelmingly approved a resolution authorizing President Lyndon Johnson to "take all necessary measures" to prevent further attacks. With the approval of Congress in hand, President Johnson acted quickly. He personally reviewed the targets for bombing North Vietnam and made a television appearance in which he announced the attacks on U.S. ships, assuring the public that "a reply is being given as I speak to you tonight." On the next day, sixty-four sorties against four North Vietnamese targets were flown, and an estimated 25 vessels were destroyed or damaged. Two American airplanes were lost and the pilot of one of those planes, Lt. Everett Alvarez, Jr., of San Jose, California, became the first American prisoner of war. At that time, opinion polls were strongly behind the administration's actions, with 85 percent of the public supporting a military response to North Vietnam.

The United States had been involved in covert actions against North Vietnam since the Geneva Convention of 1954, but these bombing raids were the first American air strikes on the North. Those directing American foreign policy had long been searching for a pretext to introduce American combat troops and air power into the conflict, and the Tonkin Gulf events provided them with the opportunity.

Although rarely talked about today, there were many reasons why direct U.S. intervention in Vietnam was necessary in 1964. After the assassination of Ngo Dinh Diem in November 1963, the stability of the government and army of South Vietnam was precarious. In a period of a few months, regimes came and went in rapid succession. When he visited South Vietnam in 1964, Secretary of Defense Robert McNamara privately worried that the government of South Vietnam might crumble at any moment. Although he issued a statement of confidence intended for public consumption, he alerted the Johnson administration to the fact that without U.S. troops becoming involved in Vietnam, it could easily come to pass that the regime in Saigon would be overrun by the NLF, an event that would cause the United States not only to lose face in the eyes of a watchful world but to lose a strategic ally in the struggle against what was perceived as Soviet expansionism.

It should also be recalled that 1964 was a presidential election year. Lyndon Johnson was seeking election against Barry Goldwater, the Republican nominee who had declared in his acceptance speech at the Republican convention in San Francisco that "extremism in the defense of liberty is no vice." Ironically it was conservatives who sought to limit the powers of the presidency by a strict reading of the Constitution. A decade earlier, Harry Truman, a Democrat, had plunged the United States into the Korean War without authorization from Congress by simply declaring U.S. intervention a police action.

Significantly, the resolution serving as a functional equivalent of a declaration of war against North Vietnam had been prepared many months before the Gulf of Tonkin incidents occurred. As early as March 1, 1964, William Bundy had proposed to the president that a way for the United States to become involved directly in supporting the government of South Vietnam would be a congressional resolution of the kind that President Eisenhower had employed in 1955 when he had used force to defend the islands of Quemoy and Matsu off the shore of China. Bundy was concerned that the extraordinary step of seeking a declaration of war against North Vietnam might spark domestic controversy, and he therefore suggested the kind of resolution that five months later was passed as the Gulf of Tonkin Resolution. Walt Rostow, then head of the State Department's policy planning staff, had proposed a legislative resolution in February, even a month earlier than Bundy.

When he was president, John Kennedy had created the Green Berets to train the South Vietnamese army, but he never approved the bombing of North Vietnam or the use of U.S. ground troops in combat. Shortly after Lyndon Johnson became president following Kennedy's assassination on November 22, 1963, he embarked on a much more ambitious plan for the war which, among other things, immediately offered the navy its first chance for involvement through a program entitled "Desoto Electronic Surveillance." Under the auspices of this program, the destroyer USS *Maddox* was assigned to provide intelligence on North Vietnamese radar installations in the Tonkin Gulf. On August 1, 1964, the ship cruised to within four miles of the islands of Hon Ngu and Hon Me. Two days earlier, South Vietnamese commando boats had bombarded the North Vietnamese radar installations on these islands. The *Maddox* had intercepted North Vietnamese radio transmissions during the attack by the South Vietnamese, thereby providing direct assistance.

On the morning of August 2, the *Maddox* was within ten miles of the Red

River delta in North Vietnam when it came into contact with hundreds of North Vietnamese junks. The captain of the *Maddox* sounded a general quarter's alarm and prepared for hostile action. After he radioed the Seventh Fleet and steered eastward, away from North Vietnam, he watched as three North Vietnamese patrol boats near the island of Hon Me attacked his ship. A *Maddox* crew member, radar man James Stankevitz, described the ensuing combat as "like trying to swat mosquitoes with a big fly swatter." Although one North Vietnamese bullet did manage to hit the *Maddox*, there were no casualties on the American ship. On the other side, two of the patrol boats were left dead in the water and the third was sunk.

President Johnson responded quickly. For the first time he used the "hot line" to send a personal message to Soviet Prime Minister Khrushchev. He warned North Vietnam not to attack U.S. vessels, a warning he reiterated in the first American diplomatic note ever sent to Hanoi. Johnson ordered the *Maddox* back into the area, and another destroyer, the USS *Turner Joy*, was sent to accompany it to "assert the right of freedom of the seas." The two destroyers were ordered within eight miles of North Vietnam's coast and four miles of its islands, although at that time international law clearly stated that there was a twelve-mile territorial limit.

Whether or not a second Tonkin Gulf incident took place is a matter of great historical importance and continuing debate. Although a few people continue to maintain that such an event occurred, there is little if any evidence to that effect. Nonetheless, at the time, President Johnson was told that a second attack *had* occurred and so were the American public and Congress. The Gulf of Tonkin Resolution was quickly and unanimously approved by the House of Representatives. By a vote of 88 to 2, it passed the Senate. Without knowing what the future would bring, Congress had given the president a blank check for military action.

Document 12 is journalist I.F. Stone's article, "International Law and the Tonkin Bay Incidents." In 1964, Stone was one of the few people who perceived the quagmire in which the United States would find itself after the escalation of its military involvement. Hanoi's position that there was never a second incident is provided in Document 13.

The Gulf of Tonkin resolution provided two American presidents with the constitutional authorization to wage an undeclared war against North Vietnam for over six years. It was not until June 24, 1970, after President Richard Nixon had ordered the invasion of Cambodia, that the Senate voted 88 to 10 to rescind the resolution. By then, the country was in the midst of a severe domestic crisis precipitated by the continuation of the war and the tragic killing of six students during antiwar protests at Kent State and Jackson State universities.

11
The Gulf of Tonkin Resolution, August 7, 1964

Source: Department of State Bulletin 51 (August 24, 1964).

To Promote the Maintenance of International Peace and Security in Southeast Asia.

Whereas naval units of the Communist regime in Vietnam, in violation of the principles of the Charter of the United Nations and of international law, have deliberately and repeatedly attacked United States naval vessels lawfully present in international waters, and have thereby created a serious threat to international peace; and

Whereas these attacks are part of a deliberate and systematic campaign of aggression that the Communist regime in North Vietnam has been waging against its neighbors and the nations joined with them in the collective defense of their freedom; and

Whereas the United States is assisting the peoples of southeast Asia to protect their freedom and has no territorial, military or political ambitions in that area, but desires only that these peoples should be left in peace to work out their own destinies in their own way: Now, therefore, be it

Resolved by the Senate and House of Representatives of the United States of America in Congress assembled.

That the Congress approves and supports the determination of the President, as Commander in Chief, to take all necessary measures to prevent further aggression.

SEC. 2. The United States regards as vital to its national interest and to world peace the maintenance of international peace and security in southeast Asia. Consonant with the Constitution of the United States and the Charter of the United Nations and in accordance with its obligations under the Southeast Asia Collective Defense Treaty, the United States is, therefore, prepared, as the President determines, to take all necessary steps, including the use of armed force, to assist any member or protocol state of the Southeast Asia Collective Defense Treaty requesting assistance in defense of its freedom.

SEC. 3. This resolution shall expire when the President shall determine that the peace and security of the area is reasonably assured by international conditions created by action of the United Nations or otherwise, except that it may be terminated earlier by concurrent resolution of the Congress.

12
International Law and the Tonkin Bay Incidents

I. F. Stone

Source: I. F. Stone's Weekly, August 24, 1964.

The American government and the American press have kept the full truth about the Tonkin Bay incidents from the American public. Let us begin with the retaliatory bombing raids on North Viet-Nam. When I went to New York to cover the U.N. Security Council debate on the affair, U.N. correspondents at lunch recalled cynically that four months earlier Adlai Stevenson told the Security Council the U.S. had "repeatedly expressed" its emphatic disapproval "of retaliatory raids, wherever they occur and by whomever they are committed." But none mentioned this in their dispatches.

When Britain Staged Reprisals

On that occasion, last April, the complaint was brought by Yemen against Britain. The British, in retaliation for attacks from Yemen into the British protectorate of Aden, decided to strike at the "privileged sanctuary" from which the raids were coming. The debate then might have been a preview of the Vietnamese affair. The British argued that their reprisal raid was justified because the Fort they attacked at Harib was "a centre for subversive and aggressive activities across the border." The Yemeni Republicans in turn accused the British of supporting raids into Yemen by the Yemeni Royalists. "Obviously," Stevenson said, "it is most difficult to determine precisely what has been happening on the remote frontiers of southern Arabia." But he thought all U.N. members could "join in expressing our disapproval of the use of force by either side as a means of solving disputes, a principle that is enshrined in the Charter," especially when such "attacks across borders" could "quickly escalate into full-scale wars." The outcome was a resolution condemning "reprisals as incompatible with the purposes and principles of the United Nations." That resolution and Stevenson's words are as applicable to Southeast Asia as to southern Arabia. Though the Czech delegate cited them in his speech to the Council on August 7 about the Vietnamese affair, no word to this appeared in the papers next day.

In the August 7 debate, only Nationalist China and Britain supported the U.S. reprisal raids. The French privately recalled the international uproar over the raid they had made under similar circumstances in February, 1958, into the "privileged sanctuary" afforded the Algerian rebels by Tunisia. They struck at the Sakiet-Sidi-Youssef camp just across the border. Senators Kennedy, Humphrey, Morse, and Knowland denounced the raid and Eisenhower warned the French the U.S. would not be able to defend their action in the Security Council.

Reprisals in peacetime were supposed to have been outlawed by the League of Nations Covenant, the Kellogg Pact and the United Nations Charter. All of them pledged peaceful settlement of disputes. Between nations, as between men, reprisals are lynch law. Some White House ghost writer deserves a literary booby prize for the mindless jingle he turned out to defend ours in Viet-Nam. "The world remembers, the world must never forget," were the words he supplied for Johnson's speech at Syracuse, "that aggression unchallenged is aggression unleashed." This gem of prose is a pretty babble. What the world (and particularly the White House) needs to remember is that aggression is unleashed and escalated when one party to a dispute decides for itself who is guilty and how he is to be punished. This is what is happening in Cyprus, where we have been begging Greeks and Turks to desist from the murderous escalation of reprisal and counterreprisal. Johnson practices in southeast Asia what he deplores in the Mediterranean.

More Reprisal Raids Coming?

Public awareness of this is essential because the tide is running strongly toward more reprisal raids in the Far East. The first was the raid by U.S. Navy planes in June on Pathet-Lao headquarters in Laos in retaliation for shooting down two reconnaissance planes. We would not hesitate to shoot down reconnaissance planes over our own territory; such overflights are a clear violation of international law. But the U.S. now seems to operate on the principle that invasion of other people's skies is our right, and efforts to interfere with it (at least by weaker powers) punishable by reprisal. This is pure "might is right" doctrine.

The very day we took the Vietnamese affair to the Security Council, Cambodia illustrated a sardonic point to be found in Schwarzenberger's *Manual of International Law*—"military reprisals are open only to the strong against the weak." The U.N. distributed to Security Council members the latest in a series of complaints from Cambodia that U.S. and South Vietnamese forces had been violating its borders. It alleged that at dawn on July 31 "elements of the armed forces of the Republic of Viet-Nam, among them Americans in uniform," opened fire "with automatic weapons and mortars," seriously wounding a peasant and killing a bull. If Cambodia could only afford a fleet large enough, we suppose it would be justified by Johnsonian standards in lobbing a few shells into the U.S.A.

The Law We Applied at Nuremberg

Even in wartime, reprisals are supposed to be kept within narrow limits. Hackworth's *Digest*, the State Department's huge Talmud of international law, quotes an old War Department manual, *Rules of Land Warfare*, as authoritative on the subject. This says reprisals are never to be taken "merely for revenge" but "only as an unavoidable last resort" to "enforce the recognized rules of civilized warfare." Even the reprisals "should not be excessive or exceed the degree of violence committed by the enemy." These were the principles we applied at the Nuremberg trials. Our reprisal raids on North Viet-Nam hardly conformed to these standards. By our own account, in self-defense, we had already sunk three or four attacking torpedo boats in two incidents. In neither were our ships damaged nor any of our men hurt; indeed, one bullet embedded in one destroyer hull is the only proof we have been able to muster that the second of the attacks even took place. To fly sixty-four bombing sorties in reprisal over four North Vietnamese bases and an oil depot, destroying or damaging twenty-five North Vietnamese PT boats, a major part of that tiny navy, was hardly punishment to fit the crime. What was our hurry? Why did we have to shoot from the hip and then go to the Security Council? Who was Johnson trying to impress? Ho Chi Minh? Or Barry Goldwater?

This is how it looks on the basis of our own public accounts. It looks worse if one probes behind them. Here we come to the questions raised by Morse of Oregon on the Senate floor August 5 and 6 during debate on the resolution giving Johnson a predated declaration of war in Southeast Asia. Morse was speaking on the basis of information given in executive session by Secretaries Rusk and McNamara to a joint session of the Senate Committee on Foreign Relations and Armed Services. Morse said he was not justifying the attacks on U.S. ships in the Bay of Tonkin but "as in domestic criminal law," he added, "crimes are sometimes committed under provocation" and this "is taken into account by a wise judge in imposing sentence."

Morse revealed that U.S. warships were on patrol in Tonkin Bay nearby during the shelling of two islands off the North Vietnamese coast on Friday, July 31, by South Vietnamese vessels. Morse said our warships were within three to eleven miles of North Vietnamese territory, at the time, although North Viet-

Nam claims a twelve-mile limit. Morse declared that the U.S. "knew that the bombing was going to take place." He noted that General Khanh had been demanding escalation of the war to the North and said that with this shelling of the islands it was escalated. Morse declared the attack was made "by South Vietnamese naval vessels—not by junks but by armed vessels of the PT boat type" given to South Viet-Nam as part of U.S. military aid. Morse said it was not just another attempt to infiltrate agents but "a well-thought-out military operation." Morse charged that the presence of our warships in the proximity "where they could have given protection, if it became necessary" was "bound to be looked upon by our enemies as an act of provocation." The press, which dropped an Iron Curtain weeks ago on the antiwar speeches of Morse and Gruening, ignored this one, too.

Yet a reading of the debate will show that Fulbright and Russell, the chairmen of the two committees Rusk and McNamara had briefed in secret session, did not deny Morse's facts in their defense of the Administration and did not meet the issue he raised. Fulbright's replies to questions were hardly a model of frankness. When Ellender of Louisiana asked him at whose request we were patrolling in the Bay of Tonkin, Fulbright replied:

> These are international waters. Our assistance to South Viet-Nam is at the request of the South Vietnamese government. The particular measures we may take in connection with that request is our own responsibility.

Senator Nelson of Wisconsin wanted to know how close to the shore our ships had been patrolling:

> MR. FULBRIGHT: It was testified that they went in at least eleven miles in order to show that we do not recognize a twelve-mile limit, which I believe North Viet-Nam has asserted.
>
> MR. NELSON: The patrolling was for the purpose of demonstrating to the North Vietnamese that we did not recognize a twelve-mile limit?
>
> MR. FULBRIGHT: That was one reason given. . . .
>
> MR. NELSON: It would be mighty risky if Cuban PT boats were firing on Florida, for Russian armed ships or destroyers to be patrolling between us and Cuba, eleven miles out.

When Ellender asked whether our warships were there to protect the South Vietnamese vessels shelling the islands, Fulbright replied:

> The ships were not assigned to protect anyone. They were conducting patrol duty. The question was asked specifically of the highest authority, the Secretary of Defense and the Secretary of State. They stated without equivocation that these ships, the *Maddox* and the *C. Turner Joy*, were not on convoy duty. They had no connection whatever with any Vietnamese ships that might have been operating in the same general area.

Fulbright did not deny that both destroyers were in the area at the time of the July 31 shelling and inside the territorial limits claimed by North Viet-Nam. He did not deny Morse's charge that the U.S. knew about the shelling of the islands before it took place. He merely denied that the warships were there to cover the operation in any way. Our warships, according to the official account, just happened to be hanging around. Morse's point—which neither Fulbright nor Russell challenged—was that they had no business to be in an area where an attack was about to take place, that this was bound to appear provocative. Indeed the only rational explanation for their presence at the time was that the Navy was looking for trouble, daring the North Vietnamese to do something about it.

Why Our Ships Moved Out to Sea

Morse made another disclosure. "I think I violate no privilege or secrecy," he declared, "if I say that subsequent to the bombing, and apparently because there was some concern about the intelligence that we were getting, our ships took out to sea." Was this intelligence that the ships were about to be attacked within the territorial waters claimed by North Viet-Nam? Morse said our warships went out to sea and "finally, on Sunday, the PT boats were close enough for the first engagement to take place." This dovetails with a curious answer given by Senator Russell at another point in the debate to Senator Scott of Pennsylvania when the latter asked whether Communist China had not published a series of warnings (as required by international law) against violations of the twelve-mile limit. Russell confirmed this but said, "I might add that our vessels had turned away from the North Vietnamese shore and were making for the middle of the gulf, *where there could be no question*, at the time they were attacked."

The italics are ours and call attention to an evident uneasiness about our legal position. The uneasiness is justified. A great many questions of international law are raised by the presence of our warships within an area claimed by another country as its territorial waters while its shores were being shelled by ships we supplied to a satellite power. There is, first of all, some doubt as to whether warships have a right of "innocent passage" through territorial waters even under peaceful circumstances. There is, secondly, the whole question of territorial limits. The three-mile limit was set some centuries ago by the range of a cannon shot. It has long been obsolete but is favored by nations with large navies. We make the three-mile limit the norm when it suits our purposes but widen it when we need to. We claim another nine miles as "contiguous waters" in which we can enforce our laws on foreign ships. While our planes on reconnaissance operate three miles off other people's shores, we enforce an Air Defense Identification Zone on our own coasts, requiring all planes to identify themselves when two hours out. In any case, defense actions may be taken beyond territorial limits. The law as cited in the U.S. Naval Academy's handbook, *International*

Law for Sea-Going Officers, is that "the right of a nation to protect itself from injury" is "not restrained to territorial limits. . . . It may watch its coast and seize ships that are approaching it with an intention to violate its laws. It is not obliged to wait until the offense is consummated before it can act."

If the Cubans Shelled Key West

More important in this case is the doctrine of "hot pursuit." The North Vietnamese radio claims that in the first attack it chased the U.S. warships away from its shores. "The right of hot pursuit," says Schwarzenberger's *Manual of International Law*, "is the right to continue the pursuit of a ship from the territorial sea into the high sea." The logic of this, our Naval Academy handbook explains, is that "the offender should not go free simply because of the proximity of the high seas." It is easy to imagine how fully these questions would be aired if we spotted Russian ships hanging around in our waters while Cuban PT boats shelled Key West. Our actions hardly fit Johnson's description of himself to the American Bar Association as a champion of world law.

There are reasons to believe that the raids at the end of July marked a new step-up in the scale of South Vietnamese operations against the North. These have been going on for some time. In fact, a detailed account in *Le Monde* (August 7) says they began three years before the rebellion broke out in South Viet-Nam. Ever since January of this year the U.S. press has been full of reports that we were planning to move from infiltration and commando operations to overt attacks against the North. *Newsweek* (March 9) discussed a "Rostow Plan No. 6" for a naval blockade of Haiphong, North Viet-Nam's main port, to be followed by PT boat raids on North Vietnamese coastal installations and then by strategic bombing raids. In the middle of July the North Vietnamese radio reported that the U.S. had given South Viet-Nam five hundred "river landing ships" and four small warships from our mine-sweeping fleet. A dispatch from Hong Kong in the *New York Times* (August 14) quoted an "informed source" as saying that the North Vietnamese had concealed the fact "that the shelling of the islands" on July 31 "had been directed at a sensitive radar installation." The shelling of radar installations would look from the other side like a prelude to a landing attempt.

How the Public Is Brain-Washed

These circumstances cast a very different light on the *Maddox* affair, but very few Americans are aware of them. The process of brain-washing the public starts with off-the-record briefings for newspapermen in which all sorts of far-fetched theories are suggested to explain why the tiny North Vietnamese navy would be mad enough to venture an attack on the Seventh fleet, one of the world's most powerful. Everything is discussed except the possibility that the attack might have been provoked. In this case the "information agencies," i.e., the propaganda apparatus of the government, handed out two versions, one for domestic, the other for foreign consumption. The image created at home was that the U.S. had manfully hit back at an unprovoked attack—no paper tiger we. On the other hand, friendly foreign diplomats were told that the South Vietnamese had pulled a raid on the coast and we had been forced to back them up. As some of the truth began to trickle out, the information agencies fell back on the theory that maybe the North Vietnamese had "miscalculated." That our warships may have been providing cover for an escalation in raiding activities never got through to public consciousness at all.

The two attacks themselves are still shrouded in mystery. The *Maddox* claims to have fired three warning shots across the bow of her pursuers; three warning shots are used to make a merchantman heave-to for inspection. A warship would take this as the opening of fire, not as a warning signal. The North Vietnamese radio admitted the first encounter but claimed its patrol boats chased the *Maddox* out of territorial waters. The second alleged attack North Viet-Nam calls a fabrication. It is strange that though we claim three boats sunk, we picked up no flotsam and jetsam as proof from the wreckage. Nor have any pictures been provided. Whatever the true story, the second incident seems to have triggered off a long-planned attack of our own. There are some reasons to doubt that it was merely that "measured response" against PT bases it was advertised to be. Bernard Fall, author of *The Two Viet-Nams*, who knows the area well, pointed out in the Washington *Post* August 9 that "none of the targets attacked" in the reprisal raids "was previously known as a regular port or base area. Hon-Gay, for example, was one of the largest open-pit coal mining operations in Asia, if not the world." Was this one of the strategic industrial targets in Rostow's "Plan No. 6"?

13
Hanoi's Statement on "Tonkin Gulf Incident," September 1964

Source: The Pentagon's Secrets and Half-Secrets (Hanoi, 1971), pp. 90–96 (excerpt).

On August 4, President L. Johnson summoned two meetings of the National Security Council, conferred with his Cabinet and General Earle Wheeler, Chairman of the Joint Chiefs of Staff, and then with Congressional leaders of both the

Democratic and Republican parties.

At 18:00 (local time), US Assistant Defense Secretary Arthur Sylvester issued to the press an announcement which read in part:

> A second deliberate attack was made during darkness by an undetermined number of North Vietnamese PT-boats on the USS *Maddox* and the USS *Turner Joy* while the two destroyers were cruising in company on routine patrol in the Tonkin gulf international waters about 65 miles from the nearest land. The attack came at 10:30 P.M. local time (10:30 A.M. August 4, Washington time, or 14:30 GMT).
>
> At 23:40 (local time), President L. Johnson announced to the American people: "The initial attack on the destroyer *Maddox*, on August 2, was repeated today by a number of hostile vessels attacking two US destroyers with torpedoes."

At about midnight, Defense Secretary McNamara affirmed in a press conference in Washington that these were "North Vietnamese surface vessels." The truth was totally different from the contentions made by the US President and the US Defense Secretary in their solemn statements to the American people and the world.

First and foremost, this is an impudent fabrication in as much as in the day and night of August 4, 1964, no naval craft of the Democratic Republic of Viet Nam was present in the area where the US destroyers were allegedly "attacked for a second time by North Vietnamese PT-boats."

The alleged "attack" was deliberately staged by the United States to have a pretext for carrying out its criminal designs against the Democratic Republic of Viet Nam.

According to reports from various sources, a task group of the Seventh Fleet including the aircraft-carrier Ticonderoga and the destroyers Berkeley, Edison, Harry Hubbard, and Samuel More, was cruising on a permanent basis in the South China Sea off Da Nang.

On August 4, 1964, the Harry Hubbard met with the HQ. 609 and HQ. 11 of the South Viet Nam Navy 60 kilometres off Da Nang. Thereafter, the South Vietnamese ships did not return to their base Tien Sa (Da Nang) as usual. On the same night, from 20:00 to 22:00 at about the time when "North Vietnamese PT-boards" allegedly "attacked the *Maddox* and the *Turner Joy*" gun shelling was heard, and flares and planes were seen off the shores of the Democratic Republic of Viet Nam on international waters.

That is what the Pentagon termed "the second deliberate attack" on the destroyers *Maddox* and *Turner Joy* or "the second Tonkin Gulf incident."

Chapter IV

The American Buildup

While it was not until 1965 that U.S. ground forces went into combat in Vietnam, the presence of uniformed Americans goes back ten years further. The Geneva Agreements of 1954 had set a limit on American troops at 685, a modest number, but one that allowed the United States to establish a presence in southern Vietnam. By 1962, there were at least 12,000 American advisers in Vietnam as President Kennedy's Green Berets were beefed up, and at the end of 1964 there were nearly twice that many.

Although these numbers appear large when compared to the Geneva limit of 685, they are minuscule considering subsequent deployments. Once the United States began bombing North Vietnam after the Tonkin Gulf incidents in 1964, American airfields in the South came under attack by the NLF. In February 1965, Gen. William Westmoreland requested two marine battalions to protect the American airfield near Danang, and on March 8, 1965, the buildup of U.S. ground forces began when 3,500 marines landed. The Pentagon assured the American public that the government of South Vietnam had requested the troops, but that regime had not even been consulted in advance. It appears that President Johnson's decision to deploy the marines was not part of a master plan for a massive buildup but merely a response to the immediate need to defend American airfields. As these newly introduced American troops came under attack, even more troops had to be sent in. Johnson tried to keep the new deployments out of public view by avoiding elaborate press briefings and only gradually introducing more troops, and at least in the beginning he was successful. As U.S. casualties mounted, however, his decision to intervene massively destroyed his presidency.

In recent years, a flurry of evidence has emerged that points to another reason why American troops were needed in 1965: it appears that the Saigon government and army were on the verge of collapse and that the NLF was going to win the war outright, an outcome judged totally unacceptable by President Johnson.

In November 1963, Ngo Dinh Diem had been killed by his own generals with the tacit approval of the United States, and in the ensuing months, none of the new governments in Saigon had been able to consolidate power. During a single week in August 1964, there were three new governments. By January 1965, there had been seven different regimes, and by the middle of that year, the number of changes of government after Diem's murder stood at thirteen.

On the other side, the NLF was stronger than ever. Analyst Douglas Pike, the U.S. government's foremost expert on the guerrillas, believes the NLF almost won the war as early as 1963, even before Diem was overthrown. In 1964, the guerrillas had stepped up their attacks, destroying six B-57 jets and damaging twenty other planes at Bienhoa airbase twelve miles from Saigon. They even brought the war into South Vietnam's capital, when they bombed the Brinks Hotel (a favorite among American officers) on Christmas Eve. On February 7, 1965, the American airbase at Pleiku in the central highlands was heavily damaged, and 8 Americans were killed and 126 wounded. Three days later, an attack on the U.S. barracks at Qui Nhom left 19 dead and 13 wounded. On May 11, more than 1,000 guerrillas overran a provincial capital fifty miles from Saigon, while in central Vietnam, two ARVN units (Army of the Republic of Vietnam) were decimated.

By the middle of June, all of the ARVN's best units had been scattered, and the government fell once again. The armed forces installed Nguyen Van Thieu as the new chief of state. Although he was able to stabilize the regime and run South Vietnam until its collapse in 1975, it required tens of thousands of American troops to prevent an immediate NLF victory. At the time, General Westmoreland estimated that he needed 180,000 troops right away since "the South Vietnamese armed forces can't stand up to this pressure without substantial U.S. combat support on the ground."

Westmoreland's request was quickly fulfilled, and by the end of the next year, as the ground war intensified, the number of U.S. troops stood at 400,000. In 1967, their number passed the half a million mark, and by the high point of the ground war in 1968, more than 540,000 U.S. servicepeople were in Vietnam. The actual number of U.S. troops involved in the war was even higher since the more than 55,000 troops of the Seventh Fleet, whose aircraft carriers and ships off the coast launched daily attacks, would have to be counted as would thousands more in Thailand (where the U.S. had some of its largest airbases), the Philippines, Taiwan, Guam, Okinawa, and Japan (medical facilities). Figuring all these troops into the U.S. effort brings their total number to over 800,000. Additionally, if the ARVN, South Korean, Thai, Australian, and New Zealand troops are included, the total allied forces numbered at least 1,593,000.

Officially, the U.S. government's justification for the presence of allied troops was to defend South Vietnam from an attack by the North, a position presented in this chapter with an excerpt from the State Department's White

Paper, "Aggression from the North" (Document 14). The problem with the government's rationale can be gleaned from its own data. Comparing the number of infiltrators from the North with the number of U.S. troops in Vietnam reveals an interesting fact: throughout the 1960s, there were more Americans than North Vietnamese in South Vietnam. Ironically, at the same time that U.S. intelligence first identified North Vietnamese troops in South Vietnam, there were even more South Korean troops there fighting on the American side!

Moreover, when journalist I.F. Stone investigated the numbers reported in the State Department's White Paper, he found that of the twenty-three specific names of people the State Department could identify as having infiltrated from North to South Vietnam, seventeen had been born in southern Vietnam. According to the American government's own analysis of infiltrators, the majority of those it could identify were actually southerners who had gone north in 1954 because of their affiliation with the Vietminh. These men were simply returning to their homes and families, something they had originally expected to do within two years (since national elections were supposed to be held in 1956). Similarly, of the 179 captured weapons that the State Department put on display as indicating a Communist invasion, only 2 percent of them were found to have come from North Vietnam. The vast majority of those weapons had been captured in the South during either the French or American phases of the war or had been manufactured in the areas of South Vietnam controlled by the NLF. Even as late as 1966, the Pentagon portrayed the guerrillas as self-sufficient, able to collect taxes and receiving 80 to 90 percent of their supplies locally.

The NLF responded to the increasing number of American troops by stepping up their attacks. Document 15 is their response to the White Paper. Although Diem's strategic hamlet program had uprooted 85 percent of the rural population, after his murder the hamlets were completely destroyed. According to American estimates, by the beginning of 1965, about two-thirds of the population and four-fifths of the territory were under solid NLF control. This meant Washington had to either make peace or escalate the war.

Part of the reason the latter option was chosen can be found in Document 16, Secretary of State Dean Rusk's speech equating wars of national liberation with Communist intervention. Rusk doubly condemned the NLF—both as agents of Hanoi and as tied to Moscow. While the argument he made was based upon the evidence contained in the White Paper, he also put forth the idea that "vital national interests of the United States" were at stake. In the final chapter of this anthology, Professor Hans Morgenthau's discussion of American national interest (Document 46) rebuts both Rusk's claim and the State Department's White Paper.

The last document in this chapter, a letter from Ho Chi Minh to the American people, like his numerous letters to American presidents, never received much publicity in the United States. It expresses faith in the desire of people for peace and a belief that justice would ultimately prevail. His optimism propelled the Vietnamese patriotic movement against the Japanese, the French, and the United States. As the American war intensified, many people in the United States were also persuaded by his quiet insistence on the need for Vietnamese independence.

14
Aggression from the North

U.S. Department of State White Paper

Source: Excerpts from Department of State Publication 7839, released February 1965.

Hanoi Supplies the Key Personnel for the Armed Aggression Against South Viet-Nam

The hard core of the Communist forces attacking South Viet-Nam are men trained in North Viet-Nam. They are ordered into the South and remain under the military discipline of the Military High Command in Hanoi. Special training camps operated by the North Vietnamese army give political and military training to the infiltrators. Increasingly the forces sent into the South are native North Vietnamese who have never seen South Viet-Nam. A special infiltration unit, the 70th Transportation Group, is responsible for moving men from North Viet-Nam into the South via infiltration trails through Laos. Another special unit, the maritime infiltration group, sends weapons and supplies and agents by sea into the South.

The infiltration rate has been increasing. From 1959 to 1960, when Hanoi was establishing its infiltration pipeline, at least 1,800 men, and possibly 2,700 more, moved into South Viet-Nam from the North. The flow increased to a minimum of 3,700 in 1961 and at least 5,400 in 1962. There was a modest decrease in 1963 to 4,200 confirmed infiltrators, though later evidence is likely to raise this figure.

For 1964 the evidence is still incomplete. However, it already shows that a minimum of 4,400 infiltrators entered the South, and it is estimated more than 3,000 others were sent in.

There is usually a time lag between the entry of infiltrating troops and the discovery of clear evidence they have entered. This fact, plus collateral evidence of increased use of the infiltration routes, suggests strongly that 1964 was probably the year of greatest infiltration so far.

Thus, since 1959, nearly 20,000 VC officers, soldiers, and technicians are known to have entered South Viet-Nam under orders from Hanoi. Additional information indicates that an estimated 17,000 more infiltrators were dispatched to the South by the regime in Hanoi during the past six years. It can reasonably be assumed that still other infiltration groups have entered the South for which there is no evidence yet available.

To some the level of infiltration from the North may seem modest in comparison with the total size of the Armed Forces of the Republic of Viet-Nam. But one-for-one calculations are totally misleading in the kind of warfare going on in Viet-Nam. First, a high proportion of infiltrators from the North are well-trained officers, cadres, and specialists. Second, it has long been realized that in guerrilla combat the burdens of defense are vastly heavier than those of attack. In Malaya, the Philippines, and elsewhere a ratio of at least 10-to-1 in favor of the forces of order was required to meet successfully the threat of the guerrillas' hit-and-run tactics.

In the calculus of guerrilla warfare the scale of North Vietnamese infiltration into the South takes on a very different meaning. For the infiltration of 5,000 guerrilla fighters in a given year is the equivalent of marching perhaps 50,000 regular troops, across the border, in terms of the burden placed on the defenders.

Above all, the number of proved and probable infiltrators from the North should be seen in relation to the size of the VC forces. It is now estimated that the Viet-Cong number approximately 35,000 so-called hard-core forces, and another 60,000–80,000 local forces. It is thus apparent that infiltrators from the North—allowing for casualties—make up the majority of the so-called hard-core Viet-Cong. Personnel from the North, in short, are now and have always been the backbone of the entire VC operation.

It is true that many of the lower-level elements of the VC forces are recruited within South Viet-Nam. However, the thousands of reported cases of VC kidnapings and terrorism make it abundantly clear that threats and other pressures by the Viet-Cong play a major part in such recruitment.

Hanoi Supplies Weapons, Ammunition, and Other War Matériel to Its Forces in the South

When Hanoi launched the VC campaign of terror, violence, and subversion in earnest in 1959, the Communist forces relied mainly on stocks of weapons and ammunition left over from the war against the French. Supplies sent in from North Viet-Nam came largely from the same source. As the military campaign progressed, the Viet-Cong depended heavily on weapons captured from the Armed Forces in South Viet-Nam. This remains an important source of weapons and ammunition for the Viet-Cong. But as the pace of the war has quickened, requirements for up-to-date arms and special types of weapons have risen to a point where the Viet-Cong cannot rely on captured stocks. Hanoi has undertaken a program to re-equip its forces in the South with Communist-produced weapons.

Large and increasing quantities of military supplies are entering South Viet-

Nam from outside the country. The principal supply point is North Viet-Nam, which provides a convenient channel for matériel that originates in Communist China and other Communist countries.

An increasing number of weapons from external Communist sources have been seized in the South. These include such weapons as 57 mm. and 75 mm. recoilless rifles, dual-purpose machineguns, rocket launchers, large mortars, and antitank mines.

A new group of Chinese Communist-manufactured weapons has recently appeared in VC hands. These include the 7.62 semiautomatic carbine, 7.62 light machinegun, and the 7.62 assault rifle. These weapons and ammunition for them, manufactured in Communist China in 1962, were first captured in December, 1964, in Chuong Thien Province. Similar weapons have since been seized in each of the four Corps areas of South Viet-Nam. Also captured have been Chinese Communist antitank grenade launchers and ammunition made in China in 1963.

One captured Viet-Cong told his captors that his entire company had been supplied recently with modern Chinese weapons. The re-equipping of VC units with a type of weapons that require ammunition and parts from outside South Viet-Nam indicates the growing confidence of the authorities in Hanoi in the effectiveness of their supply lines into the South.

Incontrovertible evidence of Hanoi's elaborate program to supply its forces in the South with weapons, ammunition, and other supplies has accumulated over the years. Dramatic new proof was exposed just as this report was being completed.

On February 16, 1965, an American helicopter pilot flying along the South Vietnamese coast sighted a suspicious vessel. It was a cargo ship of an estimated 100-ton capacity, carefully camouflaged and moored just offshore along the coast of Phu Yen Province. Fighter planes that approached the vessel met machinegun fire from guns on the deck of the ship and from the shore as well. A Vietnamese Air Force strike was launched against the vessel, and Vietnamese Government troops moved into the area. They seized the ship after a bitter fight with the Viet-Cong.

The ship, which had been sunk in shallow water, had discharged a huge cargo of arms, ammunition, and other supplies. Documents found on the ship and on the bodies of several Viet-Cong aboard identified the vessel as having come from North Viet-Nam. A newspaper in the cabin was from Haiphong and was dated January 23, 1965. The supplies delivered by the ship—thousands of weapons and more than a million rounds of ammunition—were almost all of Communist origin, largely from Communist China and Czechoslovakia, as well as North Viet-Nam. At least 100 tons of military supplies were discovered near the ship.

A preliminary survey of the cache near the sunken vessel from Hanoi listed the following supplies and weapons:

- approximately 1 million rounds of small-arms ammunition;
- more than 1,000 stick grenades;
- 500 pounds of TNT in prepared charges;
- 2,000 rounds of 82 mm mortar ammunition;
- 500 antitank grenades;
- 500 rounds of 57 mm recoilless rifle ammunition;
- more than 1,000 rounds of 75 mm recoilless rifle ammunition;
- one 57 mm recoilless rifle;
- 2 heavy machineguns;
- 2,000 7.95 Mauser rifles;
- more than 100 7.62 carbines;
- 1,000 submachineguns;
- 15 light machineguns;
- 500 rifles;
- 500 pounds of medical supplies (with labels from North Viet-Nam, Communist China, Czechoslovakia, East Germany, Soviet Union, and other sources). . . .

North Viet-Nam: Base for Conquest of the South

The Third Lao Dong Party Congress in Hanoi in September, 1960, set forth two tasks for its members: "to carry out the socialist revolution in North Viet-Nam" and "to liberate South Viet-Nam."

The resolutions of the congress described the effort to destroy the legal Government in South Viet-Nam as follows: "The revolution in the South is a protracted, hard, and complex process of struggle, combining many forms of struggle of great activity and flexibility, ranging from low to higher, and taking as its basis the building, consolidation, and development of the revolutionary power of the masses."

At the September meeting the Communist leaders in the North called for formation of "a broad national united front." Three months later Hanoi announced creation of the "Front for Liberation of the South." This is the organization that Communist propaganda now credits with guiding the forces of subversion in the South; it is pictured as an organization established and run by the people in the South themselves. At the 1960 Lao Dong Party Congress the tone was different. Then, even before the front existed, the Communist leaders were issuing orders for the group that was being organized behind the scenes in Hanoi. "This front must rally . . ."; "The aims of its struggle are . . ."; "The front must carry out . . ."—this is the way Hanoi and the Communist Party addressed the "Liberation Front" even before its founding.

The Liberation Front is Hanoi's creation; it is neither independent nor southern, and what it seeks is not liberation but subjugation of the South. . . .

Organization, Direction, Command, and Control of the Attack on South Viet-Nam Are Centered in Hanoi

The VC military and political apparatus in South Viet-Nam is an extension of an elaborate military and political structure in North Viet-Nam which directs and supplies it with the tools for conquest. The Ho Chi Minh regime has shown that it is ready to allocate every resource that can be spared—whether it be personnel, funds, or equipment—to the cause of overthrowing the legitimate Government in South Viet-Nam and of bringing all Viet-Nam under Communist rule.

Political Organization

Political direction and control of the Viet-Cong is supplied by the Lao Dong Party, i.e., the Communist Party, led by Ho Chi Minh. Party agents are responsible for indoctrination, recruitment, political training, propaganda, anti-Government demonstrations, and other activities of a political nature. The considerable intelligence-gathering facilities of the party are also at the disposal of the Viet-Cong.

Over-all direction of the VC movement is the responsibility of the Central Committee of the Lao Dong Party. Within the Central Committee a special Reunification Department has been established. This has replaced the "Committee for Supervision of the South" mentioned in intelligence reports two years ago. It lays down broad strategy for the movement to conquer South Viet-Nam.

Until March, 1962, there were two principal administrative divisions in the VC structure in the South. One was the Interzone of South-Central Viet-Nam (sometimes called Interzone 5); the other was the Nambo Region. In a 1962 reorganization these were merged into one, called the Central Office for South Viet-Nam. The Central Committee, through its Reunification Department, issues directives to the Central Office, which translates them into specific orders for the appropriate subordinate command.

Under the Central Office are six regional units (V through IX) plus the special zone of Saigon/Cholon/Gia Dinh. A regional committee responsible to the Central Office directs VC activities in each region. Each regional committee has specialized units responsible for liaison, propaganda, training, personnel, subversive activities, espionage, military bases, and the like.

Below each regional committee are similarly structured units at the province and district levels. At the base of the Communist pyramid are the individual party cells, which may be organized on a geographic base or within social or occupational groups. The elaborateness of the party unit and the extent to which it operates openly or underground is determined mainly by the extent of VC control over the area concerned. . . .

Conclusion

The evidence presented in this report could be multiplied many times with similar examples of the drive of the Hanoi regime to extend its rule over South Viet-Nam.

The record is conclusive. It establishes beyond question that North Viet-Nam is carrying out a carefully conceived plan of aggression against the South. It shows that North Viet-Nam has intensified its efforts in the years since it was condemned by the International Control Commission. It proves that Hanoi continues to press its systematic program of armed aggression into South Viet-Nam. This aggression violates the United Nations Charter. It is directly contrary to the Geneva Accords of 1954 and of 1962 to which North Viet-Nam is a party. It shatters the peace of Southeast Asia. It is a fundamental threat to the freedom and security of South Viet-Nam.

The people of South Viet-Nam have chosen to resist this threat. At their request, the United States has taken its place beside them in their defensive struggle.

The United States seeks no territory, no military bases, no favored position. But we have learned the meaning of aggression elsewhere in the postwar world, and we have met it.

If peace can be restored in South Viet-Nam, the United States will be ready at once to reduce its military involvement. But it will not abandon friends who want to remain free. It will do what must be done to help them. The choice now between peace and continued and increasingly destructive conflict is one for the authorities in Hanoi to make.

15
Statement of the South Viet Nam N.F.L. Central Committee Concerning the Intensification and Expansion of the U.S. Imperialists' Aggressive War in South Viet Nam

Source: South Viet Nam National Front for Liberation, *Documents* (Giai Phong Publishing House, December 1968), pp. 33–52 (excerpts).

For more than ten years now, the U.S. imperialists have continuously interfered in South Viet Nam and committed aggression against it. Of late, they brought into South Viet Nam many more U.S. combat units, composed of missile and marine units and B.52 strategic bombers, as well as mercenary troops from South Korea, Taiwan, the Philippines, Australia, Malaya, etc. They even ordered their air force and that of their henchmen to conduct repeated bombings against North Viet Nam and Laos. At present, they are not only stubbornly prosecuting their criminal aggressive war in South Viet Nam but also attempting to fan the flames of war throughout Indochina and Southeast Asia.

Clearly, the puppet administration in South Viet Nam, close upon the Americans' heels, is daily committing more monstrous crimes against the fatherland. These impudent traitors are bending their knees before the aggressors and "bringing in snakes to kill chickens of the home coop," inviting troops of the United States and many of its satellites into South Viet Nam to massacre their own compatriots, occupy and trample upon our sacred territory and most harshly oppress and exploit our people.

The Vietnamese people, the peoples of Indochina and Southeast Asia, and peace- and justice-loving people all over the world are highly indignant at and strongly protesting against, the criminal acts of the U.S. imperialists.

Facing this situation of utmost gravity, the South Viet Nam National Front for Liberation deems it necessary to reaffirm once again its firm and unswerving stand to carry out the war of resistance against the U.S. imperialists for national salvation.

1. *The U.S. Imperialists are the Saboteur of the Geneva Agreements, the Most Brazen Warmonger and Aggressor, and the Sworn Enemy of the Vietnamese People.*

As is known to everyone, the glorious resistance of the Vietnamese people defeated the aggressive war of the French colonialists in spite of the intervention and assistance of the U.S. imperialists. True, during this protracted resistance, the U.S. imperialists supplied to the French colonialists 2,600 million dollars, hundreds of thousands of tons of armaments, and 200 military advisers in order to strangle the aspirations for independence and freedom of the Vietnamese people. However, prompted by their indomitability and their determination to die rather than be enslaved, their courage and their strong resolve to fight, and enjoying the wholehearted support of the people around the world, the heroic Vietnamese people have won great victories, and liberated half of their beloved country from the clutches of the enemy; this led to the conclusion of international agreements in Geneva in 1954 which solemnly recognized the sovereignty, independence and territorial integrity of Viet Nam, Laos and Cambodia, restored peace in this area and laid the basis for the reunification of Viet Nam by peaceful means.

The Vietnamese people deeply understand the value of these agreements. Now as in the past, they are correctly implementing them and are resolved to make them implemented with due respect to the spirit and letter of a thoroughly legal international accord. On the other hand, the U.S. imperialists and their henchmen in South Viet Nam have, step by step and more brazenly with every passing day, trampled on the Geneva Agreements and have in fact scrapped them by openly waging an atrocious war of aggression against it for nearly eleven years in an attempt to enslave and oppress its people, turn it into a colony and military base on their own, and perpetuate the partition of Viet Nam.

Before the ink of their signature on the Geneva Agreements had dried, the U.S. imperialists induced their henchmen to set up the SEATO, a military bloc of aggression and deliberately put South Viet Nam under its "umbrella," which amounted in fact to placing this part of Viet Nam under the sway of the United States. Ever since the United States had undertaken deeper and more brazen intervention in the South. From late 1954 to 1959 the U.S. imperialists and the puppet Ngo Dinh Diem administration launched a series of barbarous terroristic raids and mop-ups such as the Truong Tan Buu and Thoai Ngoc Hau operations, frenziedly massacring patriotic and peace-loving people of all walks of life and former resistance members, and exterminating religious sects and all those who did not side with them.

Right in the first days following the restoration of peace, the blood of the South Vietnamese people already shed in Duy Xuyen, Huong Dien, Cho Duoc, Vinh Trinh and many other places, even in the streets of Saigon. In order to step up their large-scale and barbarous mop-ups, the U.S. imperialists and their henchmen enacted the fascist 10–59 law, outlawing all the South Vietnamese people, political groupings and individuals who opposed them and whom they called "Communists." At the same time, they dragged guillotines across the breadth and length of the territory. In this period, according to still incomplete figures, the U.S. hangmen and their lackeys massacred or detained hundreds of thousands of patriots for the only reason that they struggled for peace and demanded the execution of the provisions of the Geneva Agreements, and consultation on general elections between the authorities of the two zones with a view to the reunification of the country, or simply because they refused to submit to them.

The criminal acts of the U.S. imperialists and their henchmen naturally fanned the flames of anger throughout Viet Nam and aroused a wave of indignation around the world. Public opinion in Viet Nam and Asia and unbiased opinion all over the five continents severely condemned the tyrannical acts of the U.S. imperialists and their henchmen and demanded that they stop their acts of war and aggression against the South Vietnamese people and correctly implement the 1954 Geneva Agreements.

However, in defiance of the peace- and justice-loving people throughout the world, the U.S. imperialists stubbornly continued to push forward their piratical war in South Viet Nam.

In pursuing their policy of colonialist aggression here in the past eleven years, the U.S. imperialists spent 4,000 million dollars under the signboard of "aid," more than 80% of which were devoted to military expenditures. This aggressive war has earned the special attention of the U.S. ruling circles. The late President Kennedy and President Johnson, the U.S. National Security Council, the Defense Department, the State Department and the Central Intelligence Agency have daily been following the developments in South Viet Nam. Honolulu has become the site for monthly meetings of the leaders of the White House and the Pentagon and American brass hats in the Pacific to discuss plans for the invasion of South Viet Nam.

To tightly control and directly command the war of aggression against South Viet Nam, besides the military mission M.A.A.G., the American imperialists set up a U.S. military command in Saigon headed by Paul D. Harkins, and recently they rigged up the so-called "U.S.-Viet Nam Joint Command" which is in reality a military organ of the United States vested with the highest power in South Viet Nam and placed under the direct conduct of the American President and the Defense Department to prosecute the war of aggression against South Viet Nam. Nearly all the high officials of the United States, including Department secretaries and generals, have come to South Viet Nam to supervise and draw plans of aggression. To direct their predatory war on the spot the U.S. government sent to Saigon a series of well-known generals like O'Daniel, James Collins, McGarr, Robert Williams, P. D. Harkins, etc. More recently it dispatched there Maxwell Taylor, former Chairman of the Joint Chiefs of Staff, and a host of generals among whom W. G. Westmoreland and John L. Throckmorton.

The U.S. imperialists and their henchmen have used all their modern weapons and war means, except atomic bombs, to terrorize and massacre the South Vietnamese people with the hope of achieving their only goal that is to impose their domination and turn South Viet Nam into a colony and military base of their own.

For nearly eleven years, they conducted over 160,000 big and small raids, killed nearly 170,000 people, wounded or tortured to invalidity some 800,000, detained over 400,000 in more than 1,000 jails, raped tens of thousands of women, including old women, little girls and religious believers, disembowelled, plucked out livers and biles of the victims, and buried alive over 5,000 persons, razed to the ground a great many villages, herded over 5 million persons into 8,000 concentration camps disguised as "prosperity zones," "resettlement centres," and "strategic hamlets," sprayed toxic chemicals on many areas, which destroyed hundreds of thousands of hectares of food crops and fruit trees, and affected the health of tens of thousands of persons. They have also demolished thousands of pagodas, churches and temples, killing tens of thousands of religious believers. Under the iron heels of the cruel American aggressors and their lackeys, the beautiful and fertile land of South Viet Nam has been turned into a land of ruins and desolation. The barbarous, fascist rule of the U.S. imperialists and their flunkeys in South Viet Nam is still more cruel than Hitler's Nazi regime or sinister ones in the Middle Ages.

The above data written down with our blood suffice to denounce the crimes of the U.S. imperialists and their quislings, and expose their bellicose, aggressive and traitorous nature. The latter have not only violated the provisions of the Agreement on the Cessation of Hostilities and the Final Declaration of the 1954 Geneva Conference, but also blatantly and entirely scrapped all these international agreements. The Washington rulers and the Vietnamese traitors have not only flouted the Geneva Agreements but also grossly trampled upon the spirit and letter of international law and the resolutions of the Bandung Conference. These are undeniable facts. To cover up their piratical nature, the U.S. imperialists have resorted to deceitful signboards which nevertheless cannot fool the world people. It is necessary to recall the so-called "White Paper" recently issued by Washington is completely null and void. This clumsy "thief-crying-stop-thief" trick has thrown stronger lights on their intention to intensify and expand their aggressive war. At present, the reality in South Viet Nam is that the U.S. imperialists are waging a criminal war of aggression, that they are the most impudent saboteur of the Geneva Agreements, the most dangerous war provacateur and aggressor, the sworn enemy of the peoples of Viet Nam, Indochina and the rest of the world.

2. *The Heroic People of South Viet Nam Are Resolved to Drive Out the U.S. Imperialists in Order to Liberate Themselves and Achieve an Independent, Democratic, Peaceful and Neutral South Viet Nam, Pending National Reunification*

Though deeply attached to peace, the South Vietnamese people are determined not to sit back with folded arms and let the U.S. aggressors and their henchmen trample upon their homeland. Rather to die than live in slavery, the fourteen million valiant South Vietnamese have stood up like one man in an undaunted struggle to defeat the U.S. aggressors and the native traitors so as to liberate their territory and achieve independence, democracy, peace and neutrality in South Viet Nam, in contribution to the maintenance of peace in Indochina and Southeast Asia. Their war of liberation fully conforms to the most elementary and basic principles of international law concerning the people's rights to self-determination and their right to wage a patriotic war against foreign aggression. In this sacred war of liberation they have used all kinds of weapons to fight against their enemy. The chief and biggest arms purveyor of their forces is none other than the U.S. imperialists themselves, who have sustained heavy and repeated setbacks over the past years.

With bare hands at the beginning, the South Vietnamese people have achieved a great work and recorded glorious feats of arms. They are firmly convinced that with their own strength and the wholehearted support of the people throughout the world, they will certainly win complete victory. The U.S. imperialists and their lackeys find themselves in a desperate blind alley. They are being knocked down in the powerful storm of the South Vietnamese people's revolution and are madly writhing before reconciling themselves to their defeat. To retrieve this serious situation, the U.S. imperialists are plunging headlong into extremely dangerous military adventures.

The fact that they have dispatched to South Viet Nam more weapons and combat troops of the U.S. Navy, Army and Air Force, more mercenary troops from South Korea and other U.S. satellites, and undertaken air strikes against the Democratic Republic of Viet Nam and the Kingdom of Laos, etc. is no indication of their strength; these are but frenzied acts of a truculent enemy who has lost his senses and thus can intimidate nobody.

The intensification and expansion by the U.S. imperialists of their aggressive war is in itself one of their pitiful failures, and proves that the colonialist and aggressive policy carried out in South Viet Nam over the past eleven years and their so-called "special war" have gone bankrupt. Bogged down so seriously in their "special war" they will have their hands fastened still more tightly in a "limited war." And if they are rash enough to extend the war to North Viet Nam, to the whole of Indochina or farther, they will surely meet with still more shameful and quicker defeat.

3. *The Valiant People and Liberation Armed Forces of South Viet Nam Are Resolved to Fulfill Their Sacred Duty to Drive Out the U.S. Imperialists so as to Liberate South Viet Nam and Defend North Viet Nam*

Viet Nam is one country; the Vietnamese people are one nation. North and South Viet Nam are of the same family. This sentiment is loftier than mountains and deeper than the sea. This truth is shining like the rising sun; nothing can tarnish it. In this boiling situation and in this life-and-death struggle against the U.S. imperialists and their lackeys, our heart cannot but suffer when our hands are cut. That the people in North Viet Nam are resolved to accomplish their duty toward their kith and kin in the South fully conforms to sentiment and reason.

On behalf of the fourteen million South Vietnamese people, the N.F.L. conveys to their seventeen million blood-sealed compatriots in the North their unshakable confidence and unswerving commitment: "The South Vietnamese people and their heroic Liberation Armed Forces are determined to fulfill their sacred duty to drive out the U.S. imperialists, liberate the

South, defend the North and proceed toward the reunification of their fatherland."

Recently, to save their critical situation and their inevitable collapse in South Viet Nam, the U.S. imperialists and their flunkeys recklessly sent aircraft and warships to bomb, strafe and shell North Viet Nam, but they have received due punishment. Over 50 American jet planes have been shot down. The South Vietnamese Armed Forces and people greatly rejoice at, and warmly hail, those brilliant military exploits of the North Vietnamese army and people.

The heart suffers when the hand is cut! To defend the beloved North, the armed forces and people of the South have given vent to their flames of anger at the U.S. aggressors and their agents. If the U.S. imperialists strike at the North of our fatherland they will resolutely deal them blows twice or three times harder. In February 1965, when the aggressors and traitors attacked the North, in the south the Liberation Armed Forces launched stormy attacks on many of their important military bases and main forces, putting out of action 20,706 troops (among them nearly 600 U.S. aggressors killed, wounded or captured), seizing 4,144 guns of all calibers and shooting down, damaging or destroying 111 aircraft of various types.

4. *The South Vietnamese People Express Their Profound Gratitude to the Whole-hearted Support of the Peace- and Justice-Loving People around the World, and Declare Their Readiness to Receive Assistance, Including Weapons and All Other War Materials, from Their Friends in the Five Continents*

In their just, patriotic struggle the South Vietnamese people have enjoyed the sympathy, support and encouragement of the peace- and justice-loving people throughout the world. They have enlisted not only moral support but also material assistance from them. Of course, they and their representative—the National Front for Liberation—are fully entitled to accept this valuable assistance which they warmly welcome. Though the N.F.L. has always relied mainly on its own strength and capabilities, it is ready to go on accepting all moral support and material assistance, including weapons and other war materials from the socialist countries, and the newly-independent countries as well as from all international organizations and peace-loving people the world over. Besides, the Front reserves for itself the right to buy arms and matériel from all countries to strengthen the potential of its self-defence capacity.

The International Conference for Solidarity with the Vietnamese People Against U.S. Imperialist Aggression and For the Defense of Peace which was held late last year and attended by representatives from fifty countries and twelve international organizations, gave a positive response to these urgent and quite legitimate demands of ours. If the U.S. imperialists continue to commit U.S. combat troops and those of their satellites in South Viet Nam, and to extend the war to North Viet Nam and Laos, the N.F.L. will call on the peoples of all countries to send youths and armymen to South Viet Nam so as, shoulder to shoulder with the South Vietnamese people, to wipe out their common enemy.

5. *The Entire People with Arms in Hand Continue to March Forward Heroically, Resolved to Fight and Defeat the U.S. Aggressors and the Vietnamese Traitors*

The armed struggle waged by the South Vietnamese people against the U.S. aggressors and their henchmen has won very great victories.

In appearance, the U.S. imperialists and their lackeys are formidable, but in reality they have been greatly weakened; confusion prevails in their ranks, and their isolation has reached unprecedented dimensions. The South Vietnamese people, bearing in mind their vow "rather to die than live in slavery," will certainly smash the cruel and savage enemy.

The South Viet Nam N.F.L. and people are not only strong with the justice of their cause; their material and organizational strength are rapidly increasing. They have been and are the glorious victors. The more they fight, the more ardent they become and the more victories they win; and the more they win, the stronger they grow and the greater their victories. Worthy heirs to the traditions of the Dien Bien Phu fighters and of the Vietnamese people who possess a 4,000-year history of heroic struggle against foreign invasion, we have developed these traditions to a high degree. Moreover, the N.F.L. and the people of South Viet Nam are conducting their valiant fight in extremely favourable conditions afforded by the present time when the oppressed nations in Asia, Africa and Latin America have risen up like tidal waves. The socialist countries and the forces of democracy and peace around the world are an important factor stimulating the advance of mankind, overwhelming and smashing imperialism and colonialism under whatever disguise. If the U.S. imperialists and their henchmen are rash enough to fan the flames of war all over Indochina, the people of this area and Southeast Asia as a whole will resolutely stand up like one man and drive them out into the ocean.

The South Vietnamese people and their sole authentic representative—the South Viet Nam National Front for Liberation—will surely win final victory.

Having got the better of the U.S. aggressors in the past ten years, we now have still more favourable conditions to defeat them. They, who have lost during this time, will further weaken and incur still more shameful defeats, especially if they venture to extend the war to the North. We are absolutely confident that victory will be ours. We are determined to fight, strike vigorously and accurately at the U.S. aggressors and their lackeys. We are determined to liberate the South, defend the North and reunify our fatherland.

South Viet Nam, March 22, 1965
The Central Committee of the South Vietnam National Front for Liberation

---

16
American Foreign Policy and International Law

Dean Rusk

Source: Department of State Bulletin (May 10, 1965), pp. 694–700.

. . . American foreign policy is at once principled and pragmatic. Its central objective is our national safety and well-being—to "secure the Blessings of Liberty to ourselves and our Posterity." But we know we can no longer find security and well-being in defenses and policies that are confined to North America, or the Western Hemisphere, or the North Atlantic community.

This has become a very small planet. We have to be concerned with all of it—with all of its land, waters, atmosphere, and with surrounding space. We have a deep national interest in peace, the prevention of aggression, the faithful performance of agreements, the growth of international law. Our foreign policy is rooted in the profoundly practical realization that the purposes and principles of the United Nations Charter must animate the behavior of states if mankind is to prosper or is even to survive. Or at least they must animate enough states with enough will and enough resources to see to it that others do not violate those rules with impunity. . . .

Unhappily, a minority of governments is committed to different ideas of the conduct and organization of human affairs. They are dedicated to the promotion of the Communist world revolution. And their doctrine justifies any technique, any ruse, any deceit, which contributes to that end. They may differ as to tactics from time to time. And the two principal Communist powers are competitors for the leadership of the world Communist movement. But both are committed to the eventual communization of the entire world.

The overriding issue of our time is which concepts are to prevail: those set forth in the United Nations Charter or those proclaimed in the name of a world revolution.

Charter Prohibitions on Use of Force

The paramount commitment of the charter is article 2, paragraph 4, which reads:

> All Members shall refrain in their international relations from the threat or use of force against the territorial integrity or political independence of any state, or in any other manner inconsistent with the Purposes of the United Nations.

This comprehensive limitation went beyond the Covenant of the League of Nations. This more sweeping commitment sought to apply a bitter lesson of the interwar period—that the threat or use of force, whether or not called "war," feeds on success. The indelible lesson of those years is that the time to stop aggression is at its very beginning.

The exceptions to the prohibitions on the use or threat of force were expressly set forth in the charter. The use of force is legal:

—as a collective measure by the United Nations, or

—as action by regional agencies in accordance with chapter VIII of the charter, or

—in individual or collective self-defense. . . .

What Is a "War of National Liberation"?

What is a "war of national liberation"? It is, in essence, any war that furthers the Communist world revolution—what, in broader terms, the Communists have long referred to as a "just" war. The term "war of national liberation" is used not only to denote armed insurrection by people still under colonial rule—there are not many of those left outside the Communist world. It is used to denote any effort led by Communists to overthrow by force any non-Communist government.

Thus the war in South Vietnam is called a "war of national liberation." And those who would overthrow various other non-Communist governments in Asia, Africa, and Latin America are called "forces of national liberation."

Nobody in his right mind would deny that Venezuela is not only a truly independent nation but that it has a government chosen in a free election. But the leaders of the Communist insurgency in Venezuela are described as leaders of a fight for "national liberation"—not only by themselves and by Castro and the Chinese Communists but by the Soviet Communists.

A recent editorial in *Pravda* spoke of the "peoples of Latin America . . . marching firmly along the path of struggle for their national independence" and said, ". . . the upsurge of the national liberation movement in Latin American countries has been to a great extent a result of the activities of Communist parties." It added:

> The Soviet people have regarded and still regard it as their sacred duty to give support to the peoples fighting for their independence. True to their international duty the Soviet people have been and will remain on the side of the Latin American patriots.

In Communist doctrine and practice, a non-Communist government may be labeled and denounced as "colonialist," "reactionary," or a "puppet," and any state so labeled by the Communists automatically becomes fair game—while

Communist intervention by force in non-Communist states is justified as "self-defense" or part of the "struggle against colonial domination." "Self-determination" seems to mean that any Communist nation can determine by itself that any non-Communist state is a victim of colonialist domination and therefore a justifiable target for a "war of liberation."

As the risks of overt aggression, whether nuclear or with conventional forces, have become increasingly evident, the Communists have put increasing stress on the "war of national liberation." The Chinese Communists have been more militant in language and behavior than the Soviet Communists. But the Soviet Communist leadership also has consistently proclaimed its commitment in principle to support wars of national liberation. This commitment was reaffirmed as recently as Monday of this week by Mr. Kosygin [Aleksai N. Kosygin, Chairman of the U.S.S.R. Council of Ministers].

International law does not restrict internal revolution within a state or revolution against colonial authority. But international law does restrict what third powers may lawfully do in support of insurrection. It is these restrictions that are challenged by the doctrine, and violated by the practice, of "wars of liberation."

It is plain that acceptance of the doctrine of "wars of liberation" would amount to scuttling the modern international law of peace which the charter prescribes. And acceptance of the practice of "wars of liberation," as defined by the Communists, would mean the breakdown of peace itself.

South Vietnam's Right of Self-Defense

Vietnam presents a clear current case of the lawful versus the unlawful use of force. I would agree with General Giap [Vo Nguyen Giap, North Vietnamese Commander-in-Chief] and other Communists that it is a test case for "wars of national liberation." We intend to meet that test.

Were the insurgency in South Vietnam truly indigenous and self-sustained, international law would not be involved. But the fact is that it receives vital external support—in organization and direction, in training, in men, in weapons and other supplies. That external support is unlawful for a double reason. First, it contravenes general international law, which the United Nations Charter here expresses. Second, it contravenes particular international law: the 1954 Geneva accords on Vietnam and the 1962 Geneva agreements on Laos.

In resisting the aggression against it, the Republic of Vietnam is exercising its right of self-defense. It called upon us and other states for assistance. And in the exercise of the right of collective self-defense under the United Nations Charter, we and other nations are providing such assistance.

The American policy of assisting South Vietnam to maintain its freedom was inaugurated under President Eisenhower and continued under Presidents Kennedy and Johnson. Our assistance has been increased because the aggression from the

North has been augmented. Our assistance now encompasses the bombing of North Vietnam. The bombing is designed to interdict, as far as possible, and to inhibit, as far as may be necessary, continued aggression against the Republic of Vietnam.

When that aggression ceases, collective measures in defense against it will cease. As President Johnson has declared:

> . . . if that aggression is stopped, the people and Government of South Vietnam will be free to settle their own future, and the need for supporting American military action there will end. . . .

Nature of Struggle in Vietnam

I continue to hear and see nonsense about the nature of the struggle there. I sometimes wonder at the gullibility of educated men and the stubborn disregard of plain facts by men who are supposed to be helping our young to learn—especially to learn how to think.

Hanoi has never made a secret of its designs. It publicly proclaimed in 1960 a renewal of the assault on South Vietnam. Quite obviously its hopes of taking over South Vietnam from within had withered to close to zero—and the remarkable economic and social progress of South Vietnam contrasted, most disagreeably for the North Vietnamese Communists, with their own miserable economic performance.

The facts about the external involvement have been documented in white papers and other publications of the Department of State. The International Control Commission has held that there is evidence "beyond reasonable doubt" of North Vietnamese intervention.

There is no evidence that the Vietcong has any significant popular following in South Vietnam. It relies heavily on terror. Most of its reinforcements in recent months have been North Vietnamese from the North Vietnamese Army.

Let us be clear about what is involved today in Southeast Asia. We are not involved with empty phrases or conceptions that ride upon the clouds. We are talking about the vital national interests of the United States in the peace of the Pacific. We are talking about the appetite for aggression—an appetite that grows upon feeding and that is proclaimed to be insatiable. We are talking about the safety of nations with whom we are allied—and in the integrity of the American commitment to join in meeting attack.

It is true that we also believe that every small state has a right to be unmolested by its neighbors even though it is within reach of a great power. It is true that we are committed to general principles of law and procedure that reject the idea that men and arms can be sent freely across frontiers to absorb a neighbor. But underlying the general principles is the harsh reality that our own security is threatened by those who would embark upon a course of aggression whose announced ultimate purpose is our own destruction.

Once again we hear expressed the views that cost the men of my generation a terrible price in World War II. We are told that Southeast Asia is far away—but so were Manchuria and Ethiopia. We are told that, if we insist that someone stop shooting, that is asking them for unconditional surrender. We are told that perhaps the aggressor will be content with just one more bite. We are told that, if we prove faithless on one commitment, perhaps others would believe us about other commitments in other places. We are told that, if we stop resisting, perhaps the other side will have a change of heart. We are asked to stop hitting bridges and radar sites and ammunition depots without requiring that the other side stop its slaughter of thousands of civilians and its bombings of schools and hotels and hospitals and railways and buses.

Surely we have learned over the past three decades that the acceptance of aggression leads only to a sure catastrophe. Surely we have learned that the aggressor must face the consequences of his action and be saved from the frightful miscalculation that brings all to ruin. It is the purpose of law to guide men away from such events, to establish rules of conduct which are deeply rooted in the reality of experience. . . .

17
Message to the American People, December 23, 1966

Ho Chi Minh

Source: Ho Chi Minh, *Against U.S. Aggression for National Salvation* (Hanoi, 1967), pp. 137–38.

On the occasion of the New Year, I would like to convey to the American people cordial wishes for peace and happiness.

The Vietnamese and American peoples should have lived in peace and friendship. But the U.S. Government has brazenly sent over 400,000 troops along with thousands of aircraft and hundreds of warships to wage aggression on Vietnam. Night and day it has used napalm bombs, toxic gas, fragmentation bombs and other modern weapons to massacre our people, not sparing even old persons, women and children; it has burnt down or destroyed villages and towns and perpetrated extremely savage crimes. Of late, U.S. aircraft have repeatedly bombed Hanoi, our beloved capital.

It is because of the criminal war unleashed by the U.S. Government that hundreds of thousands of young Americans have been drafted and sent to a useless death far from their homeland, on the Vietnamese battlefield. In hundreds of thousands of American families, parents have lost their sons, and wives their husbands.

Nevertheless, the U.S. Government has continually clamoured about "peace negotiations" in an attempt to deceive the American and world peoples. In fact, it is daily expanding the war.

The U.S. Government wrongly believes that with brutal force it could compel our people to surrender. But the Vietnamese people will never submit. We love peace, but it must be genuine peace in independence and freedom. For independence and freedom, the Vietnamese people are determined to fight the U.S. aggressors through to complete victory, whatever the hardships and sacrifices may be.

Who has caused these sufferings and mournings to the Vietnamese and American people? It is the U.S. rulers. The American people have realized this truth. More and more Americans are valiantly standing up in a vigorous struggle, demanding that the American Government respect the Constitution and the honour of the United States, stop the war of aggression in Vietnam and bring home all U.S. troops.

I warmly welcome your just struggle and thank you for your support to the Vietnamese people's patriotic fight.

I sincerely wish the American people many big successes in their struggle for peace, democracy and happiness.

Chapter V

The 1968 Tet Offensive

The Tet offensive of 1968 was the turning point in the war. On January 31, 1968, in the early hours of the third day of *Tet* (the Vietnamese Lunar New Year, a holiday which in American terms would be something like Christmas and the Fourth of July rolled into one), the NLF and the North Vietnamese launched synchronized attacks against and within almost every major city and town in South Vietnam. Five of six major cities, thirty-nine of forty-four provincial capitals, seventy-one district capitals, and nearly every U.S. base in the country were simultaneously besieged.

In the first hours of the offensive, more than one thousand aircraft were destroyed or damaged on the ground, twice the size of the entire air force that had been assembled by the French for their war. Although the offensive unfolded in three phases over seven months, it began dramatically when 70,000 troops attacked on one night (January 31), bringing the war into the urban areas for the first time. Only about 1,000 guerrillas entered Saigon, but they seized the grounds of the newly constructed fortress-like U.S. embassy, captured the government radio station, and surrounded the presidential palace. For a full week, the capital was disrupted by fighting, and for three weeks, the attackers held off over 11,000 U.S. and ARVN troops and police.

The battle for Hue in the northern part of South Vietnam, the old imperial capital and the center of Buddhist and student revolts in 1963 and 1966, was even more intense. "Revolutionary Hue" held out for three weeks, and it was only after bloody house-to-house fighting and massive bombing that destroyed 80 percent of the city that the NLF flag was no longer flying. After Hue was retaken, the American press began to carry stories about a bloodbath inflicted by the Communists on the civilian population, and over the past twenty years debate has continued over the source of the massive civilian casualties in Hue. It appears that during the three weeks in which the Communists controlled the city between 2,000 and 3,000 people were executed (many by families exacting revenge for the murder and torture of loved ones). At the same time, approximately 18,000 of the city's 20,000 houses were destroyed by American artillery and bombs, and as many as 6,000 people were killed as a result. The ferocity of the U.S. response to the Tet offensive was not confined to Hue. Ben Tre, a city of more than 65,000 in the Mekong Delta, was completely destroyed after it was seized by guerrillas. As an American officer at the scene told journalist Peter Arnett, "We had to destroy the town to save it."

In the two months of fighting from January 29 to March 31, 1968, at least 3,895 American soldiers and possibly ten times as many guerrillas lost their lives. By February 10, the CIA reported, the enemy had accomplished its main military, political, and psychological objectives by taking over much territory, destroying the armed forces and political legitimacy of the Saigon government, and transforming the war from a rural one to one involving the cities as well.

While not as spectacular as the first phase, phase two of the offensive began on May 4 with mortar and rocket attacks on 119 towns and cities, and in August, the third phase focused mainly on American bases. In May 1990 in Ho Chi Minh City (formerly Saigon), I met with Tran Van Tra, one of the top generals of the NLF, and he revealed to me that a planned fourth phase to coincide with the November elections in the United States had been canceled.

Although American intelligence had caught wind of increased enemy activity leading up to the offensive, the U.S. high command was taken by surprise. More importantly, the American public was completely unprepared for the magnitude of the attacks. Only five weeks earlier, on December 22, 1967, President Johnson had said that "the enemy is not beaten but he knows he has met his match in the field." A few weeks before the offensive began, General William Westmoreland discussed the "spectacular success" which the marines had enjoyed against the enemy at Khe Sanh, near the Demilitarized Zone separating North and South Vietnam. The North Vietnamese had surrounded the remote U.S. base there, and thousands of troops were locked in the most intense battle of the war. Apparently, Westmoreland believed the coming offensive would be launched from the northern provinces since he had stationed over half his maneuver battalions in that region.

Not only was the offensive a tactical surprise, but at a time when the Johnson administration was desperately trying to sell the war to the American public, raising taxes to pay for it and sacrificing the "War on Poverty" to continue to fight it, the Tet offensive was also a political disruption of major proportions. The attacks themselves were timed so that American news reporters could broadcast scenes of the fighting in time to reach the evening news in the United States The precision of the attacks was such that transmission lines for television and radio were left intact. The Vietnamese were keenly aware that theirs was the first televised war, and the strategic timing of the attacks was crucial. As soon as the offensive began, it became clear to Sen. Robert Kennedy (and others) that the war could not be won. Kennedy's statement of February 8 (Document 18) called on the American people to "rid ourselves of the illusion" that they could win the war. The offensive immediately provided antiwar candidates with unexpected popular support, lifting Eugene McCarthy to a near defeat of President Johnson in the New Hampshire primaries.

The Tet offensive led to Lyndon Johnson's most famous speech (Document 23) in which he announced his decision not to run for reelection. Other consequences included the May 1968 convening in Paris of peace talks among the United States, South Vietnam, North Vietnam, and the NLF and a gradual withdrawal of U.S. combat forces—a withdrawal completed by Richard Nixon's Vietnamization of the war (see Chapter 7). In historical terms, the Tet offensive was the equivalent of a Gettysburg for the United States, marking the high point of its attempt to control the destiny of Vietnam. Although the United States remained in Vietnam for five more years, it was already clear after Tet that the United States could not win the war.

This chapter includes an account by members of the NLF of the fighting in Saigon (Document 19). This glimpse of the other side's actions reveals a level of popular support for them not generally understood in the United States. In addition, there are statements (Documents 20 and 21) from the NLF armed forces command (the People's Liberation Armed Forces) and the Lao Dong party (often called the "Communist party" but the accurate translation is the "Workers' party") of North Vietnam. Although both these documents were written by Vietnamese fighting against the United States, they reflect differing points of view. The North Vietnamese assessment is far less spirited than that of their NLF comrades and contains a list of six "deficiencies and weak points" of the offensive.

The NLF had hoped the offensive would mobilize popular uprisings which would establish dual power (parallel structures alongside the Thieu government), and to some extent this occurred. In the rural areas, of a total of 2,500 villages in South Vietnam, nearly one-quarter (about 600) established village councils to govern themselves. These councils and their urban counterparts became the basis for the Alliance of National, Democratic and Peace Forces, a "third force" in South Vietnam that called for American withdrawal, the overthrow of the Thieu government, and negotiations with the NLF.

The offensive's impact on American officials is also portrayed here. On March 30, General Wheeler, Chairman of the Joint Chiefs of Staff, issued a statement (Document 22) to his commanders in the Pacific noting decreasing U.S. public support for the war. Wheeler also informed them in advance of the forthcoming speech by the president. The final document in this chapter is an appraisal of the effects of Tet by Clark Clifford, the man who replaced Robert McNamara as secretary of defense.

18
Robert F. Kennedy Calls Vietnam an Unwinnable War, February 8, 1968

Source: Major Problems in the History of the Vietnam War, edited by Robert McMahon (D. C. Heath and Co., 1990), pp. 352–55.

Our enemy, savagely striking at will across all of South Vietnam, has finally shattered the mask of official illusion with which we have concealed our true circumstances, even from ourselves. But a short time ago we were serene in our reports and predictions of progress.

The Vietcong will probably withdraw from the cities, as they were forced to withdraw from the American Embassy. Thousands of them will be dead.

But they will, nevertheless, have demonstrated that no part or person of South Vietnam is secure from their attacks: neither district capitals nor American bases, neither the peasant in his rice paddy nor the commanding general of our own great forces.

No one can predict the exact shape or outcome of the battles now in progress, in Saigon or at Khesanh. Let us pray that we will succeed at the lowest possible cost to our young men.

But whatever their outcome, the events of the last two weeks have taught us something. For the sake of those young Americans who are fighting today, if for no other reason, the time has come to take a new look at the war in Vietnam; not by cursing the past but by using it to illuminate the future.

And the first and necessary step is to face the facts. It is to seek out the austere and painful reality of Vietnam, freed from wishful thinking, false hopes and sentimental dreams. It is to rid ourselves of the "good company," of those illusions which have lured us into the deepening swamp of Vietnam.

We must, first of all, rid ourselves of the illusion that the events of the past two weeks represent some sort of victory. That is not so.

It is said the Vietcong will not be able to hold the cities. This is probably true. But they have demonstrated despite all our reports of progress, of government strength and enemy weakness, that half a million American soldiers with 700,000 Vietnamese allies, with total command of the air, total command of the sea, backed by huge resources and the most modern weapons, are unable to secure even a single city from the attacks of an enemy whose total strength is about 250,000. . . .

For years we have been told that the measure of our success and progress in Vietnam was increasing security and control for the population. Now we have seen that none of the population is secure and no area is under sure control.

Four years ago when we only had about 30,000 troops in Vietnam, the Vietcong were unable mount the assaults on cities they have now conducted against our enormous forces. At one time a suggestion that we protect enclaves was derided. Now there are no protected enclaves.

This has not happened because our men are not brave or effective, because they are. It is because we have misconceived the nature of the war: It is because we have sought to resolve by military might a conflict whose issue depends upon the will and conviction of the South Vietnamese people. It is like sending a lion to halt an epidemic of jungle rot.

This misconception rests on a second illusion—the illusion that we can win a war which the South Vietnamese cannot win for themselves.

You cannot expect people to risk their lives and endure hardship unless they have a stake in their own society. They must have a clear sense of identification with their own government, a belief they are participating in a cause worth fighting for.

People will not fight to line the pockets of generals or swell the bank accounts of the wealthy. They are far more likely to close their eyes and shut their doors in the face of their government—even as they did last week.

More than any election, more than any proud boast, that single fact reveals the truth. We have an ally in name only. We support a government without supporters. Without the efforts of American arms that government would not last a day.

The third illusion is that the unswerving pursuit of military victory, whatever its cost, is in the interest of either ourselves or the people of Vietnam.

For the people of Vietnam, the last three years have meant little but horror. Their tiny land has been devastated by a weight of bombs and shells greater than Nazi Germany knew in the Second World War.

We have dropped 12 tons of bombs for every square mile in North and South Vietnam. Whole provinces have been substantially destroyed. More than two million South Vietnamese are now homeless refugees.

Imagine the impact in our own country if an equivalent number—over 25 million Americans—were wandering homeless or interned in refugee camps, and millions more refugees were being created as New York and Chicago, Washington and Boston, were being destroyed by a war raging in their streets.

Whatever the outcome of these battles, it is the people we seek to defend who are the greatest losers.

Nor does it serve the interests of America to fight this war as if moral standards could be subordinated to immediate necessities. Last week, a Vietcong suspect was turned over to the chief of the Vietnamese Security Services, who executed him on the spot—a flat violation of the Geneva Convention on the Rules of War.

The photograph of the execution was on front pages all around the world—leading our best and oldest friends to ask, more in sorrow than in anger, what has happened to America?

The fourth illusion is that the American national interest is identical with—or should be subordinated to—the selfish interest of an incompetent military regime.

We are told, of course, that the battle for South Vietnam is in reality a struggle for 250 million Asians—the beginning of a Great Society for all of Asia. But this is pretension.

We can and should offer reasonable assistance to Asia; but we cannot build a Great Society there if we cannot build one in our own country. We cannot speak extravagantly of a struggle for 250 million Asians, when a struggle for 15 million in one Asian country so strains our forces, that another Asian country, a fourth-rate power which we have already once defeated in battle, dares to seize an American ship and hold and humiliate her crew.

The fifth illusion is that this war can be settled in our own way and in our own time on our own terms. Such a settlement is the privilege of the triumphant: of those who crush their enemies in battle or wear away their will to fight.

We have not done this, nor is there any prospect we will achieve such a victory.

Unable to defeat our enemy or break his will—at least without a huge, long and ever more costly effort—we must actively seek a peaceful settlement. We can no longer harden our terms every time Hanoi indicates it may be prepared to negotiate; and we must be willing to foresee a settlement which will give the Vietcong a chance to participate in the political life of the country.

These are some of the illusions which may be discarded if the events of last week are to prove not simply a tragedy, but a lesson: a lesson which carries with it some basic truths.

First, that a total military victory is not within sight or around the corner; that, in fact, it is probably beyond our grasp; and that the effort to win such a victory will only result in the future slaughter of thousands of innocent and helpless people—a slaughter which will forever rest on our national conscience.

Second, that the pursuit of such a victory is not necessary to our national interest, and is even damaging that interest.

Third, that the progress we have claimed toward increasing our control over the country and the security of the population is largely illusory.

Fourth, that the central battle in this war cannot be measured by body counts or bomb damage, but by the extent to which the people of South Vietnam act on a sense of common purpose and hope with those that govern them.

Fifth, that the current regime in Saigon is unwilling or incapable of being an effective ally in the war against the Communists.

Sixth, that a political compromise is not just the best path to peace, but the only path, and we must show as much willingness to risk some of our prestige for peace as to risk the lives of young men in war.

Seventh, that the escalation policy in Vietnam, far from strengthening and consolidating international resistance to aggression, is injuring our country through the world, reducing the faith of other peoples in our wisdom and purpose and weakening the world's resolve to stand together for freedom and peace.

Eighth, that the best way to save our most precious stake in Vietnam—the lives of our soldiers—is to stop the enlargement of the war, and that the best way to end casualties is to end the war.

Ninth, that our nation must be told the truth about this war, in all its terrible reality, both because it is right—and because only in this way can any Administration rally the public confidence and unity for the shadowed days which lie ahead.

No war has ever demanded more bravery from our people and our Government—not just bravery under fire or the bravery to make sacrifices—but the bravery to discard the comfort of illusion—to do away with false hopes and alluring promises.

Reality is grim and painful. But it is only a remote echo of the anguish toward which a policy founded on illusion is surely taking us.

This is a great nation and a strong people. Any who seek to comfort rather than speak plainly, reassure rather than instruct, promise satisfaction rather than reveal frustration—they deny that greatness and drain that strength. For today as it was in the beginning, it is the truth that makes us free.

19
Fighting Saigon—Popular Uprising

Source: South Viet Nam: A Month of Unprecedented Offensive and Uprising (Giai Phong Publishing House, March 1968), pp. 67–77.

Our troops stormed across the C. bridge. A photoreporter of the *Giai Phong* Press Agency rushed ahead to take snapshots. But he was stopped by a young man carrying a submachinegun, who said he was a member of the street self-defense corps and wanted to see his papers. The flag of the South Viet Nam National Front for Liberation was flapping in the wind atop an electric pylon at the end of the bridge. On both sides of the street, from the shacks and also from the many-storeyed houses, people rushed out and stood at their doors or on their balconies watching the Liberation troops march into the city. All vehicles had pulled up along the curb to let the troops pass and also for the people riding on them to look more closely at the revolutionary fighters, those sons of Saigon whose images they had for so long cherished. From the V-shaped bridge onward, groups of young people neatly dressed and carrying submachineguns stood at intervals of a few score yards on the pavements. All were wearing red armbands with the following inscription in yellow or white letters: "Revolutionary self-defense corps." They were youngsters, school or college students, workers and labourers engaged in ensuring security for their wards and streets, and also for the revolutionary cadres and troops.

A young man in oil-stained worker's clothes was helping a friend carry a heavy bench from a house to a barricade being built. Seeing a girl with a first-aid kit pass by, he called to her: "Hey Nam, rush to the other end of the street, Bay's son has just been wounded by bullets from a helicopter." As the girl started running in the direction indicated, two armed young men hastened to follow her, probably to see to her security. The people were now masters of their wards and streets; self-defense units and first-aid people were busy all day. We had won control over these quarters for only a few days and a lot of work had to be done to put things in order. The wicked agents of the enemy had either been punished or had taken to their heels, leaving behind things to be cleaned up. Very few of the owners of big stores and factories had remained, and so self-defense units had to stand guard to protect their property. The people, including young men whom the puppet administration had labelled as "stray" or "insubordinate" elements, were keeping everything in good order. Local self-management committees were appointed to look after local affairs. The first thing to do was to set up armed self-defense units to foil all counter-attacks by the enemy and liquidate remnants of enemy agents. Then first-aid teams and fire brigades had to be organized to help cope with the damage done by enemy artillery and air raids. At the same time workers and other people were sent to take care of stores, factories and depots. Rice, firewood and foodstuffs were distributed to the people. Cadres were sent to every street and home to advise people on how to dig trenches and build shelters for their own protection against enemy bombing and shelling.

While such urgent matters were being dealt with, enemy planes turned up. Workers' huts were set afire by rocket or napalm. Reports streamed in: "Some puppet soldiers have been killed by their own planes. . . . Send men to bury them.". . . "Houses have been set afire by napalm. . . . A fire brigade should be sent immediately. . . ."

In those days in which power was in their hands, the people had to look after everything: organizing relief to stricken areas, providing help to revolutionary cadres and troops, either by hunting down enemy agents or carrying ammunition, etc.

It was the first opportunity for a very long time for the people in this ward to meet an entire unit of young and strong revolutionary troops. At Binh Thoi an elderly woman was seen stroking the hair of a young Liberation armyman, praising him for his good health and good look, and telling him how he reminded her of her own son. "Those puppets of the Americans have been saying that Viet Cong troops are all pale and sickly. What shameless liars!" She told him that her only son had been labelled as an insubordinate element by the Thieu-Ky administration. But after revolutionary troops had entered the central part of the city, she said, a local cadre had told her that her son had been given a gun and an armband with the inscription "revolutionary self-defense corps."

Everywhere, old folk, young people and even children belonging to all social strata were helping in the attack. There were instances in which revolutionary units fought for many days and nights on end without having time to look after their own supplies: the people then brought them food and drink. Cakes and balls of rice, carefully wrapped and bearing the words "Supplies for Liberation troops" were piled up in front of every house.

As the revolutionary troops penetrated deeper into the city, the fight became ever fiercer. Hard street-fighting took place. But even then, setting at defiance enemy bombs and shells, the people came out of their houses, bringing to the revolutionary troops cakes, fruit, beer and other refreshments. A young girl with permed hair was seen handing a lemonade through a window to a Liberation armyman in the street and stammering with emotion: "Drink, drink, brother . . ."

Right at this moment, her mother handed her a watermelon and told her to pass it on to the N.F.L. fighter. That day, the fight lasted until nightfall.

The N.F.L. cadre who told me the above story added: "The support and encouragement given us by the Saigon people have instilled into us even more enthusiasm and pride. And that's why we are determined to fight to the end, until the aggressors and traitors are all destroyed."

Barricades in the Streets

The tank shivered, spewed a thick cloud of bluish smoke which spread all over the street, then stopped dead. Quick as lightning, three black-clad N.F.L. fighters darted out from a back alley and rushed to the vehicle. A sharp burst of submachinegun made away with the last of its occupants. From several houses other men ran into the street, their guns slung before their chests. A young man wearing a pair of gold-rimmed spectacles and blue clothes appeared from behind a bullet-riddled door panel, carrying two wooden chairs, and staggered towards the tank. Following on his heels was a chubby dark-complexioned girl in tight-fitting black clothes; she carried on her shoulders a brand new armchair. On the other side of the street a man about thirty with a checkered scarf round his neck and a gun in his hand was pulling a few cement bags. After looking right and left he shouted, "Comrades, beware! There may be other armoured cars ahead!"

Within a matter of minutes, two barricades were erected in the street. The three black-clad men lay on their stomachs behind the smoking tank, their guns pointed forward. The other three took up position behind a second barricade made up of a fallen tree, pieces of furniture, cement bags and empty oil drums.

A roar of tank engines came from the distance. Cannon shells burst on roofs and tree tops throwing fragments of bricks and tiles and branches around the men.

It was the third day since the offensive was launched in Saigon.

The sun was beating down hard. The shadows of electric poles gradually shortened, then disappeared altogether. The roar of tanks now sounded more distant. The street was deserted, a lull that heralded more fighting. On the barricades, the men began to feel hungry. From behind the tank, a voice with a strong Trung Bo accent rose:

"I wonder whether the unit knows we've gone that far! Gosh, I've eaten two bowlfuls of rice this morning and yet I am now so damn hungry! What a big stomach I've got!"

His friends chuckled, but their shining eyes kept scanning the street carefully. One said, "This morning I saw two girls hand you a few sandwiches, but you refused! Why should you be so shy?"

The third man said in a Saigon drawl, "Don't worry, boys, I know how to get food . . ."

He winked and jerked his head in the direction of the other barricade behind which the other people were also talking. The girl was putting in order the sight of her shining submachinegun. She said in a somewhat reproachful voice:

"They just stick to principles! Before evacuating their places, the people had left plenty of food behind, for the Liberation troops. But they wouldn't touch it! Why should they refuse to eat this food? They fully deserve it. They are fighting the enemy, not just loitering around!"

The young man in gold-rimmed specs took a packet of cigarettes from his pocket and tossed it to the other barricade. "Have a smoke, boys," he shouted.

The three black-clad N.F.L. men smiled and nodded a thanks, then lit their cigarettes. The oldest man in the other group, a Chinese worker probably, looked toward the rear and said to his two friends: "It's noon and the supply team hasn't come yet. Let's invite the N.F.L. men to lunch, what do you think?"

The girl sat up, still clasping her submachinegun. She steadied a pistol holster on her hip and told him, "I'll go home and fetch some rice." But the young man in specs sprang to his feet and beat the dust off his clothes: "I'll go," he said. "I've been too long in those stuffy classrooms: lying in the sun makes me tired. I'd rather have a walk and get some fresh air . . ."

The girl knew that what he said was not quite true: for three days this young student had been fighting by their side and had given proof of his courage and ability to endure hardships (showing himself not in the least inferior to her, who, being a labourer, was much more used to a hard life); besides, what he was going to do was no pleasure walk! But she nodded her assent all the same. However, before the young man could start on his journey, the girl pulled at his shirt and made him lie down. She herself took cover behind a tree. In the distance, a figure was weaving his way toward them, running from behind a tree to the next, with things like grenades at the end of his swinging arms. The Chinese worker also lay flat on his stomach and carefully observed the approaching shadow. Then he sprang to his feet, rubbed his hands and said with a smile: "Don't shoot! It's old Nam's little boy!"

The boy was now quite near. Sweat was trickling down his chubby red cheeks. He didn't seem to be quite 14. His dark shining eyes looked right and left at the street then at the carcass of the tank. He smiled mischievously and told the people on the barricade, "He're some beer-grenades and sandwich-rockets for you! From the uncles and aunties in town!"

He let a fat knapsack bulging with all kinds of food, which he was wearing soldier-style, slip from his shoulder, lay down and seized his submachinegun. "I wish I could get one of these," he said enthusiastically. The others looked affectionately at him and smiled.

Suddenly there was an outburst of gunfire. From both barricades guns were immediately pointed forward. The girl told the young boy in a serious voice, "Take cover, Hai. Do what I say, will you?"

Bullets ripped the road. On barricade No. 1, the anti-tank gun moved to the right. The Chinese worker half rose to have a look. Bullets hit the cement bags in front of him with a sharp whizz. As he ducked for cover, a voice rang from somewhere above, "Beware! Some of those bastards have slipped into the drugstore and are firing from there!"

Everybody looked up, but only for a few seconds, for the clank of tanks was heard. The little boy was standing on the balcony of a nearby house. Grasping the railing with both hands, he craned his neck and kept vigilant watch.

"Get down, kids!" a black-clad N.F.L. man was shouting. "It's no time and place to play bo-peep!"

On the right side of the street ahead, a few enemy troops with grenades in their hands were crawling toward them.

Before the little boy could say a word, a burst of quickfire submachinegun hit the window-panes of the next house. A puppet soldier was getting nearer and nearer, taking cover behind fallen trees. All of a sudden, he sprang up and was about to lob a grenade when a burst from the girl's gun caught him and knocked him down. He lay with his arms outstretched on a heap of rubbish. A man again shouted at the boy, "Get down, those bastards are firing at you. Get down, quick!"

But the young boy seemed not to hear. He tried to reach out even further off the balcony to observe the enemy. "Tanks coming," he shouted, "with infantry behind! Shoot at them!"

But now the men in the drugstore had seen him. A burst of machinegun crashed. From the barricade a B.40 anti-tank rocket whizzed forth, hit the drugstore and silenced the gun. But on the balcony, the young boy had staggered. One of his hands had left the railing, the other, though still keeping its hold, was shaking. The people on the barricades were deeply shocked; they rose and were about to rush up to his rescue. But they stopped, bit their lips and pointed their weapons forward. A tank, cannon blazing, was rushing toward barricade No. 2, trying to crush the people defending it. But again, from barricade No. 1, the B.40 bazooka let go a rocket with a roar. The tank shook, crawled forward a few more yards, then stopped dead, fire and smoke gushing from its side. The G.I.s behind it took to their heels. Many were felled by angry bursts of submachinegun from the barricades.

The enemy beat a hasty retreat. All six people on the barricades looked up to the balcony. The girl smiled and heaved a sigh of relief. The young boy had recovered his balance, with both hands now clutching at the wooden rail. One of his sleeves was stained with blood. A gust of wind lifted a flap of his shirt and one could see a holster strapped to a black leather belt.

A N.F.L. man, the one with the Trung Bo accent, came up to him and carried him down on his back. The girl blinked and said in a warm voice, "He is a very courageous boy. Only yesterday, he meted out due punishment to two wicked agents of the enemy."

The student took off his glasses and wiped them. Trying hard to contain his emotion, he told his friends the story of Gavroche.

The heat had somewhat subsided. The two barricades had now been moved a hundred yards up the street. The little boy was now lying beside his friends, a newly-captured carbine in his hands, his pistol laid on the ground, just beneath his chest. Some distance away, a group of enemy soldiers were bracing themselves up for an attack. The battle on the streets of Saigon had only begun . . .

20
Third Special Communique, February 26, 1968

South Viet Nam P.L.A.F. Command

Source: South Viet Nam: A Month of Unprecedented Offensive and Uprising (Giai Phong Publishing House, March 1968), pp. 27–38 (excerpts).

Since the night of January 29, 1968, the People's Liberation Armed Forces, together with the entire people of South Viet Nam, have been continually stepping up their attacks and uprisings of unprecedented violence.

In nearly thirty days and nights of extremely valiant fighting, our armed forces and people have launched attacks against the enemy and risen up in all urban centres and provincial capitals of South Viet Nam, striking accurately at almost all key positions of the enemy, big and small, from the central to the local level and from Saigon and Hue cities to the provinces, seized control of many places and inflicted heavy losses on the U.S., puppet and satellite troops as well as the puppet administration. In many areas, we have struck the enemy again and again and smashed their counterattacks. Most outstanding and glorious exploits have been recorded by our armed forces and people in Saigon and Hue and the cities or provincial capitals of Da Nang, Hoi An, Da Lat, Phan Thiet, Ban Me Thuot, My Tho, Ben Tre, Vinh Long.

Our armed forces and people have

—attacked the enemy and risen up in hundreds of district towns and townships;

—attacked the enemy and risen up simultaneously in all the rural areas still under the enemy's grip and seized control of nearly all these areas;

—attacked a series of enemy command posts of various levels, U.S. operational headquarters, puppet army corps headquarters, headquarters of puppet arms and services and of U.S., puppet and satellite divisions, brigades and regiments as well as military sectors and sub-sectors of the puppet army;

—attacked a series of military bases and defense lines of the enemy, the most outstanding victory in this connection being the complete destruction of the Lang Vay position;

—attacked 45 airfields, causing to the enemy enormous losses in planes, bombs, ammunition and fuel, as well as in technical and flying personnel. The biggest U.S. airbases in South Viet Nam such as Da Nang, Chu Lai, Bien Hoa, Tan Son Nhat, Phu Bai have also been struck. Many airfields have been repeatedly attacked such as Bien Hoa, Tan Son Nhat, Da Nang, Chu Lai, Pleiku, Tra Noc, Tan Canh;

—attacked a series of enemy storages, seized or destroyed millions of tons of bombs and ammunition, fuel and other war material, among them big storage complexes such as Long Binh, Hanh Thong Tay, Nha Be, Bau Mac, Lien Chieu, Da Nang, Chu Lai, Phu Bai, Hue, Kontum, Pleiku, Ban Me Thuot, Qui Nhon, Soc Trang. Many of these dumps such as Long Binh have been attacked many times;

—attacked a series of harbours such as Cua Viet and Thu Thiem and naval bases such as Tra Vinh, Xeo Ro (Rach Gia), Dong Tam (My Tho), Nha Be and Vinh Long; attacked enemy ships and launches moving along the Huong River* and rivers in Ben Tre, An Giang, Vinh Long, Kien Tuong, My Tho, Long An, Ba Ria and Saigon. We have thus inflicted heavy losses upon the enemy in terms of warships, combat launches and other water transport means as well as in port facilities;

---

*Better known to foreigners as Perfume River.

—cut off the enemy's communication lines, including such important ones as Highways Nos. 1, 4, 14, 15, 19 and 20 which were paralyzed for many days, blew up hundreds of bridges and attacked a series of truck parks, destroying thousands of military vehicles;

—demolished dozens of jails, thereby releasing tens of thousands of patriots detained by the enemy.

The offensive and uprising of our armed forces and people is still going on.

In nearly thirty days and nights of continual fighting they have scored very great and all-sided victories.

We have wiped out a large part of the enemy's effectives. According to preliminary data, we have killed, wounded or captured more than 90,000 enemy troops, among them over 20,000 American and satellite. We have annihilated many units, including 3 armoured regiments and 39 infantry, engineer, combat-police and motorized transport battalions (mostly infantry battalions), 8 squadrons of armoured cars and 120 companies. This is a very great achievement. In only four weeks we put out of action as many enemy troops as in three months on the average in 1967. The number of enemy battalions entirely wiped out equals the average of a nine-month period in 1967, the year of biggest victories as compared with any previous year. In face of the general offensive of our armed forces and people, the puppet army has disintegrated by big chunks. In the early days of February 1968, the number of puppet troops disbanded ran into 200,000. At present, this disintegration is accelerating at an alarming rate and the enemy has no hope to stop it. Most of the puppet militia, regional and police forces have been disbanded. In Hue city, 700 functionaries of the puppet administration made public apology, the puppet troops at 14 posts surrendered while nearly 1,000 officers and men took side with the people to fight the U.S. aggressors and the puppets. In Quang Tri and Thua Thien provinces, 169 civil-guard platoons went over to the people's side to take part in the resistance against the U.S. aggressors, for national salvation. In Ben Tre, My Tho, Kien Phong and An Giang provinces, up to February 10, the puppet troops in more than 80 posts had surrendered and handed over their weapons to the revolutionary forces. In Tra Vinh province, puppet troops at 13 posts revolted. So also did puppet troops at 36 posts in Cho Lach district, Ben Tre, within six days, and those at 21 posts in Chau Thanh district, Tra Vinh. The puppet regular forces are also in a serious process of disintegration. Within a few days, 950 troops of the 7th Division in Central Nam Bo deserted. In Cai Lay district, My Tho, 500 soldiers left their ranks. The 4th Battalion of the 16th Regiment in Vinh Long has no more than 30 men.

We have destroyed a large part of the enemy war means. According to statistics available, we have shot down or destroyed on the ground more than 1,800 aircraft, knocked out more than 1,300 tanks and armoured cars, and thousands of other military vehicles, sunk or damaged 90 warships and combat launches, and destroyed millions of tons of bombs, ammunition and fuel. This is also a great achievement of our armed forces and people. Enemy losses in four weeks equal three-fifths of their total losses in 1967 in aircraft, one-third in armoured cars and two-fifths in warships or combat launches. This at the same time constitutes a very heavy defeat for the enemy. Their fire-power and mobility have been seriously weakened. Their combat units in many places are running short of ammunition, food, and fuel and are meeting with enormous difficulties in their movement just as in rescue operations. The U.S. First Airmobile Cavalry Division has only half of its normal aircraft strength left.

What the enemy regard as their strongest points and actually forms the main props of their troops has been badly hit. As a consequence, the morales of U.S., puppet and satellite troops has dropped to a new low. Our armed forces and people are continuing to bring into full play their tradition of striking accurately and continually, in day-time as at night, at the enemy airbases, ports, storages, war material and transport means, of continually cutting off their communication lines, thus landing them in a still more critical situation, in the military and economic fields, with regard to both morale and matériel.

We have dealt shattering blows at the puppet administrative machine and expanded the people's control.

The puppet regime of the Thieu-Ky clique of traitors at the centre has come under heavy attacks and is being paralyzed and disarrayed. The puppet administration at the provincial and district levels is also in a moribund state. Its machine of repression and its reactionary organizations in almost all villages and hamlets have been in the main wiped out. We have destroyed, captured, or forced enemy troops to withdraw from more than 700 posts and watch-towers. We have completely smashed the "rural pacification" plan which was so vital to the adversary. 1,200,000 more of our compatriots have been liberated from their grip. Our people have won the control of the most part of the vast countryside and many urban areas, and are speedily setting up revolutionary power at all levels. The Thua Thien-Hue People's Revolutionary Committee has come into being to assume the tasks of a provincial and municipal people's administrative organ. This is another of our far-reaching successes. Our rear, a permanent factor of our victory, and our resistance areas have been considerably expanded, stretching from the Truong Son Range and the immense High Plateaux down to the vast plains of Quang Tri and Thua Thien provinces and Central Trung Bo, from the mountain regions of Eastern Nam Bo down to the Plain of Reeds and the immense Mekong Delta. Our manpower and material resources have increased quickly and steadily.

That at the same time is another very heavy failure for the enemy. The puppet administration, one of the main props of U.S. neo-colonialism, is now merely a decaying tree on the point of being pulled down by the revolutionary storm of our armed forces and people. The enemy's rear, the area and source of their plundering activities, has been narrowed down to an extent hitherto unknown.

In short, we have won victories of very important strategic significance, both militarily and politically. The aggressors and their puppets are suffering heaviest losses, very hard to be retrieved. They have failed to achieve the strategic objectives which they had long been pursuing such as to "search and destroy" the South Vietnamese people's armed forces, "pacify" the countryside, build up the puppet administration, consolidate the puppet army. In future, having to deal with a much more difficult situation, they will have still less chance to realize these objectives.

Precisely, because they have sustained so heavy losses and so bitter a setback the Americans and Thieu-Ky have recently cooked up and told fantastic tales over and over again in the hope of making black white, bolstering up the morale of the puppet troops and administrative personnel, and deceiving public opinion. However, they cannot hide an elephant with a basket. The truth is that our armed forces and people have won unprecedented victories while the position of the Americans and their henchmen who have suffered unheard-of bitter failure, is becoming shakier with every passing hour, in everybody's eyes. That is why all their odious distortions have exploded like soap bubbles. Also to conceal their defeats and intimidate the Vietnamese people, they have used bombs and shells, toxic gas and noxious chemicals to massacre our people, set afire their houses, thus rendering tens of thousands of them homeless. Most cruel and cowardly pirates, while thus killing and burning, they call for "assistance" to those whose relatives are victims to their crimes. They want to put the blame on others, but their savage and vile acts cannot deceive our people. Neither can their bombs and shells intimidate our people. Like pouring oil on the flame, they embitter our people's hatred which will come down on their heads like thunderbolts. They will certainly have to repay ten times for their crimes. Nothing is more precious than independence and freedom; nothing can shake our people's determination to fight and to win, to die rather than live in slavery.

The glorious victories of our armed forces and people have given rise to a new situation on the battlefield, which is particularly favourable to us and unfavourable to the enemy.

Never has the unrivalled political and moral superiority of our armed forces and people reached such a high and been turned into so powerful a material force as now.

Millions of people have courageously taken to the streets to confront the enemy and set up combat units equipped with captured weapons. Our political army has become a mighty force and is more experienced than ever.

Personalities, intellectuals, students, pupils, youths, women, businessmen and people of other walks of life are actively contributing to the cause of national independence.

The "Alliance of National, Democratic, and Peace Forces" in Saigon, the "National Democratic and Peace Alliance" in Hue, and many other patriotic organizations have come into being and are siding with the entire people to step up the struggle for national liberation.

Our kith and kin in the North are supporting us with might and main and constantly encouraging the struggle of our armed forces and people.

Our people's resistance against U.S. aggression for national salvation is enjoying the warmest and greatest sympathy and support from the whole socialist camp and progressive mankind, including the progressive American people.

We are being provided with the most favourable conditions and the firmest bases to achieve our aims.

Our position and strength is growing like the radiant rising sun.

The enemy position and strength is flickering like a dying flame.

We shall certainly win complete victory.

The enemy are doomed to complete failure.

The U.S. invaders and the Thieu-Ky clique of traitors are still stubbornly resorting to many wicked schemes and tricks. The war remains hard and fierce.

Dear compatriots in rural and urban areas!

Let our compatriots in towns resolutely rise up and valiantly struggle for their vital rights, help one another and tide over difficulties caused by the enemy, be resolved to crush all their schemes and activities aimed at dividing, terrorizing and massacring them.

Let all of you resolutely stand up, kill wicked agents, break up the enemy's grip, overthrow the Thieu-Ky traitors and wrest power for the people, fight shoulder to shoulder with the Liberation Armed Forces. Everything for the front, everything for victory over the U.S. aggressors.

Dear young friends,

Enthusiastically join the militia, self-defense units, regional troops and regular forces. This is a golden opportunity for you to dedicate your strength, talent and mind to the accomplishment of our task and avenge our fatherland and your own families. Let those who are still living in the areas under the enemy's temporary control resolutely smash their draft scheme.

Officers and men, policemen and officials in the puppet army and administration,

The fate of the U.S. aggressors and the Thieu-Ky clique is sealed; our people are determined to make them repay their enormous blood debt. Dissociate yourselves from the gloomy lot of the invaders and their valets. Rise up, stage mutinies and achieve feats to save the fatherland and yourselves.

Dear fighters and compatriots!

Our people have a history of four thousand years during which they have written brilliant pages in their resistance to foreign invasion; possessed of glorious traditions, they fought against stronger and more numerous enemies and won splendid victories such as at Bach Dang, Chi Lang, Dong Da and Dien Bien Phu.

Over the past ten years South Viet Nam, the Brass Wall of our Fatherland, has repeatedly got the better of the U.S. aggressors. Clearly, they and their lackeys are doomed to complete defeat.

The charge is being sounded all over our country.

The Truong Son Range is shaking.

The Mekong River is surging.

Fighters and compatriots, heroically march forward!

21
Lao Dong Party [North Vietnam Communist Party] Document on Tet, March 1968

Source: Viet-Nam Documents and Research Notes (U.S. Embassy, Saigon, July 1968), excerpt.

1. *Great and unprecedented successes recorded in all fields during the first-month phase of the General Offensive and General Uprising.*

Since the beginning of Spring this year, the "Anti-U.S. National Salvation" resistance war of our people in the South has entered a new phase:

In this phase of General Offensive and General Uprising, after a month of continuous offensives and simultaneous uprisings conducted on all battlefields in the South, we have recorded great and unprecedented victories in all fields, inflicting on the enemy heavier losses than those he had suffered in any previous period.

> 1) We wore down, annihilated and disintegrated almost one-third of the puppet troops' strength, wore down and annihilated about one-fifth of U.S. combat forces, one-third of the total number of aircraft, one-third of the total number of mechanized vehicles, and an important part of U.S. and puppet material installations: destroyed and forced to surrender or withdrawal one-third of the enemy military posts, driving the enemy into an unprecedentedly awkward situation: from the position of the aggressor striving to gain the initiative through a two-prong tactic [military action and rural pacification], the enemy has withdrawn into a purely passive and defensive position, with his forces dispersed on all battlefields in the South for the purpose of defending the towns, cities and the main lines of communications. The struggle potential

and morale of U.S. and puppet troops have seriously weakened because our army and people have dealt thundering blows at them everywhere, even at their principal lairs, and because they are facing great difficulties in replenishing troops and replacing war facilities destroyed during the past month.

2) We attacked all U.S.-puppet nerve centers, occupied and exerted our control for a definite period and at varying degrees over almost all towns, cities and municipalities in the South, and destroyed and disintegrated an important part of puppet installations at all levels, seriously damaging the puppet administrative machinery.

3) We liberated additional wide areas in the countryside containing a population of 1.5 million inhabitants; consolidated and widened our rear areas, shifted immense resources of manpower and material, which had been previously robbed by the enemy in these areas, to the support of the front-line and of victory; encircled and isolated the enemy, and reduced the enemy's reserves of human and material resources, driving him into a very difficult economic and financial situation.

4) We have quantitatively and qualitatively improved our armed forces and political forces which have become outstandingly mature during the struggle in the past month. Our armed forces have progressed in many aspects, political organizations are being consolidated and have stepped forward, much progress has been realized in leadership activities and methods and we have gained richer experiences.

The above-mentioned great and unprecedented successes in all fields have strongly encouraged and motivated compatriots in towns and cities and areas under temporary enemy control to arise to seize the state power, have created a lively and enthusiastic atmosphere and inspired a strong confidence in final victory among compatriots in both the North and South. These successes have moreover won the sympathy and support of the socialist countries and the world's progressive people (including the U.S. progressive people) for our people's revolutionary cause, seriously isolated the U.S. imperialists and their lackeys, deepened their internal contradictions and thereby weakened the U.S. will of aggression.

The above-mentioned great successes in all fields have been recorded thanks to the clear-sighted and correct policy, line and strategic determination of the Party, the wise and resolute leadership of the Party Central Committee, the correct implementation of the Party's policy and line by Nam Truong and Party committee echelons, the sacrifice and devotion of all Party cadres and members who have in an exemplary manner carried out the Party's strategic determination, the eagerness for independence and freedom of the people in the South who are ready to shed their blood in exchange for independence and freedom, the absolute loyalty to the Party's and masses' revolution of the People's armed forces who have fought with infinite courage, the great assistance from the northern rear area and brotherly socialist countries, and the sympathy and support from the world people.

We have won great successes but still have many deficiencies and weak points:

1) In the military field—From the beginning, we have not been able to annihilate much of the enemy's live force and much of the reactionary clique. Our armed forces have not fulfilled their role as "lever" and have not created favorable conditions for motivating the masses to arise in towns and cities.

2) In the political field—Organized popular forces were not broad and strong enough. We have not had specific plans for motivating the masses to the extent that they would indulge in violent armed uprisings in coordination with and supporting the military offensives.

3) The puppet troop proselyting failed to create a military revolt movement in which the troops would arise and return to the people's side. The enemy troop proselyting task to be carried out in coordination with the armed struggle and political struggle has not been performed, and inadequate attention had been paid to this in particular.

4) There has not been enough consciousness about specific plans for the widening and development of liberated rural areas and the appropriate mobilization of manpower, material resources and the great capabilities of the masses to support the front line.

5) The building of real strength and particularly the replenishment of troops and development of political forces of the infrastructure has been slow and has not met the requirements of continuous offensives and uprisings of the new phase.

6) In providing leadership and guidance to various echelons, we failed to give them a profound and thorough understanding of the Party's policy, line and strategic determination so that they have a correct and full realization of this phase of General Offensive and General Uprising. The implementation of our policies has not been sharply and closely conducted. We lacked concreteness, our plans were simple, our coordination poor, control and prodding were absent, reporting and requests for instructions were much delayed.

The above-mentioned deficiencies and weak points have limited our successes and are, at the same time, difficulties which we must resolutely overcome.

22
Message from General Wheeler to All Pacific Commanders, March 30, 1968

Source: Document declassified by the Department of Defense.

1. The referenced message apprises you that combat air operations against North Vietnam north of 20° North Latitude will be discontinued effective 0800

hours 1 April 1968, Saigon time. The purpose of this message is to acquaint you with the reasons for the cessation of air strikes.

2. At 2100 hours, 31 March, Washington time, the President will make an address to the Nation in which he will announce deployment of additional forces to South Vietnam, including forces called to active duty from the Reserve Components. He feels it mandatory that, at the same time, he proclaim another initiative designed to achieve a peaceful settlement of the conflict in Southeast Asia in order to blunt accusations of escalation from the opposers of Administration policy in Southeast Asia.

3. The following factors are pertinent to his decision:

a. Since the Tet offensive support of the American public and the Congress for the war in SEA has decreased at an accelerating rate. Many of the strongest proponents of forceful action in Vietnam have reversed their positions, have moved to neutral ground, or are wavering. If this trend continues unchecked, public support of our objectives in SEA will be too frail to sustain the effort.

b. Weather over the northern portion of North Vietnam will continue unsuitable for air operations during the next 30 days; therefore, if a cessation of air operations is to be undertaken, now is the best time from the military viewpoint.

c. It is hoped that this unilateral initiative to seek peace will reverse the growing dissent and opposition within our society to the war.

d. The initiative will aid in countering foreign criticism.

e. President Thieu has been consulted and agrees to the cessation.

4. The Joint Chiefs of Staff have been apprised of the unilateral initiative to be taken, understand the reasons therefore, and they enjoin all commanders to support the decision of the President. In this connection, addressees, without citing the source or mentioning the President, should draw on this message in talking to subordinate commanders to solicit their understanding and support. In particular, every effort should be made to discourage military personnel from expressing criticism to news media representatives. I recognize that this is a delicate matter and one which cannot be approached on the basis of issuing fiats; rather, the attitudes of commanders will probably be most influential in guiding the reaction of their subordinates.

5. For Admiral Sharp: Secretary Rusk has been requested by Secretary Clifford to discuss fully with you the situation in this country which I have sketched above and to acquaint you fully with the problems we face here.

6. Information contained in paragraphs 1 and 2 is time-sensitive. I request you use it prior to the President's address with utmost discretion. Warm regards to all.

23
"Peace in Vietnam and Southeast Asia"; Address to the Nation (March 31, 1968)

President Lyndon Baines Johnson

Source: Public Papers of the Presidents of the United States, 1968–1969 (Washington: U.S. Government Printing Office, 1970), pp. 468–76.

Good evening, my fellow Americans:

Tonight I want to speak to you of peace in Vietnam and Southeast Asia.

No other question so preoccupies our people. No other dream so absorbs the 250 million human beings who live in that part of the world. No other goal motivates American policy in Southeast Asia.

For years, representatives of our Government and others have traveled the world—seeking to find a basis for peace talks.

Since last September, they have carried the offer that I made public at San Antonio.

The offer was:

That the United States would stop its bombardment of North Vietnam when that would lead promptly to productive discussions—and that we would assume that North Vietnam would not take military advantage of our restraint.

Hanoi denounced this offer, both privately and publicly. Even while the search for peace was going on, North Vietnam rushed their preparations for a savage assault on the people, the government, and the allies of South Vietnam.

Their attack—during the Tet holidays—failed to achieve its principal objectives.

It did not collapse the elected government of South Vietnam or shatter its army—as the Communists had hoped.

It did not produce a "general uprising" among the people of the cities as they had predicted.

The Communists were unable to maintain control of any of the more than 30 cities that they attacked. And they took very heavy casualties.

But they did compel the South Vietnamese and their allies to move certain forces from the countryside into the cities.

They caused widespread disruption and suffering. Their attacks, and the battles that followed, made refugees of half a million human beings.

The Communists may renew their attack any day.

They are, it appears, trying to make 1968 the year of decision in South Vietnam—the year that brings, if no final victory or defeat, at least a turning point in the struggle.

This much is clear:

If they do mount another round of heavy attacks, they will not succeed in destroying the fighting power of South Vietnam and its allies.

But tragically, this is also clear: Many men—on both sides of the struggle—will be lost. A nation that has already suffered 20 years of warfare will suffer once again. Armies on both sides will take new casualties. And the war will go on.

There is no need for this to be so.

There is no need to delay the talks that could bring an end to this long and this bloody war.

Tonight, I renew the offer I made last August—to stop the bombardment of North Vietnam. We ask that talks begin promptly, that they be serious talks on the substance of peace. We assume that during those talks Hanoi will not take advantage of our restraint.

We are prepared to move immediately toward peace through negotiations.

So, tonight, in the hope that this action will lead to early talks, I am taking the first step to deescalate the conflict. We are reducing—substantially reducing—the present level of hostilities.

And we are doing so unilaterally, and at once.

Tonight, I have ordered our aircraft and our naval vessels to make no attacks on North Vietnam, except in the area north of the demilitarized zone where the continuing enemy buildup directly threatens allied forward positions and where the movements of their troops and supplies are clearly related to that threat.

Some weeks ago—to help meet the enemy's new offensive—we sent to Vietnam about 11,000 additional Marine and airborne troops. They were deployed by air in 48 hours, on an emergency basis. But the artillery, tank, aircraft, medical, and other units that were needed to work with and to support these infantry troops in combat could not then accompany them by air on that short notice.

In order that these forces may reach maximum combat effectiveness, the Joint Chiefs of Staff have recommended to me that we should prepare to send—during the next 5 months—support troops totaling approximately 13,500 men.

A portion of these men will be made available from our active forces. The balance will come from reserve component units which will be called up for service.

The actions that we have taken since the beginning of the year

—to reequip the South Vietnamese forces,

—to meet our responsibilities in Korea, as well as our responsibilities in Vietnam,

—to meet price increases and the cost of activating and deploying reserve forces,

—to replace helicopters and provide the other military supplies we need, all of these actions are going to require additional expenditures.

The tentative estimate of those additional expenditures is $2.5 billion in this fiscal year, and $2.6 billion in the next fiscal year.

These projected increases in expenditures for our national security will bring into sharper focus the Nation's need for immediate action: action to protect the prosperity of the American people and to protect the strength and the stability of our American dollar.

On many occasions I have pointed out that, without a tax bill or decreased expenditures, next year's deficit would again be around $20 billion. I have emphasized the need to set strict priorities in our spending. I have stressed that failure to act and to act promptly and decisively would raise very strong doubts throughout the world about America's willingness to keep its financial house in order.

Yet Congress has not acted. And tonight we face the sharpest financial threat in the postwar era—a threat to the dollar's role as the keystone of international trade and finance in the world.

Last week, at the monetary conference in Stockholm, the major industrial countries decided to take a big step toward creating a new international monetary asset that will strengthen the international monetary system. I am very proud of the very able work done by Secretary Fowler and Chairman Martin of the Federal Reserve Board.

But to make this system work the United States just must bring its balance of payments to—or very close to—equilibrium. We must have a responsible fiscal policy in this country. The passage of a tax bill now, together with expenditure control that the Congress may desire and dictate, is absolutely necessary to protect this Nation's security, to continue our prosperity, and to meet the needs of our people.

What is at stake is 7 years of unparalleled prosperity. In those 7 years, the real income of the average American, after taxes, rose by almost 30 percent—a gain as large as that of the entire preceding 19 years.

So the steps that we must take to convince the world are exactly the steps we must take to sustain our own economic strength here at home. In the past 8 months, prices and interest rates have risen because of our inaction.

We must, therefore, now do everything we can to move from debate to action—from talking to voting. There is, I believe—I hope there is—in both Houses of the Congress—a growing sense of urgency that this situation just must be acted upon and must be corrected.

My budget in January was, we thought, a tight one. It fully reflected our evaluation of most of the demanding needs of this Nation.

But in these budgetary matters, the President does not decide alone. The Congress has the power and the duty to determine appropriations and taxes.

The Congress is now considering our proposals and they are considering reductions in the budget that we submitted.

As part of a program of fiscal restraint that includes the tax surcharge, I shall approve appropriate reductions in the January budget when and if Congress so decides that that should be done.

One thing is unmistakably clear, however: Our deficit just must be reduced. Failure to act could bring on conditions that would strike hardest at those people that all of us are trying so hard to help.

Our objective in South Vietnam has never been the annihilation of the enemy. It has been to bring about a recognition in Hanoi that its objective—taking over the South by force—could not be achieved.

We think that peace can be based on the Geneva Accords of 1954—under political conditions that permit the South Vietnamese—all the South Vietnamese—to chart their course free of any outside domination or interference, from us or from anyone else.

So tonight I reaffirm the pledge that we made at Manila—that we are prepared to withdraw our forces from South Vietnam as the other side withdraws its forces to the north, stops the infiltration, and the level of violence thus subsides.

Our goal of peace and self-determination in Vietnam is directly related to the future of all of Southeast Asia—where much has happened to inspire confidence during the past 10 years. We have done all that we knew how to do to contribute and to help build that confidence.

A number of its nations have shown what can be accomplished under conditions of security. Since 1966, Indonesia, the fifth largest nation in all the world, with a population of more than 100 million people, has had a government that is dedicated to peace with its neighbors and improved conditions for its own people. Political and economic cooperation between nations has grown rapidly.

I think every American can take a great deal of pride in the role that we have played in bringing this about in Southeast Asia. We can rightly judge—as responsible Southeast Asians themselves do—that the progress of the past 3 years would have been far less likely—if not completely impossible—if America's sons and others had not made their stand in Vietnam.

At Johns Hopkins University, about 3 years ago, I announced that the United States would take part in the great work of developing Southeast Asia, including the Mekong Valley, for all the people of that region. Our determination to help build a better land—a better land for men on both sides of the present conflict—has not diminished in the least. Indeed, the ravages of war, I think, have made it more urgent than ever.

So, I repeat on behalf of the United States again tonight what I said at Johns Hopkins—that North Vietnam could take its place in this common effort just as soon as peace comes.

Finally, my fellow Americans, let me say this:

Of those to whom much is given, much is asked. I cannot say and no man could say that no more will be asked of us.

Yet, I believe that now, no less than when the decade began, this generation of Americans is willing to "pay any price, bear any burden, meet any hardship, support any friend, oppose any foe to assure the survival and the success of liberty."

Since those words were spoken by John F. Kennedy, the people of America have kept that compact with mankind's noblest cause.

And we shall continue to keep it.

Yet, I believe that we must always be mindful of this one thing, whatever the trials and the tests ahead. The ultimate strength of our country and our cause will lie not in powerful weapons or infinite resources or boundless wealth, but will lie in the unity of our people.

This I believe very deeply.

Throughout my entire public career I have followed the personal philosophy that I am a free man, an American, a public servant, and a member of my party, in that order always and only.

For 37 years in the service or our nation, first as a Congressman, as a Senator, and as Vice President, and now as your President, I have put the unity of the people first. I have put it ahead of any divisive partisanship.

And in these times as in times before, it is true that a house divided against itself by the spirit of faction, of party, or region, of religion, of race, is a house that cannot stand.

There is division in the American house now. There is divisiveness among us all tonight. And holding the trust that is mine, as President of all the people I cannot disregard the peril to the progress of the American people and the hope and the prospect of peace for all peoples.

So, I would ask all Americans, whatever their personal interests or concern, to guard against divisiveness and all its ugly consequences.

Fifty-two months and 10 days ago, in a moment of tragedy and trauma, the duties of this office fell upon me. I asked then for your help and God's, that we might continue America on its course, binding up our wounds, healing our history, moving forward in new units, to clear the American agenda and to keep the American commitment for all of our people.

United we have kept that commitment. United we have enlarged that commitment.

Through all time to come, I think America will be a stronger nation, a more just society, and a land of greater opportunity and fulfillment because of what we have all done together in these years of unparalleled achievement.

Our reward will come in the life of freedom, peace, and hope that our children will enjoy through ages ahead.

What we won when all of our people united just must not now be lost in suspicion, distrust, selfishness, and politics among any of our people.

Believing this as I do, I have concluded that I should not permit the Presidency to become involved in the partisan divisions that are developing in this political year.

With America's sons in the fields far away, with America's future under challenge right here at home, with our hopes and the world's hopes for peace in the balance every day, I do not believe that I should devote an hour or a day of my time to any personal partisan causes or to any duties other than the awesome duties of this office—the Presidency of your country.

Accordingly, I shall not seek, and I will not accept, the nomination of my party for another term as your President.

But let men everywhere know, however, that a strong, a confident, and a vigilant America stands ready tonight to seek an honorable peace—and stands ready tonight to defend an honored cause—whatever the price, whatever the burden, whatever the sacrifice that duty may require.

Thank you for listening.

Good night and God bless all of you.

24
Clark M. Clifford Remembers His Post-Tet Questions

Source: Clark M. Clifford, "A Vietnam Reappraisal: The Personal History of One Man's View and How It Evolved," *Foreign Affairs* (July 1969), pp. 609–12, 613. Reprinted by permission of *Foreign Affairs,* July 1969.

I took office on March 1, 1968. The enemy's Tet offensive of late January and early February had been beaten back at great cost. The confidence of the American people had been badly shaken. The ability of the South Vietnamese Government to restore order and morale in the populace, and discipline and esprit in the armed forces, was being questioned. At the President's direction, General Earle G. Wheeler, Chairman of the Joint Chiefs of Staff, had flown to Viet Nam in late February for an on-the-spot conference with General Westmoreland. He had just returned and presented the military's request that over 200,000 troops be prepared for deployment to Viet Nam. These troops would be in addition to the

525,000 previously authorized. I was directed, as my first assignment, to chair a task force named by the President to determine how this new requirement could be met. We were not instructed to assess the need for substantial increases in men and matériel; we were to devise the means by which they could be provided.

My work was cut out. The task force included Secretary Rusk, Secretary Henry Fowler, Under Secretary of State Nicholas Katzenbach, Deputy Secretary of Defense Paul Nitze, General Wheeler, CIA Director Richard Helms, the President's Special Assistant, Walt Rostow, General Maxwell Taylor and other skilled and highly capable officials. All of them had had long and direct experience with Vietnamese problems. I had not. I had attended various meetings in the past several years and I had been to Viet Nam three times, but it was quickly apparent to me how little one knows if he has been on the periphery of a problem and not truly in it. Until the day-long sessions of early March, I had never had the opportunity of intensive analysis and fact-finding. Now I was thrust into a vigorous, ruthlessly frank assessment of our situation by the men who knew the most about it. Try though we would to stay with the assignment of devising means to meet the military's requests, fundamental questions began to recur over and over.

It is, of course, not possible to recall all the questions that were asked nor all of the answers that were given. Had a transcript of our discussions been made—one was not—it would have run to hundreds of closely printed pages. The documents brought to the table by participants would have totalled, if collected in one place—which they were not—many hundreds more. All that is pertinent to this essay are the impressions I formed, and the conclusions I ultimately reached in those days of exhausting scrutiny. In the colloquial style of those meetings, here are some of the principal issues raised and some of the answers as I understood them:

"Will 200,000 more men do the job?" I found no assurance that they would.

"If not, how many more might be needed—and when?" There was no way of knowing.

"What would be involved in committing 200,000 more men to Viet Nam?" A reserve call-up of approximately 280,000, an increased draft call and an extension of tours of duty of most men then in service.

"Can the enemy respond with a build-up of his own?" He could and he probably would.

"What are the estimated costs of the latest requests?" First calculations were on the order of $2 billion for the remaining four months of that fiscal year, and an increase of $10 to $12 billion for the year beginning July 1, 1968.

"What will be the impact on the economy?" So great that we would face the possibility of credit restrictions, a tax increase and even wage and price controls. The balance of payments would be worsened by at least half a billion dollars a year.

"Can bombing stop the war?" Never by itself. It was inflicting heavy personnel and matériel losses, but bombing by itself would not stop the war.

"Will stepping up the bombing decrease American casualties?" Very little, if at all. Our casualties were due to the intensity of the ground fighting in the South. We had already dropped a heavier tonnage of bombs than in all the theaters of World War II. During 1967, an estimated 90,000 North Vietnamese had infiltrated into South Viet Nam. In the opening weeks of 1968, infiltrators were coming in at three to four times the rate of a year earlier, despite the ferocity and intensity of our campaign of aerial interdiction.

"How long must we keep on sending our men and carrying the main burden of combat?" The South Vietnamese were doing better, but they were not ready yet to replace our troops and we did not know when they would be.

When I asked for a presentation of the military plan for attaining victory in Viet Nam, I was told that there was no plan for victory in the historic American sense. Why not? Because our forces were operating under three major political restrictions: The President had forbidden the invasion of North Viet Nam because this could trigger the mutual assistance pact between North Viet Nam and China; the President had forbidden the mining of the harbor at Haiphong, the principal port through which the North received military supplies, because a Soviet vessel might be sunk; the President had forbidden our forces to pursue the enemy into Laos and Cambodia, for to do so would spread the war, politically and geographically, with no discernible advantage. These and other restrictions which precluded an all-out, no-holds-barred military effort were wisely designed to prevent our being drawn into a larger war. We had no inclination to recommend to the President their cancellation.

"Given these circumstances, how can we win?" We would, I was told, continue to evidence our superiority over the enemy; we would continue to attack in the belief that he would reach the stage where he would find it inadvisable to go on with the war. He could not afford the attrition we were inflicting on him. And we were improving our posture all the time.

I then asked, "What is the best estimate as to how long this course of action will take? Six months? One year? Two years?" There was no agreement on an answer. Not only was there no agreement, I could find no one willing to express any confidence in his guesses. Certainly, none of us was willing to assert that he could see "light at the end of the tunnel" or that American troops would be coming home by the end of the year.

After days of this type of analysis, my concern had greatly deepened. I could not find out when the war was going to end; I could not find out the manner in which it was going to end; I could not find out whether the new requests for men and equipment were going to be enough, or whether it would take more and, if more, when and how much; I could not find out how soon the South Vietnamese forces would be ready to take over. All I had was the statement, given with too little self-assurance to be comforting, that if we persisted for an indeterminate length of time, the enemy would choose not to go on.

And so I asked, “Does anyone see any diminution in the will of the enemy after four years of our having been there, after enormous casualties and after massive destruction from our bombing?”

The answer was that there appeared to be no diminution in the will of the enemy. . . .

And so, after these exhausting days, I was convinced that the military course we were pursuing was not only endless, but hopeless. A further substantial increase in American forces could only increase the devastation and the Americanization of the war, and thus leave us even further from our goal of a peace that would permit the people of South Viet Nam to fashion their own political and economic institutions. Henceforth, I was also convinced, our primary goal should be to level off our involvement, and to work toward gradual disengagement.

Chapter VI

The Antiwar Movement

The American people have always been hesitant to become involved in foreign wars. During nearly every major war this country has waged, there has been a protest movement against it. Notable were the small but articulate movements against the Mexican War of 1846–1848 and the conquest of the Philippines from 1899–1901. Because of the public's unwillingness to go to war, even the country's entrances into World War I and World War II were delayed for years.

With this historical background, it should not be surprising that a powerful antiwar movement existed in the United States during the Vietnam War, a movement that increasingly affected even the most conservative (pro-military) segments of the population. One of the reasons for the vast size of the antiwar movement was the simple fact, intuitively obvious to the most casual observer, that Vietnam posed no direct danger to American lives or property. Unlike other wars in the twentieth century where the enemy attacked or threatened the United States, no case could be made at any point that Vietnamese presented any direct danger to Americans. There was never even a hint that North Vietnam or the NLF might have nuclear weapons, chemical weapons, or any of the kinds of weapons that, more recently, it was thought that Saddam Hussein possessed in 1991.

Although not well known, the impact of the antiwar movement on policymakers was critical in preventing the war's escalation. In November 1969, as we know today from Richard Nixon's memoirs, the president was prevented from using nuclear weapons against North Vietnam by the hundreds of thousands of people who marched in the United States. Years earlier, the power of protesters was felt by Lyndon Johnson. In August 1966, his military chiefs had urged massive bombing of Hanoi and Haiphong to speed the end of the war. To make their case, the generals arranged for Johnson to meet the Pentagon's computer experts, men who had calculated that three quarters of a million lives had been saved by using atomic bombs against Japan and that a similar number could be saved again through attacks on the North's urban areas. LBJ heard them out before interrupting, "I have one more problem for your computer—how long will it take 500,000 angry Americans to climb that White House wall out there and lynch their president if he does something like that?"

While there were examples of protest against the war in the early 1960s, for the most part these were isolated voices. As the body bags came home in increasing numbers, however, what had been a tiny minority espousing moral principles became an increasingly militant and popular movement. Once eighteen-year-olds were drafted and ordered to kill or be killed, the movement became based more on self-interest than moral indignation, and its actions changed from passive protest to militant rebellion.

Nowhere was this more true than among black Americans. In 1965, as the ground war heated up, black Americans increasingly did more than speak out against the war, write letters to presidents, lobby congresspeople, or sign public declarations of conscience. Labeling the war a white man's war on colored people, many blacks refused to be inducted into the armed forces. The most famous person to do so was Muhammad Ali, heavyweight champion of the world, whose boxing title was taken away from him for his refusal to be inducted.

In the mid-1960s, with the civil rights movement in the midst of its quest to end segregation, black Americans increasingly made arguments such as: "Why should we fight, kill and die in a war for the democratic rights of Vietnamese when we ourselves do not have democratic rights in the United States?" The first document in this chapter, Malcolm X's "Two Minutes on Vietnam," was transcribed in 1965, at a time when the general public knew very little about the Vietnam War. Malcolm already understood quite well that the United States had abandoned Diem, and his warning that escalation would only deepen the final defeat of the United States proved to be prophetic.

Black Americans' share of combat troops and fatalities exceeded their proportion of the general population. Their higher fatality rate was due in part to their receiving the most dangerous and dirty assignments, a level of discrimination that gave rise to conflicts within the military and handicapped its ability to fight the enemy.

Racial antagonisms within the antiwar movement also became highly pronounced during the Vietnam War. While whites marched under banners proclaiming, "We are not a nation of killers," black Americans linked the killings in Vietnam to their own experiences. On January 3, 1966, civil rights worker Samuel Younge, a member of the Student Non-Violent Coordinating Committee (SNCC), was shot and killed in Alabama when he tried to use a whites-only rest room, and SNCC's statement called his murder "no different from the murder of people in Vietnam, for both Younge and the Vietnamese sought and are seeking to secure rights guaranteed them by law. In each case, the U.S. government bears a great part of the responsibility for these deaths."

The war caused Students for a Democratic Society (SDS), an organization founded by idealistic college students in 1962, to change its focus from community organizing of poor people to opposing the war in Vietnam and the draft. Document 26 is SDS's call for the first national antiwar demonstration on April 17, 1965. The rally organizers expected very few people and were amazed when more than 15,000 showed up. In the next four years the antiwar movement grew by leaps and bounds, encompassing ever-widening segments of the population and radicalizing its activist leaders. From an idealistic organization that condemned the war as immoral in 1965, SDS by 1969 called for actions "in support of the heroic fight of the Vietnamese people and the National Liberation Front," actions designed to "bring the war home" (Document 27). Only a few hundred people went to Chicago on October 11, 1969 to fight the "pigs" (as they referred to the police) during the Days of Rage. The small turnout signaled that SDS had lost touch with its student base as it entered its final phase, one of "revolutionary" nihilism.

By 1970, SDS no longer existed, but the antiwar movement reached its high point when Richard Nixon expanded the war by ordering the invasion of Cambodia on April 30, 1970 (see Document 28). What happened in the next three weeks was the largest strike in the history of the United States, a strike involving more than four million students and faculty on the nation's college campuses. All over the country there were severe protests, and in sixteen states the National Guard had to be called out to control the campuses because of the depth of outrage over the invasion of Cambodia. At Kent State University four students were shot dead by the National Guard, and at Jackson State University two students were shot dead by the Highway Patrol.

As the movement against the war gathered momentum, dissent within the army also multiplied. In May 1970 (during the student strike), 500 GIs deserted every day in Vietnam, and some of these men went over to the side of the enemy. That year there were 65,000 deserters from the army alone. Soldiers returning from combat provided new leadership for the antiwar movement. These Vietnam veterans organized themselves into an organization called Vietnam Veterans Against the War (VVAW). In the summer of 1970, there were only 2,000 members of VVAW, but by 1972, there were 2,500 members *in Vietnam alone* and many thousands more in the United States.

In its final days, SDS had called on the movement to act in solidarity with the NLF, but the Black Panther party actually offered troops to the Vietnamese guerrillas. One demand of the Black Panther party had been that black people should not have to serve in the U.S. military, but it was a different matter to fight against that establishment. Document 30 consists of the letter that Huey Newton, head of the Black Panther party, wrote to the NLF and the reply he was sent by Nguyen Thi Dinh. The Panthers' offer reflected the wide loss of legitimacy suffered by the American government, a breakdown in patriotic values that was also manifest in the People's Peace Treaty (Document 31), a treaty of peace signed and circulated by American student governments. By 1971, a broad segment of the population felt that the government was not negotiating in good faith to end the war and that only a people-to-people effort would bring peace. As the war dragged on, people became increasingly suspicious of and even antagonistic to the government, and one response was simply to circumvent it.

The final document in this chapter, "Reflections on Calley," by philosopher Herbert Marcuse, analyzes the reasons why Americans identified with a soldier who had killed innocent Vietnamese in cold blood. In March 1968, hundreds of unarmed women, children, and old men were massacred by U.S. troops in a village named My Lai. Although the army's official report concluded that "war crimes" had been committed and recommended court martials for over two dozen officers, only Lt. William Calley was singled out for punishment. Marcuse, a refugee from Germany prior to World War II, asked how the American psyche could tolerate and even encourage such acts as those perpetrated at My Lai, ones he saw as a replication of the horrors that the Nazis had inflicted.

25
Two Minutes on Vietnam

Malcolm X

Source: Militant Labor Forum, January 7, 1965. Reprinted by permission of Pathfinder Press.

Malcolm: Address myself to Vietnam for two minutes? It's a shame—that's one second. It is, it's a shame. You put the government on the spot when you even mention Vietnam. They feel embarrassed—you notice that? They wish they would not even have to read the newspapers about South Vietnam, and you can't blame them. It's just a trap that they let themselves get into. It's John Foster Dulles they're trying to blame it on, because he's dead.

But they're trapped, they can't get out. You notice I said "they." *They* are trapped, *they* can't get out. If they pour more men in, they'll get deeper. If they pull the men out, it's a defeat. And they should have known it in the first place.

France had about 200,000 Frenchmen over there, and the most highly mechanized modern army sitting on this earth. And those little rice farmers ate them up, and their tanks, and everything else. Yes, they did, and France was deeply entrenched, had been there a hundred or more years. Now, if she couldn't stay there and was entrenched, why, you are out of your mind if you think Sam can get in over there.

But we're not supposed to say that. If we say that, we're anti-American, or we're seditious, or we're subversive, or we're advocating something that's not intelligent. So that's two minutes, sir. Now they're turning around and getting in a worse situation in the Congo. They're getting into the Congo the same way they got into South Vietnam. They put Diem over there. Diem took all of their money, all their war equipment and everything else, and got them trapped. Then they killed him.

Yes, they killed him, murdered him in cold blood, him and his brother, Madame Nhu's husband, because they were embarrassed. They found out that they had made him strong and he was turning against them. So they killed him and put big Minh in his place, you know, the fat one. And he wouldn't act right, so they got rid of him and put Khanh in his place. And he's started telling Taylor to get out. You know, when the puppet starts talking back to the puppeteer, the puppeteer is in bad shape.

26
A Call to All Students to March on Washington to End the War in Vietnam, April 17, 1965

Students for a Democratic Society

Source: Collection of George Katsiaficas.

The current war in Vietnam is being waged in behalf of a succession of unpopular South Vietnamese dictatorships, not in behalf of freedom. No American-supported South Vietnamese regime in the past few years has gained the support of its people, for the simple reason that the people overwhelmingly want peace, self-determination, and the opportunity for development. American prosecution of the war has deprived them of all three.

• The war is fundamentally a *civil* war, waged by South Vietnamese against their government; it is not a "war of aggression." Military assistance from North Vietnam and China has been minimal; most guerrilla weapons are home-made or are captured American arms. The areas of strongest guerrilla control are not the areas adjacent to North Vietnam. And the people could not and cannot be isolated from the guerrillas by forced settlement in "strategic hamlets"; again and again Government military attacks fail because the people tip off the guerrillas; the people and the guerrillas are inseparable. Each repressive Government policy, each napalm bomb, each instance of torture, creates more guerrillas. Further, what foreign weapons the guerrillas have obtained are small arms, and are no match for the bombers and helicopters operated by the Americans. The U.S. government is the only foreign government that has sent major weapons to Vietnam.

• It is a *losing* war. Well over half of the area of South Vietnam is already governed by the National Liberation Front—the political arm of the "Viet Cong." In the guerrillas the peasants see relief from dictatorial Government agents; from the United States they get napalm, the jellied gasoline that burns into the flesh. The highly touted "counter-insurgency" the U.S. is applying in its "pilot project war" is only new weaponry, which cannot substitute for popular government. Thousands of Government troops have defected—the traditional signal of a losing counter-guerrilla war. *How many more lives must be lost before the Johnson Administration accepts the foregone conclusion*?

• It is a *self-defeating* war. If the U.S. objective is to guarantee self-determination in South Vietnam, that objective is far better served by allowing the South Vietnamese to choose their own government—something provided for by the 1954 Geneva Agreement but sabotaged in 1956 by the American-supported dictator Ngo Dinh Diem and never allowed since. The Diem government that invited U.S. intervention was thus illegitimate, having violated the agreement that established it. The Vietnamese, North and South, have no taste for Chinese domination—these two countries have fought one another for over a thousand years. Moreover, South Vietnam is not a "domino"—the "threat" to it is internal, not Chinese, and the greater threat to stability in other Southeast Asian countries is U.S.-inspired provocation of China, not China's own plans.

• It is a *dangerous* war. Every passing month of hostilities increases the risk of America escalating and widening the war. Since the '50s U.S.-trained South Vietnamese commando teams have been penetrating North Vietnam, considerably provoking the North Vietnamese. We all know of the presence of American destroyers in the Tonkin Gulf, a body of water surrounded on three sides by North Vietnamese and Chinese territory. How calm would the United States be if Cuban commandos were being sent into Florida, and Chinese ships were "guarding" Cape Cod Bay?

• It is a war never declared by Congress, although it costs almost two million dollars a day and has cost billions of dollars since the U.S. began its involvement. The facts of the war have been systematically concealed by the U.S. government for years, making it appear as if those expenditures have been helping the Vietnamese people. These factors erode the honesty and decency of American political life, and make democracy at home impossible. We are outraged that two million dollars a day is expended for a war on the poor in Vietnam, while government financing is so desperately needed to abolish poverty at home. *What kind of America is it whose response to poverty and oppression in South Vietnam is napalm and defoliation, whose response to poverty and oppression in Mississippi is . . . silence?*

• It is a hideously *immoral* war. America is committing pointless murder.

But the signs are plain that Americans are increasingly disaffected by this state of affairs. To draw together, express and enlarge the number of these voices of protest and to make this sentiment visible, Students for a Democratic Society (SDS) is calling for a

MARCH ON WASHINGTON TO END THE WAR IN VIETNAM

We urge the participation of all students who agree with us that the war in Vietnam injures both Vietnamese and Americans, and should be stopped.

The March, to be held on Saturday, April 17, 1965, will include a picketing of the White House, a march down the Mall to the Capitol Building to present a statement to Congress, and a meeting with both student and adult speakers. Senator Ernest Gruening of Alaska and I. F. Stone have already agreed to address the body.

Thousands of us can be heard. We dare not remain silent.

27
Bring the War Home!

Students for a Democratic Society

Source: Collection of George Katsiaficas.

It has been almost a year since the Democratic Convention, when thousands of young people came together in Chicago and tore up pig city for five days. The action was a response to the crisis this system is facing as a result of the war, the demand by black people for liberation, and the ever-growing reality that this system just can't make it.

This fall, people are coming back to Chicago: more powerful, better organized, and more together than we were last August.

SDS is calling for a National Action in Chicago on October 11. We are coming back to Chicago, and we are going to bring those we left behind last year.

Look At It: America, 1969: The war goes on, despite the jive double-talk about troop withdrawals and peace talks. Black people continue to be murdered by agents of the fat cats who run this country, if not in one way, then in another: by the pigs or the courts, by the boss or the welfare department. Working people face higher taxes, inflation, speed-ups, and the sure knowledge—if it hasn't happened already—that their sons may be shipped off to Vietnam and shipped home in a box. And young people all over the country go to prisons that are called schools, are trained for jobs that don't exist or serve no one's real interest but the boss's, and, to top it all off, get told that Vietnam is the place to defend their "freedom."

None of this is very new. The cities have been falling apart, the schools have been bullshit, the jobs have been rotten and unfulfilling for a long time.

What's new is that today not quite so many people are confused, and a lot more people are angry: angry about the fact that the promises we have heard since first grade are all jive; angry that, when you get down to it, this system is nothing but the total economic and military put-down of the oppressed peoples of the world.

And more: it's a system that steals the goods, the resources, and the labor of poor and working people all over the world in order to fill the pockets and bank accounts of a tiny capitalist class. (Call it imperialism.) It's a system that divides white workers from blacks by offering whites crumbs off the table, and telling them that if they don't stay cool the blacks will move in on their jobs, their homes, and their schools. (Call it white supremacy.) It's a system that divides men from women, forcing women to be subservient to men from childhood, to be slave labor in the home and cheap labor in the factory. (Call it male supremacy.) And it's a system that has colonized whole nations within this country—the nation of black people, the nation of brown people—to enslave, oppress, and ultimately murder the people on whose backs this country was built. (Call it fascism.)

But the lies are catching up to America—and the slick rich people and their agents in the government bureaucracies, the courts, the schools, and the pig stations just can't cut it anymore.

Black and brown people know it.

Young people know it.

More and more white working people know it.

And you know it.

Last Year, There Were Only about 10,000 of Us in Chicago

The press made it look like a massacre. All you could see on TV were shots of the horrors and blood of pig brutality. That was the line that the bald-headed businessmen were trying to run down—"If you mess with us, we'll let you have it." But those who were there tell a different story. We were together and our power was felt. It's true that some of us got hurt, but last summer was a victory for the people in a thousand ways.

Our actions showed the Vietnamese that there were masses of young people in this country facing the same enemy that they faced.

We showed that white people would no longer sit by passively while black communities were being invaded by occupation troops every day.

We showed that the "democratic process" of choosing candidates for a presidential election was nothing more than a hoax, pulled off by the businessmen who really run this country.

And we showed the whole world that in the face of the oppressive and exploitative rulers—and the military might to back them up—thousands of people are willing to fight back.

SDS Is Calling the Action This Year

But it will be a different action. An action not only against a single war or a "foreign policy," but against the whole imperialist system that made that war a necessity. An action not only for immediate withdrawal of all U.S. occupation troops, but in support of the heroic fight of the Vietnamese people and the National Liberation Front for freedom and independence. An action not only to bring "peace to Vietnam," but beginning to establish another front against imperialism right here in America—to "bring the war home."

We are demanding that all occupational troops get out of Vietnam and every other place they don't belong. This includes the black and brown communities, the workers' picket lines, the high schools, and the streets of Berkeley. No longer will we tolerate "law and order" backed up by soldiers in Vietnam and pigs in the communities and schools; a "law and order" that serves only the interests of those in power and tries to smash the people down whenever they rise up.

We are demanding the release of all political prisoners who have been victimized by the ever-growing attacks on the black liberation struggle and the people in general. Especially the leaders of the black liberation struggle like Huey P. Newton, Ahmed Evans, Fred Hampton, and Martin Sostre.

We are expressing total support for the National Liberation Front and the newly formed Provisional Revolutionary Government of South Vietnam. Throughout the history of the war, the NLF has provided the political and military leadership to the people of South Vietnam. The Provisional Revolutionary Government, recently formed by the NLF and other groups, has pledged to "mobilize the south Vietnamese armed forces and people" in order to continue the struggle for independence. The PRG also has expressed solidarity with "the just struggle of the Afro-American people for their fundamental national rights," and has pledged to "actively support the national independence movements of Asia, Africa, and Latin America."

We are also expressing total support for the black liberation struggle, part of the same struggle that the Vietnamese are fighting, against the same enemy.

We are demanding independence for Puerto Rico, and an end to the colonial oppression that the Puerto Rican nation faces at the hands of U.S. imperialism.

We are demanding an end to the surtax, a tax taken from the working people of this country and used to kill working people in Vietnam and other places for fun and profit.

We are expressing solidarity with the Conspiracy 8 who led the struggle last summer in Chicago. Our action is planned to roughly coincide with the beginning of their trial.

And we are expressing support for GIs in Vietnam and throughout the world who are being made to fight the battles of the rich, like poor and working people have always been made to do. We support those GIs at Fort Hood, Fort Jackson, and many other army bases who have refused to be cannon fodder in a war against the people of Vietnam.

It's Almost Hard to Remember When the War Began

But, after years of peace marches, petitions, and the gradual realization that this war was no "mistake" at all, one critical fact remains: the war is not just happening in Vietnam.

It is happening in the jungles of Guatemala, Bolivia, Thailand, and all oppressed nations throughout the world.

And it is happening here. In black communities throughout the country. On college campuses. And in the high schools, in the shops, and on the streets.

It is a war in which there are only two sides; a war not for domination but for an end to domination, not for destruction, but for liberation and the unchaining of human freedom.

And it is a war in which we cannot "resist"; it is a war in which we must fight.

On October 11, tens of thousands of people will come to Chicago to bring the war home. Join us.

All power to the people!

28
Address by President Nixon on Cambodia, April 30, 1970

Source: U.S. Senate Committee on Foreign Relations, *Background Information Relating to Southeast Asia and Vietnam* (December 1974), pp. 345–47.

Good evening, my fellow Americans. Ten days ago, in my report to the Nation on Viet-Nam, I announced a decision to withdraw an additional 150,000 Americans from Viet-Nam over the next year. I said then that I was making that decision despite our concern over increased enemy activity in Laos, in Cambodia, and in South Viet-Nam.

At that time, I warned that if I concluded that increased enemy activity in any of these areas endangered the lives of Americans remaining in Viet-Nam I would not hesitate to take strong and effective measures to deal with that situation.

Despite that warning, North Viet-Nam has increased its military aggression in all these areas, and particularly in Cambodia.

After full consultation with the National Security Council, Ambassador Bunker, General Abrams, and my other advisers, I have concluded that the actions of the enemy in the last 10 days clearly endanger the lives of Americans who are in Viet-Nam now and would constitute an unacceptable risk to those who will be there after withdrawal of another 150,000.

To protect our men who are in Viet-Nam and to guarantee the continued success of our withdrawal and Vietnamization programs, I have concluded that the time has come for action.

* * *

North Viet-Nam in the last 2 weeks has stripped away all pretense of respecting the sovereignty or the neutrality of Cambodia. Thousands of their soldiers are invading the country from the sanctuaries; they are encircling the Capital of Phnom Penh. Coming from these sanctuaries, as you see here, they have moved into Cambodia and are encircling the Capital.

Cambodia, as a result of this, has sent out a call to the United States, to a number of other nations, for assistance. Because if this enemy effort succeeds, Cambodia would become a vast enemy staging area and a springboard for attacks on South Viet-Nam along 600 miles of frontier, a refuge where enemy troops could return from combat without fear of retaliation.

North Vietnamese men and supplies could then be poured into that country, jeopardizing not only the lives of our own men but the people of South Viet-Nam as well.

Now, confronted with this situation, we have three options.

First, we can do nothing. Well, the ultimate result of that course of action is clear. Unless we indulge in wishful thinking, the lives of Americans remaining in Viet-Nam after our next withdrawal of 150,000 would be gravely threatened.

Let us go to the map again. Here is South Viet-Nam. Here is North Viet-Nam. North Viet-Nam already occupies this part of Laos. If North Viet-Nam also occupied this whole band in Cambodia, or the entire country, it would mean that South Viet-Nam was completely outflanked and the forces of Americans in this area, as well as the South Vietnamese, would be in an untenable military position.

Our second choice is to provide massive military assistance to Cambodia itself. Now, unfortunately, while we deeply sympathize with the plight of 7 million Cambodians, whose country is being invaded, massive amounts of military assistance could not be rapidly and effectively utilized by the small Cambodian Army against the immediate threat.

With the other nations, we shall do our best to provide the small arms and other equipment which the Cambodian Army of 40,000 needs and can use for its defense. But the aid we will provide will be limited to the purpose of enabling Cambodia to defend its neutrality and not for the purpose of making it an active belligerent on one side or the other.

Our third choice is to go to the heart of the trouble. That means cleaning out major North Vietnamese and Viet Cong occupied territories—these sanctuaries which serve as bases for attacks on both Cambodia and American and South Vietnamese forces in South Viet-Nam. Some of these, incidentally, are as close to Saigon as Baltimore is to Washington. This one, for example *[indicating]*, is called the Parrot's Beak. It is only 33 miles from Saigon.

Now, faced with these three options, this is the decision I have made.

In cooperation with the armed forces of South Viet-Nam, attacks are being launched this week to clean out major enemy sanctuaries on the Cambodian-Viet-Nam border.

A major responsibility for the ground operations is being assumed by South Vietnamese forces. For example, the attacks in several areas, including the Parrot's Beak that I referred to a moment ago, are exclusively South Vietnamese ground operations under South Vietnamese command, with the United States providing air and logistical support.

There is one area, however, immediately above Parrot's Beak, where I have concluded that a combined American and South Vietnamese operation is necessary.

Tonight American and South Vietnamese units will attack the headquarters for the entire Communist military operation in South Viet-Nam. This key control center has been occupied by the North Vietnamese and Viet Cong for 5 years in blatant violation of Cambodia's neutrality.

This is not an invasion of Cambodia. The areas in which these attacks will be launched are completely occupied and controlled by North Vietnamese forces. Our purpose is not to occupy the areas. Once enemy forces are driven out of these sanctuaries and once their military supplies are destroyed, we will withdraw.

These actions are in no way directed at the security interests of any nation. Any government that chooses to use these actions as a pretext for harming relations with the United States will be doing so on its own responsibility and on its own initiative, and we will draw the appropriate conclusions.

29
History of the Organization

Vietnam Veterans Against the War

Source: Collection of George Katsiaficas.

With a membership now approaching 20,000 and with chapters chartered or forming in all 50 states and Vietnam, the Vietnam Veterans Against the War has come a long way in the four years since it was founded in the spring of 1967 by six young veterans living in New York City.

By the beginning of 1968 the VVAW had established chapters in states as far flung as Alabama and California, Ohio and Oregon. Actually there were dozens, if not hundreds, of Nam veterans across the country speaking out as concerned individuals, just waiting for something organized to happen.

With a base of 500–600 members, the fledgling veterans' organization opened a national office in New York, began publishing a serviceman's newspaper from Chicago, "Vietnam GI" and filling speaking engagements across the country.

By the summer of 1968, through the fall-off of public support for the peace movement after President Johnson's April 1 abdication speech and the draining of energies by the political campaigns, the VVAW was nearly broke and had to close its New York office. We sent 50 veterans to the Democratic National Convention—one from each state—to lobby with the delegates in support of an anti-war platform, and instead of being listened to, the vets were teargassed along with everyone else.

With the renewed activity of the peace movement and the popular response to the first two Moratoriums, the VVAW found itself back together again. As it had before, the revived organization concentrated on speaking and debating engagements, newspaper advertisements and radio and television talk show appearances. By the beginning of 1970 the national membership was approaching 1500 members. However, with the slump in peace activities and public support through the winter, the VVAW was again at low ebb by early spring.

A new direction, which would presently bear fruit, had been taken during the winter by a small group within the VVAW. Following the press expose of the My Lai massacre in November 1969, and the Administration's contentions that the shootings at Song My had been an "isolated incident," a number of Vietnam veterans who knew otherwise from their own experience, helped form a series of war crimes hearings that brought forth Vietnam veterans to testify to American atrocities they had witnessed. The first of these hearings was held in Annapolis, Maryland in February 1970; the second, six weeks later in Springfield, Massachusetts.

Then in May came the invasion of Cambodia, the shootings at Jackson and Kent State, and the national student strikes. Once again the VVAW was revived by fresh energies and new applications for membership. Members of the VVAW led student strikes on major campuses throughout the country. And, for the first time, Vietnam veteran patients in VA hospitals got involved in the peace movement in large numbers. Some of them also got into trouble with hospital authorities, and the VVAW national office found itself in a new role of pressuring and lobbying for veterans rights.

Over the summer of 1970 the VVAW gradually grew in membership to the 2000 mark. Then over Labor Day weekend the Vietnam veterans group staged an action that catapulted it toward national recognition. The action was "Operation Rapid American Withdrawal (RAW)"; a four-day, 86-mile simulated search-and-destroy mission from Morristown, New Jersey to Valley Forge, Pennsylvania. Conducted by actual combat veterans wearing their old jungle battle gear and carrying plastic toy M–16s, "Operation RAW" was a mixture of peace march, mobile speak-out and guerrilla theater. Sweeping through the rural back counties of New Jersey and Eastern Pennsylvania, the 150 veterans on the march (who held 110 Purple Hearts among them) distributed leaflets, "cordoned" villages and small towns, "interrogated" and "shot" local civilians (pre-arranged groups of actors), and, in general, tried to recreate the brutal realities of the war.

At the rally at Valley Forge on Labor Day, 1500 local supporters watched the vets sweep "on line" down a long, grassy slope—the last three hundred yards chanting "Peace . . . Now"—and carrying five body bags with numbers of US and Vietnamese dead and wounded on them. After an afternoon of speeches, the veterans massed in company formation and, on command, broke their plastic weapons to symbolize their determination for peace.

Then, through the fall, the growing veterans group planned its most ambitious effort yet. After having held hearings into war crimes in a dozen cities on the East Coast and Mid-West, VVAW decided to hold national hearings involving over one hundred Nam vets. The name chosen for the national hearings was the "Winter Soldier Investigation"; a reference to Tom Paine's 1776 remark about the "summer soldiers and sunshine patriots" who shrink from the service of their country in times of crisis. As Vietnam veterans we know the Administration is cynically seeking to shift its own guilt to the lower grade field officers, the non-coms, and the enlisted men, for war crimes that originate in Washington, D.C.

The Winter Soldier Investigation was held in Detroit, Michigan on January 31, February 1 and 2, 1971. This, coupled with a free full-page ad published in the February issue of *Playboy,* increased our membership considerably.

The next action planned by VVAW was "Operation Dewey Canyon III"; a five-day operation in Washington, D.C. from April 19 to 23, 1971. Veterans of all wars were invited to join us to protest not only U.S. involvement in Southeast

Asia, but also the domestic, social, political and economic conditions that have caused and permitted the continuance of the war, the deplorable conditions in VA and military hospitals, the inadequacy of the GI benefits, and the extraordinary rate of unemployment among Vietnam veterans.

Some 2000 veterans participated in what was regarded by most of the press and public as the most important event to have occurred in the peace movement in a long while. The frustrations, however, were many. During the week prior to VVAW's arrival in Washington, government attorneys appeared before a Federal judge where they requested, and were granted, an injunction to forbid the vets from camping on the Mall. The injunction was rescinded three days later by the US Court of Appeals. The next day the government took its case to the Supreme Court and got an order restraining the original injunction. Veterans expected to be arrested at any time, but when no move was made to enforce the injunction Justice Department attorneys appeared before the Federal judge and got him to dismiss the earlier order. Earlier in the week the gates of Arlington Cemetery had been slammed shut in the face of veterans and Gold Star mothers when they attempted to lay two wreaths. The following day the gates were opened. The response of the Washington community and the nation to America's veterans was overwhelmingly sympathetic. Food, clothing, legal help and money for bail were freely given. Lobbying, guerrilla theater and testimony were presented daily to the Congress. It was a great week.

Since Dewey Canyon III VVAW has expanded its services to veterans on a national basis. We have formed both a Veterans Action Group and a lobbying office in Washington, D.C. The Action Group is involved in research and the drafting of legislation relative to veterans' services and benefits. The lobbying office is doing the advance work and mapping the strategy for maneuvering the legislation through the Congress. . . .

In keeping with the objectives of our organization, VVAW has started a "Lifeline to Cairo." We have moved to the offensive against the forces of racism and economic exploitation in this country. Our continuing convoys of food and clothing to Cairo, Illinois will enable our brothers and sisters to continue their struggle against the racist power structure that seeks to exploit poor and third-world people throughout the country.

Winter Soldier Investigations are being conducted by our chapters across the country (with some twenty-eight planned in the next two months) as a part of our continuing effort to bring the truth to the U.S.

Our members are regularly appearing on radio and TV shows and speaking at gatherings, large and small, throughout this country and around the world.

We have sent delegates to the World Peace Council Conferences in Budapest and Stockholm, the Seventeenth World Conference Against Atomic and Hydrogen Bombs in Hiroshima and to Hanoi and Paris to meet with our Indochinese brothers and sisters. Domestically we have participated in the

Southern Christian Leadership Conference in New Orleans, the National Student Association Congress in Ft. Collins, Colorado, the National Welfare Rights Organization's convention in Providence, Rhode Island and the People's Coalition for Peace and Justice Convention in Milwaukee, to name a few.

In August 1971 we published the first edition of the new VVAW newspaper, "The 1st Casualty." "The New Soldier," a book about Dewey Canyon III, published by Macmillan, will be released in September 1971. Another book, "The Winter Soldier Investigation" (testimony from the Detroit hearings), published by Beacon Press, was released in February 1972. The WSI film opened in February 1972 at the Whitney Museum in New York. The 90-minute feature film has received outstanding reviews from all the major critics in New York. We are looking forward to national distribution in the near future. September and October of 1971 saw VVAW in the communities of America, marching and rapping with the people on the street. Veterans Day 1971 saw over 300 Vietnam veterans arrested for exercising their right of free speech. Their "crime"? attempting to change the traditional glorification of militarism now emphasized by the establishment veterans organizations.

Thanksgiving was non-celebrated by VVAWs presence at state capitols across the country. Fasts and memorial services were on the schedule as the veterans were joined by members of the communities for this day of un-thanks.

Operation Peace on Earth, with encampments in Berkeley, Ca.; Killeen, Texas; Chicago, Illinois; and Valley Forge, Pennsylvania, saw VVAW participating in "protective reaction strikes" around the country:

—The Statue of Liberty in New York
—The Travis Air Force Base Drug War
—St. Patrick's Cathedral on Christmas Eve
—The Betsy Ross House in Philadelphia
—The South Vietnamese Consulate in San Francisco
—The Chicago Stock Exchange
—The Air Force Recruiting Station in Dorchester, Mass.
—The Connecticut National Guard Headquarters in Hartford, Conn.
—The Lincoln Memorial in Washington, DC
—Fort Hood, Texas
—Times Square on New Year's Eve
—Visits to VA and Military Hospitals around the country

VVAW reacted to the Administration's latest evidence of their low regard for human life. VVAW will continue to bring the realities of the everyday atrocities of the air war and the continuing ground war home.

Guided by a national steering committee of 26 regional coordinators, the VVAW is run day-to-day by a five-member national coordinating committee, under a charter of incorporation from the State of New York as a non-profit, educational organization.

Never, in the history of American warfare, have veterans of that war protested it while the war they participated in was still in progress. Another, and greater precedent has now been set: VVAW currently has 2500 members on active duty in Vietnam. The membership is increasing at the rate of 50 to 75 each day. The Nam members are from every service and every job classification, from Grunts to Doctor, from Battery Commander to Nurse, from IV Corps to I Corps, from Laos to Cambodia to Thailand to the South China Sea.

"When the spoils are worth the victory,
the battle must be fought."

Objectives of Vietnam Veterans Against the War, Inc.

1. To demand an immediate cessation of fighting and the withdrawal of all American troops from Indochina. We cannot allow one more human being to be killed in Indochina.

2. To demand Congress enact legislation for the immediate termination of all funds being utilized by the United States government, its allies and the Central Intelligence Agency to support their illegal operations in Latin America, Africa, China, Europe and the countries of Vietnam, Cambodia, Laos and Thailand.

3. To demonstrate that our military tactics dehumanize soldiers and civilians, and to make clear the United States government is prosecuting an illegal, unjust and immoral war in Indochina.

4. To show Americans that their society is structured by a racism which lets us view all non-whites as less than human. This racism pushes our minorities through inferior schools and into the combat arms. Thus, we send our minorities off to die in disproportionately high numbers while we kill Asians indiscriminately. We demand that the military recognize its complicity in America's domestic and international racism.

5. To make clear that the United States has never undertaken an extensive open investigation of American war crimes in Indochina. We demand that the United States government, in its war in Indochina, affirm the principles of Nuremberg. As former GIs, we recognize the responsibility of the individual soldier to refrain from committing war crimes. We also recognize the responsibility and guilt of war crimes committed in the name of America lies with our policy-makers at all levels.

6. To demand that all active-duty servicemen and women be afforded the rights as citizens that are guaranteed by the United States Constitution and Bill of Rights that are presently denied them by the Uniform Code of Military Justice. We are appalled that servicemen and women are treated as less than first-class

citizens. We endorse the efforts of our active duty sisters and brothers in their struggle to democratize the military.

7. To support all military personnel refusing to serve in wars of aggression at home and abroad. We demand Congress enact legislation for the immediate repatriation with full amnesty to those brothers and sisters who are in prison or in self-exile by reason of their refusal to serve in the military. We support all persons refusing to be drafted.

8. To demand immediate legislation to provide proper care and services for all veterans in VA hospitals; to make available job training and placement for every returning veteran; and to provide the funds and means necessary for their educational and vocational endeavors.

9. To affirm that the membership is not only concerned with ending this war, but changing the domestic social, political and economic institutions that have caused and permitted the continuance of war.

30
Letter to the National Liberation Front of South Vietnam (with Reply)

Huey P. Newton

Source: To Die for the People, pp. 290–93, by Huey P. Newton. Copyright © 1970 by Huey P. Newton. Reprinted by permission of Random House, Inc.

August 29, 1970

In the spirit of international revolutionary solidarity the Black Panther Party hereby offers to the National Liberation Front and Provisional Revolutionary Government of South Vietnam an undetermined number of troops to assist you in your fight against American imperialism. It is appropriate for the Black Panther Party to take this action at this time in recognition of the fact that your struggle is also our struggle, for we recognize that our common enemy is the American imperialist who is the leader of international bourgeois domination. There is not one fascist or reactionary government in the world today that could stand without the support of United States imperialism. Therefore our problem is international, and we offer these troops in recognition of the necessity for international alliances to deal with this problem.

Such alliances will advance the struggle toward the final act of dealing with American imperialism. The Black Panther Party views the United States as the "city" of the world, while we view the nations of Africa, Asia and Latin America as the "countryside" of the world. The developing countries are like the Sierra Maestra in Cuba and the United States is like Havana. We note that in Cuba the people's army set up bases in the Sierra Maestra and choked off Havana because it was dependent upon the raw materials of the countryside. After they won all the battles in this countryside the last and final act was for the people to march upon Havana.

The Black Panther Party believes that the revolutionary process will operate in a similar fashion on an international level. A small ruling circle of seventy-six major companies controls the American economy. This elite not only exploits and oppresses Black people within the United States; they are exploiting and oppressing everyone in the world because of the overdeveloped nature of capitalism. Having expanded industry within the United States until it can grow no more, and depleting the raw materials of this nation, they have run amuck abroad in their attempts to extend their economic domination. To end this oppression we must liberate the developing nation—the countryside of the world—and then our final act will be the strike against the "city." As one nation is liberated elsewhere it gives us a better chance to be free here.

The Black Panther Party recognizes that we have certain national problems confined to the continental United States, but we are also aware that while our oppressor has domestic problems these do not stop him from oppressing people all over the world. Therefore we will keep fighting and resisting within the "city" so as to cause as much turmoil as possible and aid our brothers by dividing the troops of the ruling circle.

The Black Panther Party offers these troops because *we are the vanguard party of revolutionary internationalists who give up all claim to nationalism.* We take this position because the United States has acted in a very chauvinistic manner and lost its claim to nationalism. *The United States is an empire which has raped the world to build its wealth here. Therefore the United States is not a nation.* It is a government of international capitalists and inasmuch as they have exploited the world to accumulate wealth this country belongs to the world. The Black Panther Party contends that the United States lost its right to claim nationhood when it used its nationalism as a chauvinistic base to become an empire.

On the other hand, the developing countries have every right to claim nationhood, because they have not exploited anyone. The nationalism of which they speak is simply their rightful claim to autonomy, self-determination and a liberated base from which to fight the international bourgeoisie.

The Black Panther Party supports the claim to nationhood of the developing countries and we embrace their struggle from our position as revolutionary internationalists. We cannot be nationalists when our country is not a nation but an empire. We contend that it is time to open the gates of this country and share the technological knowledge and wealth with the peoples of the world.

History has bestowed upon the Black Panther Party the obligation to take these steps and thereby advance Marxism-Leninism to an even higher level along the path to a socialist state, and then a non-state. This obligation springs both from the dialectical forces in operation at this time and our history as an oppressed Black colony. The fact that our ancestors were kidnapped and forced to come to the United States has destroyed our feeling of nationhood. Because our long cultural heritage was broken we have come to rely less on our history for guidance, and seek our guidance from the future. Everything we do is based upon functionalism and pragmatism, and because we look to the future for salvation we are in a position to become the most progressive and dynamic people on the earth, constantly in motion and progressing, rather than becoming stagnated by the bonds of the past.

Taking these things under consideration, it is no accident that the vanguard party—without chauvinism or a sense of nationhood—should be the Black Panther Party. Our struggle for liberation is based upon justice and equality for all men. Thus we are interested in the people of any territory where the crack of the oppressor's whip may be heard. We have the historical obligation to take the concept of internationalism to its final conclusion—the destruction of statehood itself. This will lead us into the era where the withering away of the state will occur and men will extend their hand in friendship throughout the world.

This is the world view of the Black Panther Party and in the spirit of revolutionary internationalism, solidarity and friendship we offer these troops to the National Liberation Front and Provisional Government of South Vietnam, and to the people of the world.

A Reply: Letter From Nguyen Thi Dinh, October 31, 1970

To: Mr. Huey P. Newton
Minister of Defense
Black Panther Party

Dear Comrade:

We are deeply moved by your letter informing us that the Black Panther Party is intending to send to the National Liberation Front and the Provisional Revolutionary Government of the Republic of South Vietnam an undetermined number of troops, assisting us in our struggle against the U.S. imperialist aggressors.

This news was communicated to all the cadres and fighters of the PLAF in South Vietnam; and all of us are delighted to get more comrades-in-arms, so brave as you, on the very soil of the United States.

On behalf of the cadres and fighters of the SVN PLAF I would welcome your noble deed and convey to you our sincere thanks for your warm support to our struggle against U.S. aggression for national salvation. We consider it as a great contribution from your side, an important event of the peace and democratic movement in the United States giving us active support, a friendly gesture voicing your determination to fight side-by-side with the South Vietnamese people for the victory of the common cause of revolution.

In the spirit of international solidarity, you have put forward your responsibility towards history, towards the necessity of uniting actions, sharing joys and sorrows, participating in the struggle against U.S. imperialism.

You have highly appreciated the close relation between our both uncompromising struggles against U.S. imperialism, our common enemy. It is well known now that the U.S. government is the most warlike, not only oppresses and exploits the American people, especially the Black and the coloured ones, but also oppresses and exploits various peoples the world over by all means, irrespective of morality and justice. They have the hunger of dollars and profits which they deprived by the most barbarous ways, including genocide, as they have acted for years in South Vietnam.

In the past years, your just struggle in the U.S. has stimulated us to strengthen unity, and rush forward toward bigger successes. . . . Dear Comrades, our struggle yet faces a lot of hardships, but we are determined to overcome all difficulties, unite with all progressive forces, to heighten our revolutionary vigilance, to persist in our struggle, resolutely to fight and win. We are sure to win complete victory.

So are our thinkings: At present, the struggles, right in the United States or on the SVN battle-fields, are both making positive contributions for national liberation and safeguarding the world peace. Therefore, your persistent and ever-developing struggle is the most active support to our resistance against U.S. aggression for national salvation.

With profound gratitude, we take notice of your enthusiastic proposal; when necessary, we shall call for your volunteers to assist us.

We are firmly confident that your just cause will enjoy sympathy, warm and strong support of the people at home and abroad, and will win complete victory; and our ever closer coordinated struggle surely stop the bloody hands of the U.S. imperialists and surely contribute winning independence, freedom, democracy and genuine peace.

Best greetings for "unity, militancy, and victory" from the SVN people's liberation fighters.

Nguyen Thi Dinh,
Deputy Commander
of the SVN People's
Liberation Armed Forces.
Republic of South Vietnam

31
Joint Treaty of Peace between the People of the United States, South Vietnam, and North Vietnam

People's Peace Treaty

Source: Collection of George Katsiaficas

PREAMBLE

Be it known that the American and Vietnamese people are not enemies. The war is carried out in the names of the people of the United States and South Vietnam, but without our consent. It destroys the land and people of Vietnam. It drains America of its resources, its youth, and its honor.

We hereby agree to end the war on the following terms, so that both peoples can live under the joy of independence and can devote themselves to building a society based on human equality and respect for the earth. In rejecting the war we also reject all forms of racism and discrimination against people based on color, class, sex, national origin, and ethnic grouping which form the basis of the war policies, past and present, of the United States government.

TERMS OF THE PEACE TREATY

1. THE AMERICANS AGREE TO IMMEDIATE AND TOTAL WITHDRAWAL FROM VIETNAM, AND PUBLICLY SET THE DATE BY WHICH ALL U.S. MILITARY FORCES WILL BE REMOVED.

2. The Vietnamese pledge that as soon as the U.S. government sets a date for total withdrawal:

They will enter discussions to secure the release of all American prisoners, including pilots captured while bombing North Vietnam.

3. There will be an immediate cease-fire between U.S. forces and those led by the Provisional Revolutionary Government of South Vietnam.

4. They will enter discussions on the procedures to guarantee the safety of all withdrawing troops.

5. THE AMERICANS PLEDGE TO END THE IMPOSITION OF THIEU-KY-KHIEM ON THE PEOPLE OF SOUTH VIETNAM IN ORDER TO INSURE THEIR RIGHT TO SELF-DETERMINATION AND SO THAT ALL POLITICAL PRISONERS CAN BE RELEASED.

6. The Vietnamese pledge to form a provisional coalition government to organize democratic elections. All parties agree to respect the results of elections

in which all South Vietnamese can participate freely without the presence of any foreign troops.

7. The South Vietnamese pledge to enter discussions of procedures to guarantee the safety and political freedom of those South Vietnamese who have collaborated with the U.S. or with the U.S.-supported regime.

8. The Americans agree to respect the independence, peace, and neutrality of Laos and Cambodia in accord with the 1954 and 1962 Geneva Conventions and not to interfere in the internal affairs of these two countries.

9. Upon these points of agreement, we pledge to end the war and resolve all other questions in the spirit of self-determination and mutual respect for the independence and political freedom of the people of Vietnam and the United States.

PLEDGE

BY RATIFYING THIS AGREEMENT, WE PLEDGE TO TAKE WHATEVER ACTIONS ARE APPROPRIATE TO IMPLEMENT THE TERMS OF THIS JOINT TREATY AND TO INSURE ITS ACCEPTANCE BY THE GOVERNMENT OF THE UNITED STATES.

32
Reflections on Calley

Herbert Marcuse

Source: New York Times, May 31, 1971. Copyright © 1971 by the New York Times Company.

LA JOLLA, Calif.—The obscene haste with which a large part of the American people rushed to the support of a man convicted of multiple premeditated murder of men, women and children, the obscene pride with which they even identified themselves with him is one of those rare historical events which reveal a hidden truth.

Behind the television faces of the leaders, behind the tolerant politeness of the debates, behind the radiant happiness of the commercials appear the real people: men and women madly in love with death, violence and destruction.

For this massive rush was not the result of organization, management, machine politics—it was entirely spontaneous: an outburst of the unconscious, the soul. The silent majority has its hero: a convicted war criminal—convicted of killing at close range, smashing the head of a 2-year-old child; a killer in whose defense it was said that he did not feel that he was killing "humans," a killer who did not express regret for his deeds; he only obeyed orders and killed only "dinks" or "gooks" or "V.C." This majority has its hero—it has found its martyr, its Horst Wessel whose name was sung by hundreds of thousands of marching Nazis before they marched into war. "Lieutenant Calley's Battle Hymn Marches On," the record, sold 300,000 copies in three days.

How do Calley's worshipers justify their hero?

• "The act which Calley is accused of was committed in warfare and is thus subject to special consideration." Now Calley was tried and convicted, after long deliberation, by a military tribunal of his peers, of whom it may be assumed that they knew that he acted in war. In fact, he was tried and convicted under the international rules of warfare. The rules of his own army stipulate the duty of disobedience to illegal orders (a disobedience which, as the hearings showed, was actually practiced by other American soldiers at Mylai).

• "What Calley did was widespread practice." Scores of men have come forth denouncing themselves as having done the same Calley did. Now the fact that one murderer was caught and brought to trial while others were not, does not absolve the one who was brought to trial. On the contrary, the others, having voluntarily confessed, should also be tried. The man who wrote on the windshield of his automobile: "I killed in V.N. Hang me too!" may well have meant it. People madly in love with death, including their own.

• "Everyone knows there are few genuine civilians in Vietnam today." A most revealing statement, which admits that the war is waged against a whole people: genocide.

• "Society is to blame." This is perhaps the only weighty argument. It moves on several levels:

(a) If society alone is to blame, nobody is to blame. For "society" is an abstract which cannot be brought to trial. It is true that this society is (and must be) training its young citizens to kill. But this same society operates under the rule of law, and recognizes rights and duties of the individual. Thus it presupposes individual responsibility, that is to say the ability of the "normal" individual to distinguish between criminal and noncriminal behavior (Calley was declared "normal").

(b) If the argument implies that all individual members of society are to blame, it is blatantly false and only serves to protect those who are responsible.

The reason for the "paroxysm in the nation's conscience" is "simply that Calley is all of us. He is every single citizen in our graceless land," said the Very Rev. Francis B. Sayre, Jr. Blatantly false, and a great injustice to the Berrigans, to all those who have, at the risk of their liberty and even their life, openly and actively fought the genocidal war.

To be sure, in a "metaphysical" sense, everyone who partakes of this society is indeed guilty—but the Calley case is not a case study in metaphysics. Within the general framework (restrictive enough) of individual responsibility there are definite gradations which allow attribution of specific responsibility. If it is true that Calley's action was not isolated, but an all but daily occurrence in Vietnam (which would corroborate the findings of the Russel War Crime Tribunal and call for the prosecution of all cases recorded there), then responsibility would rest with the field commanders, and, in the last analysis, with the Supreme Commander of the United States armed forces. However, this would not eliminate the responsibility of the individual agents.

(c) Technical progress in developing the capacity to kill has led to "death in the abstract"; killing that does not dirty your hands and clothes, that does not burden you with the agony of the victims—invisible death, dealt by remote controls. But technical perfection does not redeem the guilt of those who violate the rules of civilized warfare.

* * *

What does this all add up to? Perhaps Governor Maddox gave it away when he exclaimed at a rally in support of Calley: "Thank God for Lieutenant Calley and thank God for people like you." Blasphemy or religious madness? The convicted war criminal an avatar of Jesus, the Christ? "He has been crucified," shouted a woman, berating the court-martial in a German accent (one wonders?!). "Calley killed 100 Communists single-handed. He should get a medal. He should be promoted to general." And a Reverend Lord (!) told a rally: "There was a crucifixion 2,000 years ago of a man named Jesus Christ. I don't think we need another crucifixion of a man named Rusty Calley."

Has the lieutenant taken our sins upon himself, will he redeem our sins? What sins? Could it be the wish to kill, kill without being punished? Has the Lieutenant become the national model for a new Super Ego, less exacting than the traditional one, which still preserved a trace of thou shalt not kill?

The old Super Ego still stuck to the memory of this prohibition even in war. The new Super Ego is up to date. It says: you can kill. No—you can waste and destroy. Calley never used the word "kill." He told a psychiatrist that the military avoided the word "kill" because it "caused a very negative emotional reaction among the men who had been taught the commandment "Thou shalt not kill." Instead, Lieutenant Calley employed the word "destroy" or the phrase "waste 'em." A pardon for Calley, who did not kill but only destroyed and wasted 'em would, according to some, be a "constructive step to restore the morale of our armed forces and the public at large."

The mad rush away from individual responsibility, the easy-going effort to vest guilt in anonymity is the desperate reaction against a guilt which threatens to become unbearable. Infantile regression: Billy cannot be punished because Maxie and Charlie and many others did the same thing; they do it daily and they are not punished. People incapable of the simplest adult logic: if Maxie and Charlie did the same thing, they are equally guilty and Billy is not innocent.

Has the sense of guilt, the guilt of a society in which massacres and killing and body counts have become part of the normal mental equipment, become so strong that it can no longer be contained by the traditional, civilized defense mechanisms (individual defense mechanisms)? Does the sense of guilt turn into its opposite: into the proud, sado-masochistic identification with the crime and the criminal?

Has the hysteria also gripped the left, the peace movement which finds in the indictment of Calley an indictment of the war? A strange indictment indeed which regards the war criminal as a scapegoat—scapegoat for anonymous, for other scapegoats? Even Telford Taylor, who spoke so eloquently at the Nuremberg trials, thinks that the sentence may have been too harsh. And Dr. Benjamin Spock thinks that it is unjust to punish one man for the brutality of war.

Compassion. But has it ever occurred to all those understanding and compassionate liberals that clemency for Calley might indeed "strengthen the morale of the army" in killing with a good conscience? Has it ever occurred to them that compassion may be due the men, women and children who are the victims of this "morale"? Once again, we are confronted with that principle of diseased justice which was pronounced at Kent State and which expresses so neatly the perversion of the sense of guilt: "not the murderer but the murdered one is guilty."

Chapter VII

Vietnamization, the Paris Peace Treaty, and the Fall of Saigon

After the Tet offensive of 1968, American policymakers realized that the United States could not win a ground war. Nonetheless, after he was elected president in 1968, Richard Nixon insisted he would not be the first president to preside over an American military defeat. He promised "peace with honor," a phrase whose meaning included various objectives at various times, as part of a "Nixon Doctrine" designed to "prevent future Vietnams." Nixon devised a new strategy for fighting the Vietnam War, one that relied heavily on increased aerial bombardment and "Vietnamization" of the ground fighting (Document 33). Nixon gambled that so long as the rate of American fatalities was decreasing, neither Congress nor public opinion would compel him to abandon the Thieu regime.

Considered by many to be more responsive to political expediency than ethical concerns about truthfulness, Nixon was a master at disguising facts in rhetorical devices. In the November 1969 speech reprinted in this chapter, he maintained that "our air operations have been reduced by over 20 percent," yet even before his reelection in 1972, the U.S. had dropped 3.2 million tons of bombs on Indochina—more than the total dropped under Presidents Eisenhower, Kennedy, and Johnson—an average of more than a ton for every minute he was in office. In the same speech, the president assured the public that "U.S. casualties have declined during the last two months to the lowest point in three years." While that fragment of information may have been comforting, in the first six months of 1969, each week an average of 200 American soldiers were killed and 600 wounded. During Nixon's presidency, almost as many Americans were killed as in all the previous years of the war—and Nixon had been elected after promising to end the war.

In 1972, Richard Nixon was reelected, despite the facts that the majority of people wanted the war ended and his Democratic opponent, Sen. George McGovern, had long stood for an immediate end to U.S. involvement (see Document 34). A week before the election, Secretary of State Henry Kissinger announced on national television that "peace is at hand." On election day, Nixon swept the country, winning majorities in nearly every state.

For their part, the North Vietnamese understood Vietnamization not as a way for the war to end but as a way for the United States to continue fighting the war by "changing the color of the corpses." Document 35, a speech by Truong Chinh, presents the North Vietnamese interpretation of and response to the Nixon Doctrine. During the 1950s, Truong Chinh (actually a pseudonym meaning "Long March") was one of the hardliners who led the land reform program in North Vietnam during which thousands of people perished. He was personally criticized by Ho Chi Minh and demoted for the violent excesses of his policy. By 1971, he had reemerged as one of Hanoi's key strategists.

Although peace talks in Paris had begun in May 1968, their pace was agonizingly slow. It took more than six months for Washington and Hanoi to agree to the participation of the NLF and the Saigon regime. In July 1971, the Provisional Revolutionary Government (PRG), which had been formed out of the NLF, put forth its seven-point peace plan (Document 36), one point of which demanded that the United States "put an end to its interference in the internal affairs of South Viet Nam, [and] cease to support the bellicose group headed by Nguyen Van Thieu in Saigon." Three months later, the U.S. peace proposal (Document 37) agreed that Thieu should resign prior to general elections in the South. As can easily be imagined, the reaction in Saigon's presidential palace was anger. Moreover, although the Thieu government was included in the public negotiations, it was not part of the secret meetings that Henry Kissinger and Le Duc Tho (representing Hanoi) had been conducting since February 1970. In the final analysis, the intransigence of the Saigon regime proved to be a significant obstacle to peace, particularly since its spokespersons believed that Hanoi should be compelled to negotiate directly with Saigon, not solely with the United States (see Document 38). Although the South Vietnamese government recognized "the US have [sic] all the right to conduct secret talks with the other side," their exclusion from the Kissinger/Tho meetings clearly bothered them.

By early October 1972 (one month before the U.S. presidential election), Hanoi and Washington had agreed on the fundamental points of a peace agreement based on a compromise leaving both the Thieu government and North Vietnamese troops in place in South Vietnam. This is what prompted Kissinger to announce that "peace is at hand." After the election, however, Nixon and Kissinger demanded sixty-nine changes in the draft agreement. For two months the negotiations faltered, and while Kissinger threatened the North Vietnamese with "savage" bombing, the Nixon administration rushed nearly two billion dollars worth of heavy military equipment to the Thieu government, shipments which included enough air power to make the South Vietnamese air force the fourth largest in the world.

The leadership in Hanoi saw the handwriting on the wall and began to evacuate the capital. By December 16, one-third of Hanoi's population (about half a million people) had been moved out of the city, and on December 18, 129 U.S. B-52s began eleven days of bombardment of Hanoi and Haiphong. During these raids, the Bach Mai hospital in Hanoi was destroyed and, for the first time, residential areas of Hanoi were subjected to carpet bombings. According to Vietnamese sources, twenty-two B-52s and a total of eighty-one aircraft were shot down, and hundreds of pilots were captured or missing. The Pentagon publicly maintained that fifteen B-52s were shot down, but privately losses were reported to be higher, and in any event, were too high to be maintained for long. Although the United States reported civilian losses smaller than the numbers given by Hanoi, the casualties were unnecessary, and certainly resulted in little, if any, gain in the terms for peace. The differences between the U.S. proposal of October 11, 1971, and the final version of the treaty signed on January 27, 1973 (Document 39), are minimal. By bombing Hanoi, however, Nixon made it appear that he had compelled the North Vietnamese to make important concessions, and he therefore claimed that he had achieved peace with honor.

As one example of how similar the January peace treaty was to the original proposal of the PRG (the seven-point plan), the latter had demanded that the United States "bear full responsibility for the losses and destruction" throughout Vietnam, while the final treaty committed the United States to "contribute to healing the wounds of war and to postwar reconstruction" throughout Indochina. In a letter to North Vietnamese Premier Pham Van Dong less than a week after the ceasefire began (Document 40), Nixon promised to provide North Vietnam more than 3.25 billion dollars over five years for postwar reconstruction. None of that money has ever been paid.

Paul Feeny's article, "The Ecological Impact of the Air War" (Document 42), provides details on how the prolongation of the war increased the destruction of Vietnam, thereby making it an example of what would happen to countries attempting to escape control by the United States. Written during the war, this article demonstrates that even then there was considerable evidence that the herbicide Agent Orange would have severe long-term effects since it contains dioxin, one of the most deadly substances known to humans. More than 20 million gallons of Agent Orange were sprayed on South Vietnam, affecting even American servicemen, who were paid 180 million dollars in 1984 by seven chemical companies that had produced it.

During this period of time, no controversy was more intense than over the issue of whether or not the United States committed war crimes (or crimes against humanity) through its conduct of the war. While there is no doubt that the United States used many new weapons whose legality under international law was dubious (chemicals like Agent Orange as well as phosphorus bombs, several types of gas, and a wide variety of new antipersonnel weapons), at the same time millions of tons of conventional bombs (amounting to the equivalent of more than 700 Hiroshimas) were dropped, causing casualties equivalent to hundreds of My Lai's. In 1970, Gen. Telford Taylor, a retired lawyer who had been the chief American prosecutor at Nuremberg, published a book making the case that a disturbing historic parallel existed between what the Nazis did in Europe and what the United States was doing in Vietnam. As he put it:

> U.S. Chief of Staff General Westmoreland could be convicted and hanged if the standards established after World War II were applied to his conduct of the war in Vietnam. By the same logic, the top civilian leaders of the United States could be convicted of the same offense.

The statistics on the destruction wreaked by the United States on Indochina are truly staggering. For every South Vietnamese man, woman, and child, more than 1,000 pounds of bombs, a gallon of Agent Orange, forty pounds of napalm, and half a ton of CS gas (a very strong tear gas) were used by the United States. The total tonnage of bombs dropped on Vietnam by the United States was more than three times the tonnage dropped on Europe, Asia, and Africa during all of World War II. Out of a population of 20 million, ten million were made refugees. The tremendous damage that was done to Vietnam severely limited the postwar options available to the country and continues to have an impact on its people.

Despite the massive destruction aimed at the guerrillas and the supply of arms to the Thieu regime, after the withdrawal of American ground troops it was only a matter of time before Saigon's army was defeated. When the southern regime finally collapsed in 1975, it occurred much more rapidly than anyone, including the North Vietnamese, had expected. Six months after the Paris peace treaty was signed, Congress had voted to cut funds for all American military operations in Indochina, and while hundreds of millions of dollars were allocated to the Thieu government, corruption and inefficiency severely limited that government's capabilities. In the context of rapidly advancing North Vietnamese and PRG armed forces, it appeared that the overthrow of the Thieu government was imminent. Henry Kissinger, then secretary of state, appealed to Congress (Document 43) on April 15, 1975, for hundreds of millions of dollars in emergency aid for the government of South Vietnam. Congress never took action on his request, and two weeks later Saigon fell.

The final document in this chapter, "Joys and Sorrows," was written by Truong Nhu Tang, a former treasurer of the NLF who played a prominent role in the new government of South Vietnam after the war. He eventually became a "boat person," leaving Vietnam surreptitiously and making his way to Paris. Few people had been better placed to judge how the northerners who came south after the war treated their southern compatriots. Tang's account conveys well the bittersweet character the 1975 victory has had for many NLF members.

33
Vietnamization Will Shorten the War

Richard M. Nixon

Source: Richard M. Nixon, speech delivered on national television, November 3, 1969.

Fifteen years ago North Vietnam, with the logistical support of Communist China and the Soviet Union, launched a campaign to impose a Communist government on South Vietnam by instigating and supporting a revolution.

In response to the request of the government of South Vietnam, President Eisenhower sent economic aid and military equipment to assist the people of South Vietnam in their efforts to prevent a Communist takeover. Seven years ago, President Kennedy sent 16,000 military personnel to Vietnam as combat advisors. Four years ago, President Johnson sent American combat forces to South Vietnam. . . .

For these reasons, I rejected the recommendation that I should end the war by immediately withdrawing all our forces. I chose instead to change American policy on both the negotiating front and the battlefront. . . .

Obstacle to Peace

It has become clear that the obstacle in negotiating an end to the war is not the President of the United States. And it is not the South Vietnamese.

The obstacle is the other side's absolute refusal to show the least willingness to join us in seeking a just peace. It will not do so while it is convinced that all it has to do is to wait for our next concession, and the next until it gets everything it wants.

There can now be no longer any question that progress in negotiation depends only on Hanoi's deciding to negotiate, to negotiate seriously.

I realize that this report on our efforts on the diplomatic fronts is discouraging to the American people, but the American people are entitled to know the truth—the bad news as well as the good news, where the lives of our young men are involved.

Now let me turn, however, to a more encouraging report on another front.

At the time we launched our search for peace I recognized we might not succeed in bringing an end to the war through negotiation. I, therefore, put into effect another plan to bring peace—a plan which will bring the war to an end regardless of what happens on the negotiating front.

The Nixon Doctrine

It is in line with a major shift in U.S. foreign policy which I described in my press conference at Guam on July 25. Let me briefly explain what has been described as the Nixon Doctrine—a policy which not only will help end the war in Vietnam, but which is an essential element of our program to prevent future Vietnams.

We Americans are a do-it-yourself-people. We are an impatient people. Instead of teaching someone else to do a job, we like to do it ourselves. And this trait has been carried over into our foreign policy.

In Korea and again in Vietnam, the United States furnished most of the money, most of the arms, and most of the men to help the people of those countries defend their freedom against the Communist aggression.

Before any American troops were committed to Vietnam, a leader of another Asian country expressed this opinion to me when I was traveling in Asia as a private citizen. He said, "When you are trying to assist another nation defend its freedom, U.S. policy should be to help them fight the war but not to fight the war for them."

Well, in accordance with this wise counsel, I laid down in Guam three principles as guidelines for future American policy toward Asia:

First, the United States will keep all of its treaty commitments.

Second, we shall provide a shield if a nuclear power threatens the freedom of a nation allied with us or of a nation whose survival we consider vital to our security.

Third, in cases involving other types of aggression, we shall furnish military and economic assistance when requested in accordance with our treaty commitments. But we shall look to the nation directly threatened to assume the primary responsibility of providing the manpower for its defense.

After I announced this policy, I found that the leaders of the Philippines, Thailand, Vietnam, South Korea, and other nations which might be threatened by Communist aggression, welcomed this new direction in American foreign policy.

Vietnamization

The defense of freedom is everybody's business—not just America's business. And it is particularly the responsibility of the people whose freedom is threatened. In the previous Administration, we Americanized the war in Vietnam. In this Administration, we are Vietnamizing the search for peace.

The policy of the previous Administration not only resulted in our assuming the primary responsibility for fighting the war but even more significantly did not adequately stress the goal of strengthening the South Vietnamese so that they could defend themselves when we left.

The Vietnamization Plan was launched following Secretary Laird's visit to Vietnam in March. Under the plan, I ordered first a substantial increase in the training and equipment of South Vietnamese forces.

In July, on my visit to Vietnam, I changed General Abrams' orders so that they were consistent with the objectives of our new policies. Under the new orders, the primary mission of our troops is to enable the South Vietnamese forces to assume the full responsibility for the security of South Vietnam.

Our air operations have been reduced by over 20 percent.

And now we have begun to see the results of this long overdue change in American policy in Vietnam.

Significant Results

After five years of Americans going into Vietnam, we are finally bringing American men home. By December 15, over 60,000 men will have been withdrawn from South Vietnam—including 20 percent of all of our combat forces.

The South Vietnamese have continued to gain in strength. As a result they have been able to take over combat responsibilities from our American troops.

Two other significant developments have occurred since this Administration took office.

Enemy infiltration, infiltration which is essential if they are to launch a major attack, over the last three months is less than 20 percent of what it was over the same period last year.

Most important—United States casualties have declined during the last two months to the lowest point in three years.

Let me now turn to our program for the future.

We have adopted a plan which we have worked out in cooperation with the South Vietnamese for the complete withdrawal of all U.S. combat ground forces, and their replacement by South Vietnamese forces on an orderly scheduled timetable. This withdrawal will be made from strength and not from weakness. As South Vietnamese forces become stronger, the rate of American withdrawal can become greater.

No Timetable for Withdrawal

I have not and do not intend to announce the timetable for our program. There are obvious reasons for this decision which I am sure you will understand. As I have indicated on several occasions, the rate of withdrawal will depend on developments on three fronts.

One of these is the progress which can be or might be made in the Paris talks. An announcement of a fixed timetable for our withdrawal would completely remove any incentive for the enemy to negotiate an agreement.

They would simply wait until our forces had withdrawn and then move in.

The other two factors on which we will base our withdrawal decisions are the level of enemy activity and the progress of the training program of the South Vietnamese forces. I am glad to be able to report tonight progress on both of these fronts has been greater than we anticipated when we started the program in June for withdrawal. As a result, our timetable for withdrawal is more optimistic now than when we made our first estimates in June. This clearly demonstrates why it is not wise to be frozen in on a fixed timetable.

We must retain the flexibility to base each withdrawal decision on the situation as it is at that time rather than on estimates that are no longer valid.

Along with this optimistic estimate, I must—in all candor—leave one note of caution.

If the level of enemy activity significantly increases we might have to adjust our timetable accordingly.

No Misunderstandings

However, I want the record to be completely clear on one point.

At the time of the bombing halt just a year ago, there was some confusion as to whether there was an understanding on the part of the enemy that if we stopped the bombing of North Vietnam they would stop the shelling of cities in South Vietnam. I want to be sure that there is no misunderstanding on the part of the enemy with regard to our withdrawal program.

We have noted the reduced level of infiltration, the reduction of our casualties, and are basing our withdrawal decisions partially on those factors.

If the level of infiltration or our casualties increase while we are trying to scale down the fighting, it will be the result of a conscious decision by the enemy.

Hanoi could make no greater mistake than to assume that an increase in violence will be to its advantage. If I conclude that increased enemy action jeopardizes our remaining forces in Vietnam, I shall not hesitate to take strong and effective measures to deal with that situation.

This is not a threat. This is a statement of policy which as Commander-in-Chief of our Armed Forces I am making in meeting my responsibility for the protection of American fighting men wherever they may be.

Only Two Choices

My fellow Americans, I am sure you recognize from what I have said that we really only have two choices open to us if we want to end this war.

I can order an immediate, precipitate withdrawal of all Americans from Vietnam without regard to the effects of that action.

Or we can persist in our search for a just peace through a negotiated settlement if possible, or through continued implementation of our plan for Vietnamization if necessary—a plan in which we will withdraw all of our forces from Vietnam on a schedule in accordance with our program, as the South Vietnamese become strong enough to defend their own freedom.

I have chosen the second course.

It is not the easy way.

It is the right way.

It is a plan which will end the war and serve the cause of peace—not just in Vietnam but in the Pacific and in the world.

In speaking of the consequences of a precipitate withdrawal, I mentioned that our allies would lose confidence in America.

Far more dangerous, we would lose confidence in ourselves. The immediate reaction would be a sense of relief that our men were coming home. But as we saw the consequences of what we had done, inevitable remorse and divisive recrimination would scar our spirit as a people.

We have faced other crises in our history and have become stronger by rejecting the easy way out and taking the right way in meeting our challenges. Our greatness as a nation has been our capacity to do what had to be done when we knew our course was right.

34
Vietnamization Will Extend the War (1970)

George S. McGovern

Source: George S. McGovern, statement before U.S. Senate Committee on Foreign Relations, February 4, 1970.

Mr. Chairman, and members of the committee, the resolution that I have submitted with the cosponsorship of Senators Church, Cranston, Goodell, Hughes, McCarthy, Moss, Nelson, Ribicoff, and Young of Ohio calls for the withdrawal from Vietnam of all U.S. forces, the pace to be limited only by these three considerations: the safety of our troops during the withdrawal process, the mutual release of prisoners of war, and arrangements for asylum in friendly countries for any Vietnamese who might feel endangered by our disengagement. (I have recently been advised by the Department of Defense that the 484,000 men we now have in Vietnam could be transported to the United States at a total cost of $144,519,621.)

This process of orderly withdrawal could be completed, I believe, in less than a year's time.

Such a policy of purposeful disengagement is the only appropriate response to the blunt truth that there will be no resolution of the war so long as we cling to the Thieu-Ky regime. That government has no dependable political base other than the American military presence and it will never be accepted either by its challengers in South Vietnam or in Hanoi.

We can continue to pour our blood and substance into a neverending effort to support the Saigon hierarchy or we can have peace, but we cannot have both General Thieu and an end to the war.

Barrier to Peace and Healing

Our continued military embrace of the Saigon regime is the major barrier, both to peace in Southeast Asia and to the healing of our society. It assures that the South Vietnamese generals will take no action to build a truly representative government which can either compete with the NLF or negotiate a settlement of the war. It deadlocks the Paris negotiations and prevents the scheduling of serious discussions on the release and exchange of prisoners of war. It diverts our energies from critical domestic needs. It sends young Americans to be maimed or killed in a war that we cannot win and that will not end so long as our forces are there in support of General Thieu.

I have long believed that there can be no settlement of the Vietnam struggle until some kind of provisional coalition government assumes control in Saigon. But this is precisely what General Thieu will never consider. After the Midway conference last June he said, "I solemnly declare that there will be no coalition government, no peace cabinet, no transitional government, not even a reconciliatory government."

Although President Nixon has placed General Thieu as one of the two or three greatest statesmen of our age, Thieu has brushed off the suggestion that he broaden his government and has denounced those who advocate or suggest a negotiated peace as pro-Communist racketeers and traitors. A coalition government means death, he has said.

Prescription for Endless War

Mr. Chairman, let us not delude ourselves. This is a clear prescription for an endless war, and changing its name to Vietnamization still leaves us tied to a regime that cannot successfully wage war or make peace.

When administration officials expressed the view that American combat forces might be out of Vietnam by the end of 1970, General Thieu called a press conference last month and insisted that this was an "impossible and impractical goal" and that instead withdrawal "will take many years."

And yet there is wide currency to the view that America's course in Southeast Asia is no longer an issue, that the policy of Vietnamization promises an early end of hostilities. That is a false hope emphatically contradicted not only by our ally in Saigon but by the tragic lessons of the past decade.

As I understand the proposal, Vietnamization directs the withdrawal of American troops only as the Saigon armed forces demonstrate their ability to take over the war. Yet a preponderance of evidence indicates that the Vietnamese people do not feel the Saigon regime is worth fighting for. Without local support, "Vietnamization" becomes a plan for the permanent deployment of American combat troops, and not a strategy for disengagement. The President has created a fourth branch of the American Government by giving Saigon a veto over American foreign policy.

If we follow our present policy in Vietnam, there will still be an American Army in my opinion, of 250,000 or 300,000 men in Southeast Asia 15 or 20 years hence or perhaps indefinitely. Meanwhile American firepower and bombardment will have killed more tens of thousands of Vietnamese who want nothing other than an end of the war. All this to save a corrupt, unrepresentative regime in Saigon.

Any military escalation by Hanoi or the Vietcong would pose a challenge to American forces which would require heavier American military action and, therefore, heavier American casualties, or we would be faced with the possibility of a costly, forced withdrawal.

False Premises for Vietnamization

The Vietnamization policy is based on the same false premises which have doomed to failure our previous military efforts in Vietnam. It assumes that the Thieu-Ky regime in Saigon stands for freedom and a popularly backed regime. Actually, the Saigon regime is an oppressive dictatorship which jails its critics and blocks the development of a broadly based government. Last June 20, the Saigon minister for liaison for parliament, Von Huu Thu, confirmed that 34,540 political prisoners were being held and that many of those people were non-Communists who were guilty of nothing more than advocating a neutral peaceful future for their country. In proportion to population the political prisoners held by Saigon would be the equivalent of a half million political prisoners in the United States.

The Thieu-Ky regime is no closer to American ideals than its challenger, the National Liberation Front. Indeed self-determination and independence are probably far stronger among the Vietnamese guerrillas and their supporters than within the Saigon Government camp.

I have never felt that American interests and ideals were represented by the Saigon generals or their corrupt predecessors. We should cease our embrace of this regime now and cease telling the American people that it stands for freedom.

I should like to make clear that I am opposed to both the principle and the practice of the policy of Vietnamization. I am opposed to the policy, whether it works by the standard of its proponents or does not work. I oppose as immoral and self-defeating a policy which gives either American arms or American blood to perpetuate a corrupt and unrepresentative foreign regime. It is not in the interests of either the American or the Vietnamese people to maintain such a government.

I find it morally and politically repugnant for us to create a client group of Vietnamese generals in Saigon and then give them murderous military technology to turn against their own people.

Vietnamization is basically an effort to tranquilize the conscience of the American people while our Government wages a cruel and needless war by proxy.

An enlightened American foreign policy would cease trying to dictate the outcome of an essentially local struggle involving various groups of Vietnamese. If we are concerned about a future threat to Southeast Asia from China, let us have the common sense to recognize that a strong independent regime even though organized by the National Liberation Front and Hanoi would provide a more dependable barrier to Chinese imperialism than the weak puppet regime we have kept in power at the cost of 40,000 American lives and hundreds of thousands of Vietnamese lives.

Even if we could remove most of our forces from Vietnam, how could we justify before God and man the use of our massive firepower to continue a slaughter that neither serves our interests nor the interests of the Vietnamese.

The policy of Vietnamization is a cruel hoax designed to screen from the American people the bankruptcy of a needless military involvement in the affairs of the Vietnamese people. Instead of Vietnamizing the war let us encourage the Vietnamization of the government in South Vietnam. We can do that by removing the embrace that now prevents other political groups from assuming a leadership role in Saigon, groups that are capable of expressing the desire for peace of the Vietnamese people.

35
To Mobilize and Unite All Anti-U.S. Forces in the Country and World to Defeat the U.S. Aggressors

Truong Chinh

Source: Speech by Truong Chinh to the Vietnam Fatherland Front (Asia Information Group, 1972), excerpts.

Our people throughout the country are resisting the U.S. aggressors and building socialism in the North, contributing thereby to defending the socialist camp, stimulating the revolutionary movement of the people of other countries and safeguarding peace.

Our people's resistance is aimed at not only national but also international goals. The U.S. war of aggression in Vietnam is an act aimed at implementing the global strategy of U.S. imperialism—the number one enemy of mankind. The Vietnamese revolution is an inseparable part of the world revolution.

Since World War II, the U.S. imperialists have been carrying out an extremely reactionary, brutal and perfidious global strategy aimed at undermining the socialist camp; repressing the international communist and workers' movement, the national liberation movement and the democratic movement; wrecking peace; realizing U.S.-type neo-colonialism; and preparing for a new world war to seize world hegemony.

U.S. imperialism is the most bellicose imperialism. For that reason, we must study the military aspect of its global strategy. Since World War II, U.S. imperialism has set up aggressive military alliances in Europe (NATO), Asia (SEATO), the Middle East and Near East (CENTO), etc., built thousands of military bases in foreign countries, and set up a multi-ringed defense system to encircle the socialist camp and prevent the spread of the movement for national independence, stepped up the arms race, created modern weapons, including nuclear weapons, devised three different types of war: special war, local war, and total war, and waged special and local wars, while preparing for total war, which is also a nuclear showdown.

To prepare and wage a new World War, the U.S. imperialists have revived West German revanchist militarism and Japanese militarism, using them as their shock forces, and they have given aid to the reactionary rulers in Israel in provoking wars according to their plan in the Middle and Near East.

During the past 25 years, U.S. imperialism has re-adjusted its global strategy four times:

a) 1945–1950: The U.S. imperialists applied the Truman Doctrine and strategy which consists in using nuclear blackmail against the world peoples, and checking and repulsing the communist movement chiefly to defend Western Europe, an old bulwark of capitalism. However, the U.S. failed to check the revolutionary movements in Eastern Europe, North Korea, Vietnam and China.

b) 1950–1960: The period of the "cold war" in which the U.S. imperialists carried out Eisenhower's strategy of "massive retaliation." With their nuclear superiority, the U.S. imperialists applied a foreign policy known as "brinkmanship" to browbeat the socialist camp and other countries, launched the arms race, and deployed their military and economic forces on a world scale.

Also during this period, the U.S. gave military aid to the French colonialists in their aggression against Vietnam, together with other countries in its camp triggered the Korean war, and perpetrated adventurous military acts against Arab countries in the Middle and Near East. At the same time it put into practice the so-called strategy of freeing "imprisoned countries" in Eastern Europe, and engineered the counter-revolutionary putsch in Hungary (1956).

c) 1961–1968: The U.S. imperialists applied Kennedy's "strategy for peace." Militarily, they carried out the "flexible response" strategy which was later complimented by Johnson's "escalation strategy." By this time, the Soviet Union had gained nuclear parity with the U.S. Therefore the United States sought a temporary détente with the Soviet Union, tried to make full use of the differences of lines within the socialist camp and in the international communist and workers movement, especially those between the Soviet Union and China, launched a special war and then a local war in Vietnam, and instigated Israel to wage a war of aggression against a number of Arab countries, mainly against the United Arab Republic (1967).

But most disadvantageous to the U.S. in this period was the failure of its war of aggression against Vietnam, a failure that has weakened U.S. imperialism, lowered its prestige, and upset its global strategy.

d) Since 1969: The U.S. imperialists have been implementing the "Nixon Doctrine," which is precisely the global strategy of U.S. imperialism under the Nixon administration. It was born at a time when the world balance of power between revolution and counter-revolution has changed in favor of revolution. In spite of the dissension among socialist countries, the socialist system has been continually strengthened and consolidated and has exerted a decisive effect on the trend of development of human society.

The colonial system of imperialism continues its process of disintegration under the crushing blows of the national liberation movements in Asia, Africa and Latin America. The struggle of the working class and the democratic movement in the capitalist countries continue developing. More than ever before, the U.S., the ring-leader of imperialism, has been weakened militarily and isolated politically. U.S. imperialism and the other imperialist powers are in the throes of an economic and monetary crisis. The general capitalist crisis is becoming more serious. The contradictions between the U.S. and the other imperialist powers are sharpening day by day.

Under such unfavorable conditions, Nixon cannot help but readjust the U.S. global strategy. Politically, he has dished up the so-called "new strategy for peace." Militarily, he has applied the strategy of "realistic deterrence." Nixon's aim is to reduce U.S. international commitments so as to lighten the military and economic burden of the U.S., stabilize the situation at home and appease the American people, to strengthen its forces to regain a position of strength, to continue the drive for world hegemony, and to preserve U.S. interests in the various continents while continuing to play the role of international gendarme toward the revolutionary movement of people in various countries.

The main contents of Nixon's strategy consist of the following:

1. To stabilize and increase U.S. economic and military strength in order to achieve some degree of superiority over the socialist countries, especially the Soviet Union, and to use this strength to intimidate and win over a number of countries or to wage wars in one place or another.

2. To settle its differences and contradictions with its allies so as to "share responsibility" with them, use those countries as a shock force of the U.S. in each specific region, build up satellite countries as stooges to oppose and undermine the revolutionary movement of the world people, and make war with other people's blood for its own interests.

3. On this basis, it is "ready to negotiate" with a number of countries—especially the Soviet Union and China—with a view to "deterring" and "containing" these two biggest socialist countries, make the fullest use of the contradictions between these two countries and sow discord among the socialist countries in general in a bid to create favorable conditions for the U.S., to strive for "détente" among the big powers and continue to bully smaller nations.

The Nixon Doctrine applied to Asia has become Nixon's "New Doctrine on Asia." Relying on the Asian and Pacific Organization (ASPAC) with Japan as the core, this new doctrine is intended to suppress the national and democratic movement in Asia and dam up the spread of Socialism to other countries in this region.

Applying the "new doctrine on Asia" to Vietnam and Asia, Nixon has worked out the policy of "Vietnamization" of the war and "Indochinazation" of the war.

The essence of this doctrine and policy is to make Vietnamese fight Vietnamese and Indochinese fight Indochinese, and Asians fight Asians with U.S. bombs, dollars, shells and under the command of the U.S. Militarists.

"Vietnamization of the war" obviously is a perfidious move to prolong and widen the war, not to end it. "Vietnamization of the war," or "de-Americanization of the war" in no way means that the U.S. will withdraw all its troops from South Vietnam. Instead it will leave a residual force for a long-term occupation on a number of military bases to be used as bridgeheads for helping the Saigon puppet army to continue its criminal persecution and massacre of our people, and turn South Vietnam into a U.S. neo-colony and military base.

U.S. imperialism is using the Vietnam and Indochina battlefields as a testing ground for the Nixon Doctrine and for various military strategies, tactics and modern weapons of the U.S. with a view to preparing for a new world war.

The anti-U.S. resistance of the Vietnamese people and the other Indochinese peoples is not only a test of strength between our people on the one hand, and U.S. imperialism and its lackeys on the other, but also a struggle between the socialist countries and the bellicose imperialists, between the national liberation forces and the aggressive imperialist forces, between the peace-loving forces and the world's war-mongering forces led by U.S. imperialism.

The fight against U.S. aggression for national salvation of the Vietnamese and other Indochinese peoples is not only aimed at defending their fundamental rights, but also has a great international significance since it contributes positively to foiling the counter-revolutionary global strategy of U.S. imperialism, to defeating the very perfidious "Nixon Doctrine," to defending the socialist system at the cost of our blood, to encouraging the revolutionary movements of Asia, Africa and Latin America and to safeguarding peace and democracy in the world.

In the face of such a cruel and crafty enemy as the U.S. imperialist aggressors, what should we Vietnamese people do? We must struggle in all forms—politically, military and diplomatic—to drive the aggressors out of our country.

On the military front our people and people's armed forces must annihilate as much of the U.S.-puppet's potential as possible, especially their mobile strategic forces. At the same time we must smash their rural "pacification" plan; foil their policies aimed at scraping up manpower and material resources for Vietnamization; destroy "strategic hamlets" and their coercive system as a whole; wipe out, decimate, and disband the enemy's "territorial forces"; expand the liberated areas; and maintain and develop the resistance bases of our people.

Our army and people in the North must always keep high vigilance, organize well the civil defense, stand ready to fight and with the resolve to smash all military adventures of the U.S. that violate the sovereignty and security of the DRVN.

On the political front, our southern compatriots must mobilize and rally all forces that are eager for peace, independence and neutrality, especially in the cities, combining various forms of struggle and achieve unity of action in demanding the total and rapid withdrawal of all U.S. troops from South Vietnam and the ouster of the Nguyen Van Thieu administration, protest against fraudulent elections, demand the people's right to life and democracy, protest against the depraved culture of the U.S. and urge the restoration of peace. The rising political struggles in the urban centers will have the effect of shaking the enemy right in its lair and will be an excellent coordination with the armed struggle of our entire people and nation.

On the diplomatic front, our people warmly support the 7-point plan of the Provisional Revolutionary Government of the Republic of South Vietnam put forth at the four-party conference in Paris on July 1, 1971. The armed and political struggle of the popular masses at home must create a firm base for the diplomatic struggle. The latter must highlight our people's just goals, promptly lay bare all maneuvers and acts of the enemy and their deceitful and demagogic contentions, point to the certainty of our victory and the enemy's failure, contribute to winning the sympathy, support and assistance of the world's peoples for the anti-U.S. patriotic war of our people.

To lead our struggle on all of these three fronts to ever greater successes and ultimate total victory, an important thing is to mobilize and rally all the peace-loving forces. We advocate a three-layered United Front to encircle and defeat the U.S. imperialist aggressors.

In Vietnam

Our country is victim of direct aggression by the U.S. imperialists. To resist the U.S. and save the country is the duty of the entire Vietnamese people and nation. To persevere in and step up our resistance till complete victory we stand for the union of the entire people in a National United Front against U.S. aggression to struggle on three fronts—military, political and diplomatic—in order to liberate the South, defend and build the socialist North, proceed toward the peaceful reunification of the Fatherland, and build a peaceful, united, independent democratic and prosperous Vietnam, thus making a worthy contribution to the revolutionary cause of the world people. In furthering their policy of "Vietnamizing" the war, the U.S. imperialists are using Vietnamese to fight Vietnamese with a view to turning South Vietnam into a new-type colony and military base of the U.S. Therefore the entire Vietnamese people must unite millions as one to persevere in and step up the resistance and smash this vicious scheme of the U.S. aggressors.

At present, our country is temporarily divided into two zones under two different social systems. The North is under a socialist regime. The South itself has two different parts—one under the U.S. neo-colonialist regime, and the other (the liberated zone) under the people's democratic regime. The people in both the South and North Vietnam must resist U.S. aggression and save the country.

Besides this common mission, each zone has strategic revolutionary tasks suited to its conditions. The North is carrying out the socialist revolution, including socialist construction and socialist transformation. The South is waging a people's national democratic revolution to sweep away the U.S. imperialist aggressors, topple their stooges—the pro-U.S. imperialist compradors and feudal landlords, and win back national independence and democracy for the people.

Therefore, each zone has its own front. The North has the Vietnam Fatherland Front with its own program. The South has the South Vietnam National Liberation Front with its own program, and also the Vietnam Alliance of National Democratic and Peace forces with its appropriate program to rally and unite people of various strata in the urban centers under the Alliance's responsibility. The three programs differ from one another, but have this in common: they aim to unite the entire people, resist U.S. aggression, and win independence and reunification of the fatherland.

In Indochina

Under the Kennedy and Johnson administrations, the U.S. imperialists carried out an aggressive war not only in Vietnam but also in Laos. Under the Nixon administration, the U.S. imperialists have taken another step by widening the war to Cambodia. The three Indochinese countries have thus become a single battlefield. The Nixon administration is carrying out the policy of "Indochinizing the war" by using Indochinese to fight Indochinese in an attempt to turn the whole peninsula into a new-type colony and military base of the U.S.

The flame of the people's war is burning throughout Indochina. The three fraternal peoples of Vietnam, Laos and Cambodia are closely uniting in the struggle to drive the U.S. aggressors out of Indochina, overthrow the puppet administrations, henchmen of the U.S. in their countries, and win back and defend their sacred national rights. The joint declaration of the Indochinese People's Summit Conference (April 24, 1970) pointed out:

"At this historic moment, the Summit Conference of the Indochinese Peoples earnestly calls on the three peoples to strengthen their solidarity and wage a heroic and tenacious fight, to overcome all hardships and accept all sacrifice with the firm resolve to defeat the U.S. imperialists and their agents, to defend their sacred national rights, to defend the fundamental principles of the 1954 and 1962 Geneva Agreements so as to make Indochina a truly independent and peaceful area, in accordance with the aspirations of the three peoples and the interests of peace in Southeast Asia and the world."

To defeat the U.S. aggressors, the people of the three Indochinese countries assist and respect one another. During the fight against the U.S. and its henchmen as well as after their total victory, the people of each country will build their fatherland according to their own will.

To strengthen and broaden the United Front of the Indochinese people against the U.S. imperialists and their henchmen, the people of each country must strive for the consolidation and broadening of their own front: The Vietnam Fatherland Front of the DRVN, the South Vietnam National Front for Liberation and the Vietnam Alliance of National, Democratic and Peace Forces in the Republic of South Vietnam, the Lao Patriotic Front in Laos, and the National United Front of Kampuchea in Cambodia. All these organizations are members of the United Front of the Indochinese Peoples against the U.S. imperialist aggressors.

In the World

It is necessary to rally all forces in the world against the U.S. imperialists. We are elated to note that over the recent years, a world peoples' front to support the Vietnamese and the other Indochinese peoples against the U.S. imperialist aggressors actually has been taking shape. This is a front for united actions with concrete and limited objectives.

Who are the targets of that front? The U.S. imperialists and their henchmen. Its goal of struggle is to foil the aggressive and war-seeking policy of the imperialists and defend national independence and world peace.

The forces of peace, national independence, democracy and social progress have joined and are joining that front in increasing numbers. If the three torrential streams of world revolution—the great force of the socialist countries, the movement for national liberation in Asia, African and Latin American countries, and the movement of the working class and other laboring people in the capitalist countries—keep on pouring into the great river which is the World United Front, then they can sweep away both the U.S. aggressors and their henchmen.

Relying on the core forces and firmly grasping the goal of struggle, that is, to defend national independence and peace, the World People's Front against the U.S. aggressors should unite any force that can be united, win over any force that can be won over, split the imperialist ranks to the highest degree, isolate the U.S. imperialists and their henchmen, and spearhead the struggle at the cruelest enemy—U.S. imperialism.

To support the Vietnamese and Indochinese peoples' patriotic war against U.S. aggression has become the key question in the world people's struggle against U.S. imperialism. The world peoples are responding to this question to take unity of action against U.S. imperialism in various sections, branches, countries, regions (such as Asian, African and Latin American regions) of the world, from low to high, from local to global. The United Front of the Indochinese

Peoples against the U.S. aggressors and the World Peoples Front in support of the Vietnamese people against the U.S. imperialists are important reinforcements to our people's resistance against U.S. aggression, for national salvation.

We take this opportunity to express the heartfelt thanks of the Vietnamese people and the Vietnam Fatherland Front to the peoples of the fraternal socialist countries, the Lao people, the Khmer people, and the peoples in the rest of the world, including the progressive people in the United States, for their sympathy and their great support and assistance to our people's patriotic war against U.S. aggression.

In short, the anti-U.S. National United Front in Vietnam, the anti-U.S. United Front of the Indochinese Peoples, and the World Peoples' United Front against U.S. imperialism and for defending national independence and peace, are the three layers of a front encircling and defeating aggressive U.S. imperialism. With the formation of such a three-layered front, the U.S. aggressors will be hemmed in by ring after ring of steel net, and they cannot escape total defeat.

36
Seven-Point Statement

The Provisional Revolutionary Government of the Republic of South Viet Nam, made public by Minister Madame Nguyen Thi Binh at the 119th session of the Paris Conference on Viet Nam (July 1st, 1971)

Source: Collection of George Katsiaficas.

Responding to the Vietnamese people's aspirations for peace and national independence, considering the American and the world peoples' desire for peace, showing its goodwill to make the Paris Conference on Viet Nam progress, basing itself on the 10-point over-all solution, and following up the September 17, 1970, eight-point and the December 10, 1970, three-point statements, the Provisional Revolutionary Government of the Republic of South Viet Nam declares the following:

1. Regarding the Terminal Date for the Total Withdrawal of U.S. Forces

The U.S. Government must end its war of aggression in Viet Nam, stop the policy of "Vietnamization" of the war, withdraw from South Viet Nam all troops, military personnel, weapons, and war materials of the United States and of the foreign countries in the U.S. camp, and dismantle all U.S. bases in South Viet Nam, without posing any conditions whatsoever.

The U.S. Government must set a terminal date for the withdrawal from South Viet Nam of the totality of U.S. forces and those of the other foreign countries in the U.S. camp.

If the U.S. Government sets a terminal date for the withdrawal from South Viet Nam in 1971 of the totality of U.S. forces and those of the other foreign countries in the U.S. camp, the parties will at the same time agree on the modalities of

(a) the withdrawal in safety from South Viet Nam of the totality of U.S. forces and those of the other foreign countries in the U.S. camp;

(b) the release of the totality of militarymen of all parties and of the civilians captured during the war (including American pilots captured in North Viet Nam), so that they may all rapidly return to their homes.

These two operations will begin on the same date and will end on the same date.

A cease-fire will be observed between the South Viet Nam People's Liberation Armed Forces and the armed forces of the United States and of the other foreign countries in the U.S. camp as soon as the parties reach agreement on the withdrawal from South Viet Nam of the totality of U.S. forces and those of the other foreign countries in the U.S. camp.

2. Regarding the Question of Power in South Viet Nam

The U.S. Government must really respect the South Viet Nam people's right to self-determination, put an end to its interference in the internal affairs of South Viet Nam, cease to support the bellicose group headed by Nguyen Van Thieu now in office in Saigon, and stop all manœuvres, including tricks on elections, aimed at maintaining the puppet Nguyen Van Thieu.

By various means, the political, social, and religious forces in South Viet Nam aspiring to peace and national concord will form in Saigon a new administration favoring peace, independence, neutrality and democracy. The Provisional Revolutionary Government of the Republic of South Viet Nam will immediately enter into talks with that administration in order to settle the following questions:

(a) to form a broad three-segment government of national concord that will assume its functions during the period between the restoration of peace and the holding of general elections and that will organize general elections in South Viet Nam.

A cease-fire will be observed between the South Viet Nam People's Liberation Armed Forces and the armed forces of the Saigon administration as soon as a government of national concord is formed.

(b) to take concrete measures with the necessary guarantees to prohibit all acts of terror, reprisal and discrimination against persons having collaborated with one or the other party; to ensure every democratic liberty to the South Viet Nam people; to release all persons jailed for political reasons; to dissolve all concentration camps and to liquidate all forms of constraint and coercion so as to permit the people to return to their native places in complete freedom and to freely engage in their occupations.

(c) To see that the people's conditions of living are stabilized and gradually improved, to create conditions allowing everyone to contribute his talents and efforts to heal the war wounds and rebuild the country.

(d) to agree on measures to be taken to ensure the holding of genuinely free, democratic, and fair general elections in South Viet Nam.

3. Regarding the Question of Vietnamese Armed Forces in South Viet Nam

The Vietnamese parties will together settle the question of Vietnamese armed forces in South Viet Nam in a spirit of national concord, equality, and mutual respect, without foreign interference, in accordance with the post-war situation and with a view to lightening the people's contributions.

4. Regarding the Peaceful Re-Unification of Viet Nam and the Relations between the North and the South Zones

(a) The re-unification of Viet Nam will be achieve step by step, by peaceful means, on the basis of discussions and agreements between the two zones, without constraint and annexation from either party, and without foreign interference.

Pending the re-unification of the country, the North and the South zones will re-establish normal relations, guarantee free movement, free correspondence, free choice of residence, and establish economic and cultural relations on the principle of mutual interests and mutual assistance.

All questions concerning the two zones will be settled by qualified representatives of the Vietnamese people in the two zones on the basis of negotiations, without foreign interference.

(b) In keeping with the provisions of the 1954 Geneva Agreements on Viet Nam, during the present temporary partition of the country into two zones the North and the South zones of Viet Nam will refrain from joining any military alliance with any foreign countries, from allowing any foreign country to maintain military bases, troops, and military personnel on their soil, and from recognizing the protection of any country or of any military alliance or bloc.

5. Regarding the Foreign Policy of Peace and Neutrality of South Viet Nam

South Viet Nam will pursue a foreign policy of peace and neutrality, establish relations with all countries regardless of their political and social system, in accordance with the five principles of peaceful coexistence, maintain economic and cultural relations with all countries, accept the cooperation of foreign countries in the development of the resources of South Viet Nam, accept the economic and technical aid of any country without any political conditions attached, and participate in regional plans for economic cooperation.

On the basis of these principles, after the end of the war South Viet Nam and the United States will establish relations in the political, economic, and cultural fields.

6. Regarding the Damages Caused by the United States to the Vietnamese People in the Two Zones

The U.S. government must bear full responsibility for the losses and the destruction it has caused to the Vietnamese people in the two zones.

7. Regarding the Respect and the International Guarantee of the Accords to be Concluded

The parties will reach agreement on the forms of respect and international guarantee of the accords that will be concluded.

37
U.S. Peace Proposal, October 11, 1971

Source: Viet Nam News Agency, January 31, 1972.

1. The United States agrees to a total withdrawal from South Vietnam of all U.S. forces and other foreign forces allied with the Government of South Vietnam. The withdrawal will be carried out in the following manner:

—The U.S. and allied forces, except for a small number of personnel necessary for technical advice, logistics and observation of the cease-fire mentioned in Point 6, will be withdrawn by 1 July 1972 at the latest, on the condition that this declaration of principle is signed between now and 1 December 1971. In no case will the final date for these withdrawals exceed a period of 7 months after the signing of this declaration of principle.

—The remaining personnel will be progressively withdrawn, beginning 1 month before the presidential election mentioned in Point 3 and simultaneously with the resignation of the present president and vice president of South Vietnam also provided for in Point 3. These withdrawals will be completed before the date of the presidential election.

2. The release of all militarymen and innocent civilians captured throughout Indochina will be carried out in parallel with the troop withdrawals mentioned in Point 1. Both sides will present a complete list of militarymen and innocent civilians held throughout Indochina on the day this declaration of principle is signed. This release will begin on the same day the troop withdrawal begins and will be completed on 1 July 1972, on the condition that this declaration is signed by 1 December 1971 at the latest. The completion of this release will not be later than 7 months after the signing of this declaration.

3. The following principles will govern the political future of South Vietnam.

The political future of South Vietnam will be left for the South Vietnamese people to decide for themselves, free from outside interference.

There will be free and democratic presidential elections in South Vietnam within 6 months after the signing of the final agreement based on the principles of this declaration.

These elections will be organized and run by an independent body representing all political forces in South Vietnam which will assume its responsibilities on the date of the final agreement. This body will, among other responsibilities, determine the qualifications of candidates. All political forces in South Vietnam can participate in the elections and present candidates. There will be international supervision of these elections.

One month before the presidential election takes place, the present president and vice president of South Vietnam will resign. A caretaker government, headed by the chairman of the senate, will assume administrative responsibilities except for those pertaining to the election, which will remain with the independent election body.

The United States, for its part, declares that:

—It will support no candidate and will remain completely neutral in the election.

—It will abide by the outcome of this election and any other political processes shaped by the South Vietnamese people themselves.

—It is prepared to define its military and economic assistance relationships with any government that exists in South Vietnam.

Both sides agree that:

—South Vietnam, together with the other Indochinese countries, should adopt a foreign policy of neutrality.

—The reunification of Vietnam should be decided on the basis of discussions and agreements between North and South Vietnam without constraint or annexation from either party and without foreign interference.

4. Both sides will respect the 1954 Geneva agreements on Indochina and those of 1962 on Laos. There will be no foreign intervention in the Indochinese countries and the Indochinese people will be able to settle their own affairs by themselves.

5. The problems existing among the Indochinese countries will be settled by the Indochinese parties on the basis of mutual respect for their independence, sovereignty and territorial integrity and noninterference in each other's affairs. Among the problems that will be settled is the implementation of the principle that all armed forces of the Indochinese countries must remain within their national frontiers.

6. There will be a general cease-fire throughout Indochina, to begin when the final agreement is signed. Apart from the cease-fire, there will be no further infiltration of outside forces into any of the Indochinese countries.

7. There will be international supervision of the military aspects of this agreement, including the cease-fire and its provisions, the release of prisoners of war and innocent civilians and the withdrawal of outside forces from Indochina.

8. There will be an international guarantee for the fundamental national rights of the Indochinese people, for the neutrality of all Indochinese countries and for a lasting peace in this region.

Both sides express their willingness to participate in an international conference for this and other appropriate purposes.

38
Top Secret [South Vietnamese] Memorandum Re Communist Proposals and US Memorandum of September 19, 1972

As Dr. Kissinger is about to meet with Le Duc Tho we would like to stress the following points:

1. The Communist September 15 proposals are even more arrogant than their August 1 proposals. The September 15 proposals show clearly the intention of the Communists who simply seek to force us to surrender unconditionally. Furthermore, they reveal the Communists' dark schemes which they have tried to conceal at the time of their August 1 proposals.

The Government of the Republic of Viet-Nam strongly rejects the Communist September 15 proposals, and considers that it does not serve any purpose to go over them.

2. We recognize that the US has all the right to conduct secret talks with the other side; and we recognize also that any subject could be brought up in those exploratory talks. However, as far as the GVN is concerned, we wish to stress that our views with regard to the US counter-proposals are contained in our September 13 Memorandum. These views are to be interpreted restrictively.

3. When the time is appropriate for the publication of the counter-proposals to the Communist 10 points, we suggest that these counter-proposals would reflect the common stand of the USG and GVN on this subject to avoid the exploitation by the other side of possible variances between our two Governments.

If the US counter-proposals, to be published, go beyond the GVN stand as embodied in the GVN Memo of September 13, we shall be obliged to clarify and defend publicly our views on this subject.

We feel that the suggestions we made in our Memo of Sept. 13 are sufficiently forthcoming, and contain important new elements in comparison with our proposals of January 27, and are convinced that they will earn the support of public opinion for the GVN and USG in the face of the stubbornness and arrogance of the Communist aggressors.

4. The GVN considers that the North Vietnamese proposals of September 15, 1972 are even harsher and even more absurd than their proposals of August 1. Their "proposals" amount to requiring from our side unconditional surrender while they are the aggressors and are unable to achieve their aims on the battlefields.

This attitude of Hanoi shows that they are not willing and ready to have a negotiated settlement of this conflict. The North Vietnamese Communists demonstrate again that they only try to obtain maximum concession from the USG in this electoral year in the US, on the basis of their experience in this matter in 1968.

On the fundamentals of a negotiated settlement of the Viet-Nam conflict, especially on the political aspects of it, it is the considered view of the GVN that an honorable settlement could be achieved only if parallel to the Vietnamization of the war there is also the *Vietnamization of peace*. In other words, the other side should be brought to accept that the protagonist in the settlement is the GVN, and that it *should negotiate directly with the GVN for a negotiated solution.*

This is neither simply a matter of prestige or "face" for SVN, nor a "peripheral" question of forums. This is, in our view, the indispensable condition to break the deadlock generated by the circumstances under which the Paris talks began in their exploratory stage in early 1968. In our opinion, those "exploratory" talks should have been conducted by the GVN, or at least by the GVN concurrently with the USG, facing the Hanoi representatives.

We believe that by conducting the 1968 "exploratory" talks without the participation of the GVN, the USG lent itself to the description of the role which Communist propaganda has portrayed for many years, namely that the US is an aggressor in both South and North Viet-Nam, and that the GVN is only a "puppet" creature of the US, put up to materialize US "neo-colonialism."

Our common position, of course, is quite different. We consider that, pending reunification of the Viet-Nams by peaceful means, there are 2 international entities demarcated by the 17th parallel. In fact, the RVN has been recognised by a large number of countries, and is a member of numerous international organizations. Therefore the sending of troops and subversive cadres by NVN into SVN is an aggression, no less than the North Korean invasion across the 38th parallel in 1950.

Our position has also been backed up by the Geneva 1954 Agreements whose main features are the establishment of a demarcation line along the 17th parallel, and the strict obligation for the Administrations of each Zone in the North and in the South not to use force against each other, and not to interfere in the internal affairs of each other.

The participation of the US in this conflict and the presense of US troops in Viet-Nam are based on the request of the GVN which exercised its right of collective self-defense, recognised by the United Nations Charter.

In short, our position as a whole is very rational, reasonable, and quite defendable.

The "exploratory" Paris talks which began in March 1968, in which the GVN was excluded, has placed the USG, in our view, in an awkward position and allowed Hanoi to take continuously the offensive in portraying the US as the "aggressor."

Instead of having to answer on its aggression of SVN, Hanoi has been able to revert the roles, and assumes for itself the role of an "heroic" victim of "US aggression." As a result of this, Hanoi has systematically refused the principle of reciprocity in the deescalation of the war, because to be consistent with itself Hanoi said that the US "aggressor" has no right to ask for reciprocity, a phraseology which corresponds to our statements that "aggression should not be rewarded."

These illogical foundations of the Paris talks led to the opening of the so-called "expanded" talks which materialized in January 1969. In these "expanded" talks the "inclusion" of the legal Government of the RVN was considered a "concession" by NVN, to be compensated by the participation of the NLF which, therefore, was a very pale and shadowy façade organization, and whose nature as an instrument created by Hanoi had been clearly established.

Aside from the cessation of bombing of NVN which followed the "expanded" talks (the GVN preferred the term "new" talks to indicate a new phase), the net gain for the Communists was the officialized presence of the "NLF" at the talks. It is on that basis that a number of "non-aligned" governments have given recognition to the "NLF," and later to the so-called "PRG" after it has assumed that new name.

We understand the Anglo-Saxon pragmatism which seems to guide the US approach: This is a protracted conflict which should be terminated as soon as possible. As a beginning step, the opponents have to come to talk together, and we shall see what will develop. The modalities of the forum are considered of little importance.

In fact, as we have pointed out above, the circumstances leading to the official Paris talks, in which the GVN played no active part, have allowed Hanoi to take a "righteous" attitude of a victim of aggression and a most intransigent stand which seriously hinders a negotiated settlement, as almost four years of completely fruitless exchanges in Paris have amply demonstrated.

On the other hand, the participation of the "NLF" in the official Paris talks helped the Communists to achieve one of their major political goals: the recognition of their political arm in SVN.

The Communist side does not even bother to be consistent with its own stand. It repeatedly proclaimed, as late as the NLF statement of Sept. 11, 1972, that the Paris talks is a "four sides" talks. It dwelled on that description in order to emphasize the official presence of the NLF at the talks. However, in contradiction with that version of the talks, both Hanoi and the NLF pretend not to talk to the GVN, but only to the USG.

It is not difficult to understand this self-serving contradiction of the Communists: As long as Hanoi succeeds in placing the USG in the position of a protagonist in this war, it will be able to pursue its line in portraying the US as the "aggressor," and requiring the USG to make unilateral concessions.

Nothing illustrates better this approach of Hanoi to "negotiations" than its concept, in its latest "Proposals," on the "conduct of negotiations" in which Hanoi and the USG will settle all the major questions, including the political problem of South Viet-Nam.

It is the view of the GVN that this formula is utterly unacceptable because it is severely detrimental to the common interests of the GVN and the USG, and will distort beyond recognition the role of the US in the Viet-Nam war.

As we pointed out in the beginning of this Memo, we are convinced that a chance for a negotiated settlement of the Viet Nam conflict, fair and honorable to both sides, lies in *the Vietnamization of peace,* in which the Communists must seek the talks with the legal Government of the RVN.

We shall not consider their acceptance to talk with us, when it materializes itself as a "concession" from them or an "honor" to us. But when they are brought to accept the realistic facts that there is a legal, elected Government of the RVN with which they must deal as the main protagonist, they will find us willing and ready to discuss the termination of this senseless war, and the ways to achieve national reconciliation.

The Communist "proposals" of September 15 are an insolent demand for surrender. It is our view that it does not serve any useful purpose by going over it point by point.

The GVN earnestly believes that a breakthrough in the negotiated settlement will be achieved when Hanoi finds that it has to discuss the major issues with the legal government of the RVN.

International public opinion will have an opportunity to judge when we publish our suggestions to the US counter-proposals in the various Memoranda we have given to the United States, the last of which is the September 13 Memorandum, and the Communist arrogant demands of August 1 and September 15, 1972.

39
The Paris Agreements on Viet Nam—Agreement on Ending the War and Restoring Peace in Viet Nam

Source: United States Treaties and Other International Agreements, compiled and edited under the direction of the U.S. Secretary of State (U.S. Government Printing Office, 1974), excerpts.

The parties participating in the Paris Conference on Viet Nam,

With a view to ending the war and restoring peace in Viet Nam on the basis of respect for the Vietnamese people's fundamental national rights and the South Vietnamese people's right to self-determination, and to contributing to the consolidation of peace in Asia and the world,

Have agreed on the following provisions and undertake to respect and to implement them:

Chapter 1. The Vietnamese People's Fundamental National Rights

Article 1. — The United States and all other countries respect the independence, sovereignty, unity, and territorial integrity of Viet Nam as recognized by the 1954 Geneva Agreements on Viet Nam.

Chapter 2. Cessation of Hostilities—Withdrawal of Troops

Article 2. — A ceasefire shall be observed through South Viet Nam as of twenty-four hours G.M.T. on this twenty-seventh day of January, one thousand nine hundred and seventy-three.

At the same hour, the United States will stop all its military activities against the territory of the Democratic Republic of Viet Nam by ground, air and naval forces, wherever they may be based, and end the mining of the territorial waters, ports, harbours, and waterways of the Democratic Republic of Viet Nam. The United States will remove, permanently deactivate or destroy all the mines in the territorial waters, ports, harbours, and waterways of North Viet Nam as soon as this Agreement goes into effect.

The complete cessation of hostilities mentioned in this Article shall be durable and without limit of time.

Article 3. — The parties undertake to maintain the ceasefire and to ensure a lasting and stable peace.

As soon as the ceasefire goes into effect:

(a) The United States forces and those of the other foreign countries allied with the United States and the Republic of Viet Nam shall remain in place pending the implementation of the plan of troop withdrawal. The Four-Party Joint Military Commission described in Article 16 shall determine the modalities.

(b) The armed forces of the two South Vietnamese parties shall remain in place. The Two-Party Joint Military Commission described in Article 17 shall determine the areas controlled by each party and the modalities of stationing.

(c) The regular forces of all services and arms and the irregular forces of the parties in South Viet Nam shall stop all offensive activities against each other and shall strictly abide by the following stipulations:

— All acts of force on the ground, in the air, and on the sea shall be prohibited;

— All hostile acts, terrorism, and reprisals by both sides will be banned.

Article 4. — The United States will not continue its military involvement or intervene in the internal affairs of South Viet Nam.

Article 5. — Within sixty days of the signing of this Agreement, there will be total withdrawal from South Viet Nam of troops, military advisers, and military personnel, including technical military personnel and military personnel associated with the pacification programme, armaments, munitions, and war material of the United States and those of the other foreign countries mentioned in Article 3(a). Advisers from the above-mentioned countries to all paramilitary organizations and the police force will also be withdrawn within the same period of time.

Article 6. — The dismantlement of all military bases in South Viet Nam of the United States and of the other foreign countries mentioned in Article 3(a) shall be completed within sixty days of the signing of the Agreement.

Article 7. — From the enforcement of the ceasefire to the formation of the government provided for in Articles 9(b) and 14 of this Agreement, the two South Vietnamese parties shall not accept the introduction of troops, military advisers, and military personnel including technical military personnel, armaments, munitions, and war material into South Viet Nam.

The two South Vietnamese parties shall be permitted to make periodic replacement of armaments, munitions and war material which have been destroyed, damaged, worn out or used-up after the ceasefire, on the basis of piece-for-piece, of the same characteristics and properties, under the supervision of the Joint Military Commission of the two South Vietnamese parties and of the International Commission of Control and Supervision.

Chapter 3. The Return of Captured Military Personnel and Foreign Civilians, and Captured and Detained Vietnamese Civilian Personnel

Article 8. — (a) The return of captured military personnel and foreign civilians of the parties shall be carried out simultaneously with and completed not later than the same day as the troop withdrawal mentioned in Article 5. The parties shall exchange complete lists of the above-mentioned captured military personnel and foreign civilians on the day of the signing of this Agreement.

(b) The parties shall help each other to get information about those military personnel and foreign civilians of the parties missing in action, to determine the location and take care of the graves of the dead so as to facilitate the exhumation and repatriation of the remains, and to take any such other measures as may be required to get information about those still considered missing in action.

(c) The question of the return of Vietnamese civilian personnel captured and detained in South Viet Nam will be resolved by the two South Vietnamese parties on the basis of the principles of Article 21(b) of the Agreement on the Cessation of Hostilities in Viet Nam of July 20, 1954. The two South Vietnamese parties will do so in a spirit of national reconciliation and concord, with a view to ending hatred and enmity, in order to ease suffering and to reunite families. The two South Vietnamese parties will do their utmost to resolve this question within ninety days after the ceasefire comes into effect.

Chapter 4. The Exercise of the South Vietnamese People's Right to Self-Determination

Article 9. — The Government of the Democratic Republic of Viet Nam and the Government of the United States of America undertake to respect the following principles for the exercise of the South Vietnamese people's right to self determination:

(a) The South Vietnamese people's right to self-determination is sacred, inalienable, and shall be respected by all countries.

(b) The South Vietnamese people shall decide themselves the political future of South Viet Nam through genuinely free and democratic general elections under international supervision.

(c) Foreign countries shall not impose any political tendency or personality on the South Vietnamese people.

Article 10. — The two South Vietnamese parties undertake to respect the ceasefire and maintain peace in South Viet Nam, settle all matters of contention through negotiations, and avoid all armed conflict.

Article 11. — Immediately after the ceasefire, the two South Vietnamese parties will:

— Achieve national reconciliation and concord, end hatred and enmity, prohibit all acts of reprisal and discrimination against individuals or organizations that have collaborated with one side or the other;

— Ensure the democratic liberties of the people: personal freedom, freedom of speech, freedom of the press, freedom of meeting, freedom of organization, freedom of political activities, freedom of residence, freedom of work, right to property ownership, and right to free enterprise.

Article 12. — (a) Immediately after the ceasefire, the two South Vietnamese parties shall hold consultations in a spirit of national reconciliation and concord, mutual respect, and mutual non-elimination to set up a National Council of National Reconciliation and Concord of three equal segments. The Council shall operate on the principle of unanimity. After the National Council of National Reconciliation and Concord has assumed its functions, the two South Vietnamese parties will consult about the formation of councils at lower levels. The two South Vietnamese parties shall sign an agreement on the internal matters of South Viet Nam as soon as possible and do their utmost to accomplish this within ninety days after the ceasefire comes into effect, in keeping with the South Vietnamese people's aspirations for peace, independence, and democracy.

(b) The National Council of National Reconciliation and Concord shall have the task of promoting the two South Vietnamese parties' implementation of this

Agreement, achievement of national reconciliation and concord and ensurance of democratic liberties. The National Council of National Reconciliation and Concord will organize the free and democratic general elections provided for in Article 9(b) and decide the procedures and modalities of these general elections. The institutions for which the general elections are to be held will be agreed upon through consultations between the two South Vietnamese parties. The National Council of National Reconciliation and Concord will also decide the procedures and modalities of such local elections as the two South Vietnamese parties agree upon.

Article 13. — The question of Vietnamese armed forces in South Viet Nam shall be settled by the two South Vietnamese parties in a spirit of national reconciliation and concord, equality and mutual respect, without foreign interference, in accordance with the postwar situation. Among the questions to be discussed by the two South Vietnamese parties are steps to reduce their military effectives and to demobilize the troops being reduced. The two South Vietnamese parties will accomplish this as soon as possible.

Article 14. — South Viet Nam will pursue a foreign policy of peace and independence. It will be prepared to establish relations with all countries irrespective of their political and social systems on the basis of mutual respect for independence and sovereignty and accept economic and technical aid from any country with no political conditions attached. The acceptance of military aid by South Viet Nam in the future shall come under the authority of the Government set up after the general elections in South Viet Nam provided for in Article 9(b).

Chapter 5. The Reunification of Viet Nam and the Relationship between North and South Viet Nam

Article 15. — The reunification of Viet Nam shall be carried out step by step through peaceful means on the basis of discussions and agreements between North and South Viet Nam, without coercion or annexation by either party, and without foreign interference. The time for reunification will be agreed upon by North and South Viet Nam.

Pending reunification:

(a) The military demarcation line between the two zones at the 17th parallel is only provisional and not a political or territorial boundary, as provided for in Paragraph 6 of the Final Declaration of the 1954 Geneva Conference.

(b) North and South Viet Nam shall respect the demilitarized zone on either side of the provisional military demarcation line.

(c) North and South Viet Nam shall promptly start negotiations with a view to re-establishing normal relations in various fields. Among the questions to be negotiated are the modalities of civilian movement across the provisional military demarcation line.

(d) North and South Viet Nam shall not join any military alliance or military bloc and shall not allow foreign powers to maintain military bases, troops, military advisers, and military personnel on their respective territories, as stipulated in the 1954 Geneva Agreements on Viet Nam.

Chapter 8. The Relationship between the Democratic Republic of Viet Nam and the United States

Article 21. — The United States anticipates that this Agreement will usher in an era of reconciliation with the Democratic Republic of Viet Nam as with all the peoples of Indochina. In pursuance of its traditional policy, the United States will contribute to healing the wounds of war and to postwar reconstruction of the Democratic Republic of Viet Nam and throughout Indochina.

Article 22. — The ending of the war, the restoration of peace in Viet Nam, and the strict implementation of the Agreement will create conditions for establishing a new, equal, and mutually beneficial relationship between the Democratic Republic of Viet Nam and the United States on the basis of respect for each other's independence and sovereignty, and non-interference in each other's internal affairs. At the same time this will ensure stable peace in Viet Nam and contribute to the preservation of lasting peace in Indochina and Southeast Asia.

40
Letter from President Nixon to Premier Pham Van Dong, February 1, 1973

Source: Aid to North Vietnam. Hearing before the Subcommittee on Asia and Pacific Affairs of the Committee on International Relations, House of Representatives, 95th Congress, 1st Session (Washington: Government Printing Office, 1979). Appendix 2, p. 25.

The President wishes to inform the Democratic Republic of Vietnam of the principles which will govern United States participation in the postwar reconstruction of North Vietnam. As indicated in Article 21 of the Agreement on Ending the War and Restoring Peace in Vietnam signed in Paris on Jan. 27, 1973, the United States undertakes this participation in accordance with its traditional policies. These principles are as follows:

1. The Government of the United States of America will contribute to postwar reconstruction in North Vietnam without any political conditions.

2. Preliminary United States studies indicate that the appropriate programs

for the United States contribution to postwar reconstruction will fall in the range of $3.25 billion of grant aid over five years. Other forms of aid will be agreed upon between the two parties. This estimate is subject to revision and to detailed discussion between the Government of the United States and the Government of the Democratic Republic [of] Vietnam.

3. The United States will propose to the Democratic Republic of Vietnam the establishment of a United States–North Vietnamese Joint Economic Commission within 30 days from the date of this message.

4. The function of the commission will be to develop programs for the United States contribution to reconstruction of North Vietnam. This United States contribution will be based upon such factors as:

(a) The needs of North Vietnam arising from the dislocation of war;

(b) The requirements for postwar reconstruction in the agricultural and industrial sectors of North Vietnam's economy.

5. The Joint Economic Commission will have an equal number of representatives from each side. It will agree upon a mechanism to administer the program which will constitute the United States contribution to the reconstruction of North Vietnam. The commission will attempt to complete this agreement within 60 days after its establishment.

6. The two members of the commission will function on the principle of respect for each other's sovereignty, noninterference in each other's internal affairs, equality and mutual benefit. The offices of the commission will be located at a place to be agreed upon by the United States and the Democratic Republic of Vietnam.

7. The United States considers that the implementation of the foregoing principles will prompt economic, trade and other relations between the United States of America and the Democratic Republic of Vietnam and will contribute to the spirit of Chapter VIII of the Agreement on Ending the War and Restoring Peace in Vietnam which was signed in Paris on Jan. 27, 1973.

Understanding Regarding Economic Reconstruction Program

It is understood that the recommendations of the Joint Economic Commission mentioned in the President's note to the Prime Minister will be implemented by each member in accordance with its own constitutional provisions.

Note Regarding Other Forms of Aid

In regard to other forms of aid, United States studies indicate that the appropriate programs could fall in the range of $1 billion to $1.5 billion, depending on food and other commodity needs of the Democratic Republic of Vietnam.

41
Ten Years Ago: The Aerial Dien Bien Phu Battle Against the US Air Force

Vu Can

Source: Viet Nam Courier (Hanoi, 1982), no. 12, pp. 13–15.

The strategic air attack of the US Air Force against North Vietnam lasted twelve days and nights from December 18 to December 29, 1972, and on the least expected occasion, the Christmas season. In earlier years, at this time, it had been customary to agree, tacitly if not formally, to a cease-fire so that the Catholic community in Vietnam could celebrate together with their fellow believers throughout the world. Moreover, the Paris talks were nearing their final stage and the hopes for "a peace at hand" had never been so great in Vietnam, in the United States and elsewhere in the world.

For twelve days and nights on end the US Air Force sent from 500–700 sorties of tactical aircraft and 130–150 sorties of B.52 strategic bombers daily to North Vietnam. Apart from the two main targets which were Hanoi and Haiphong, US planes showered bombs on 11 towns including Thai Nguyen, Viet Tri, and Vinh, 14 district towns and 300 villages. The 1972 Christmas "present" of the White House to the Vietnamese people included 100,000 tons of bombs which represented an explosive force five times that of the atomic bomb dropped on Hiroshima. And the ordnance used was very diversified. There were airborne rockets, bombs of 2,000–3,000 pounds to obliterate whole industrial projects, lazer-guided "smart" bombs to destroy isolated targets with surgical accuracy, anti-tank perforating bombs to destroy shelters deep in the ground, fragmentation and flechette bombs under the generic name of anti-personnel ordnance. These did not include the CS-gas bombs which caused widespread intoxication in the provinces of Quang Binh, Ha Tinh, Thanh Hoa, Son La and elsewhere.

In addition to the customary aircraft such as the A–6, A–7, F–105 and F–4 which had daily sown death and destruction in Vietnam for a dozen years, the Pentagon this time sent into action two of its "trumps," the F–111 swing-wing fighter-bomber, the latest model in the arsenal of the US Air Force which could fly very low at supersonic speed to avoid detection by ground radar without losing its capacity for accurate strike. (These aircraft, capable of carrying nuclear warheads, are now deployed in US bases in Britain.)

But the main weapon the Pentagon counted on remained the intercontinental strategic B.52 bombers taken from the basic weapons arsenal of the US Air Force which came into production in the mid-fifties.

This machine of extermination can carry 30 tons of bombs including nuclear bombs, can fly at a maximum altitude of 16 kilometres and is equipped with electronic devices to escape radar detection as well as with means to detect and destroy enemy planes from a long distance. Each B.52 sortie is accompanied by a squadron of support attack aircraft. In terms of money, each plane costs 9 million dollars, the cost of training a member of the 6-member crew is valued at 70 kilos of gold and the cost of each sortie, excluding the cost of support and ordnance, stands at 41,000 dollars. Of course, Washington planned its crime with utmost lucidity. It maintained absolute secrecy, meaning to inflict a crippling blow on the adversary without a word being said, and on the other hand, to muzzle its victims by obliterating the Voice of Vietnam Radio right in the first raid. If things had happened as planned by the strategists and electronic computers of the Pentagon, this would have been a very swift and definitive blow that would have given Vietnam no time to react and would have presented the world with a fait accompli when the news finally reached the outside.

Anyone who witnessed the strategic attack of the US Air Force against North Vietnam cannot help shudder even now as they recollect those days. Daylight was the time for the operation of the tactical air force. The attack aircraft would bomb or search out aircraft, radar stations, flak emplacements, rocket launchers, MIG shelters, fuel and ammunition depots, infantry gun nests of the militia . . . in short, all the targets which were either constantly on the move or were carefully camouflaged and defended and as such posed a deadly threat to the American pilots. The B.52 fleets usually operated at night. For consecutive nights from December 18 the population of Hanoi and Haiphong could see these monsters coming from the west where lies neighbouring Thailand. In the inky night they flew in broad V-formation defiantly blinking their signals while moving slowly, inexorably to their targets.

In the shelters deep underground one could hear their arrival from a great distance. At first they sounded like the roar of the sea, ominous, mysterious and oppressive. Then when the bombs began raining, the shelter would rock and roll like a ship on a rough sea. The moment seemed interminable.

"Whose turn would be next?" everyone was asking themselves because nobody thought they could possibly survive if they were in the area of a carpet bombing.

In Hanoi alone, during those 12 frightful days and nights, the B.52s carpet-bombed 353 places inside and outside the city, causing particularly heavy destruction at Van Dien, Me Tri, An Duong, Luong Yen, Kham Thien, Gia Lam, Yen Vien, Co Loa . . . The compound of the Bach Mai hospital, a major treatment and research centre of the country with 1,200 sick beds and 50 laboratories was virtually obliterated. Some foreign embassies were also hit. In the stricken areas mangled bodies lay in different positions evoking the scene painted by Picasso in his famous "Guernica," that city of 7,000 souls destroyed by Nazi aircraft during the Spanish war. Some visitors also thought of Dresden where 30,000 people were massacred in one night in the last days of the Second World War when 3,000 sorties of 1,000 Allied aircraft staged an extermination bombing allegedly to deal a finishing blow to Nazism but actually to check the stormy advance of the Soviet army into the last refuge of Hitler's regime.

Perhaps, their deaths at least had taught Vietnamese to be ever aware of the butcher mentality which comes in the fore in times of war. Immediately after Washington started its war escalation against North Vietnam all the cities and towns had, by a general order, organized a large-scale evacuation. Together with the factories, government offices, schools and hospitals, everyone whose presence in the towns was not strictly necessary left for the countryside where they lived under the protection of the peasants. Among the victims of the US strategic air blitz not a few died because they had ignored the order of evacuation, in the false belief that Washington might give them a chance for family reunion during Christmas Day. They thought that the leaders of America were also pious worshippers of God and that the then president of the United States, when placing his hand on the Bible in his swearing-in ceremony, would not dare to make a fool of God even though he might gamble on the people's credulity.

The Collapse of a Myth

The B.52 stratofortresses were first used in the Vietnam war on the 18th of June 1965 seven years six months before the air blitz on Hanoi and Haiphong. They had made regular bombings against the stationing areas of the South Vietnam Liberation Armed Forces deep in the jungle. But these were mostly ineffective due to the elusiveness of their adversary. These giant bombers are not visible to naked eye because they fly at a very high altitude. They can be detected from the ground by sheer experience, and can be firmly identified only when the first carpet of bombs shakes the earth like rolling thunder. As for the B.52 crews, they had the self-confidence of an executioner in front of his tied-up victim. They knew perfectly that they were out of harm's way and any danger to their lives could only come from some technical trouble in the air.

The same confidence remained intact as they were ordered to fly into North Vietnam, until the results of the electronic computers of the Pentagon proved to be too simplistic. First there were several elements of surprise for the F.111s when they were detected by ground radar and met with a dense fire network from the machine-guns and other infantry rifles specifically posted on flat ground or on flat-roofed buildings to ambush low-flying aircraft. The flak emplacements were so positioned to weave a crossfire around aircraft flying at medium altitude. But the surprise was completed for the B.52 armada by SAM 2 missiles which had been improved right on the Vietnamese soil to attain the necessary range.

And only a few minutes after these "fire-spitting dragons" went into action, the "MIG" interceptors from their ambush places shot into the high sky thanks to a system of rocket-propulsion and did the remaining job. The first night of the blitz also witnessed the first downing of the supposedly invincible B.52 flying fortresses. The fall of a super bomber in the night sky of Hanoi is something to be remembered for life. From very high a ball of fire flared up and grew gradually until it became a blaze lighting up a wide area that made a newspaper readable one kilometre away.

Also on that first night, amidst the thunder of bombs and gunfire, at the Thong Nhat Hotel, which was called "Metropole" in French times, a waitress hurriedly took off her apron and picked up a rifle to join the militia in shooting at low-flying aircraft on top of the hotel. "Aren't you afraid?" a foreign reporter asked. "Don't you see that houses are falling down all around?" "Houses may go down," she replied, "but the Vietnamese will never fall." At other times this might sound a bit high-flown but it did not at that moment, especially when the first B.52 was set ablaze over the sky in Hanoi and the public address system of the city announced that the suburban militia had captured the first B.52 airmen. More and more B.52s were shot down on the following nights, reaching a record of five planes on the single night of December 26 over Hanoi alone. People danced and cheered at the gun emplacements and in air-raid shelters, and flocked together to ferret out the fugitive downed airmen while fragments of the shattered aircraft fell all over the city. The White House and the Pentagon had intended to engineer a tragedy right in the cradle of the Vietnamese nation, a wound that would be remembered for life by every Vietnamese. But the riposte was so severe, so surprising and so effective that the enemy himself was dumbfounded.

In those days the world press made frequent references to the "Hanoi Hilton," a humourous name for the Vietnamese prison for American airmen. During the strategic air blitz an average of a dozen or so B.52 airmen who used to be the idols of their lesser colleagues were taken to the "Hanoi Hilton" daily.

Lieutenant John Harry Yuill, 38, brought to the "Hanoi Hilton" on the night of December 21, may be regarded as a typical case. He had flown into Hanoi aboard a B.52 taking off from the Utapao airbase in Thailand. His record would impress any flyer: 5,500 hours of flight, 3,200 of which aboard B.52 bombers. He said: "My aircraft was hit by a rocket at an altitude of 25,000 feet. This is one of the worst Christmas I've ever lived. I have seen in Life magazine many pilots of tactical aircraft imprisoned here. I knew full well that their number is very, very big. But I never thought that we pilots of strategic bombers would one day share their fate." Statements in the same vein could be heard from many other captured US airmen. All of them before take-off were assured by their commanders that there would be nothing to fear. "Your's will be a night raid from very high. The Communist SAMs and MIGs will be of no use. Just fly in single line and come back. You'll return safely to base without a single plane missing."

Were the US commanders fooling their subalterns? Were they fooling themselves? Maybe both. At any rate, the strategic air blitz ended in a complete fiasco. Within 12 days and nights the US Air Force lost 81 aircraft including 23 B.52 stratofortresses and five tactical F.111 fighter-bombers. Hundreds of US pilots were either captured or reported missing. These were almost the last US aircraft downed over North Vietnam because the United States was to declare a bomb halt on January 15, 1973. By then the cemetary for US aircraft in North Vietnam had already gathered the wrecks of 5,000 planes of 47 different types. A myth estimated at billions of dollars—to borrow a favourite American way of reckoning—had just collapsed: the invincibility of the US Air Force in general and of the B.52 armada in particular.

42
The Ecological Impact of the Air War

Paul Feeny with Jim Allaway

ONLY WE CAN PREVENT FORESTS
—Motto over the door to headquarters, Operation Ranch Hand, Saigon

Source: From *The Air War in Indochina,* edited by Raphael Littauer and Norman Uphoff.

A. Defoliants and Herbicides

Use of defoliants in South Vietnam began on an experimental basis in 1961 and became fully operational the following year. This program had two major objectives. The first was *defoliation* (operation RANCH HAND), in which forests, roadsides, base perimeters, etc., were sprayed in order to remove the foliage cover which had afforded concealment to the enemy. At low concentrations these chemicals do indeed act merely as defoliants; at the concentrations used in Vietnam, however, they normally act also as herbicides, killing a significant fraction of the plants in addition to defoliating them. The second major objective was the *destruction of crops,* mostly rice, carried out in the hope of denying food to the enemy. Crop destruction was largely confined to the mountainous areas of northern and western South Vietnam, where the impact was felt most severely by the small population of about one million, mostly Montagnards. Crop destruction may also have had the objective of driving South Vietnamese civilians into the "strategic hamlets" set up for them by the South Vietnamese Government.

Though some spraying in Vietnam has been done with helicopters or ground equipment, the principal means of application has been the twin-engine C–123 cargo plane. In the years 1962 through 1968 these aircraft made more than 19,000 individual spray flights. Each plane is fitted with a 950-gallon tank from which the herbicide is pumped to spray booms under each wing and at the tail. When the herbicide hits the airstream it is dispersed into fine droplets. One aircraft flying at about 150 feet above the tree tops produces a swath of affected vegetation about 300 feet wide and ten miles long. Precautions must be taken that the sprayed chemical does not drift into adjacent, non-target areas. Occasional incidents occur in which an aircraft is forced to dump its herbicide quickly; it can pump out the entire 950 gallons in about 30 seconds.

Three formulations account for almost all the herbicides used in Indochina: agents Orange, White, and Blue. The composition and mode of action of these agents are discussed in greater detail in Appendix E [not reprinted here—ed.], which also contains a listing of appropriate references; a summary of the main facts is given below.

Orange: Composition, 2,4-D and 2,4,5-T; an oily liquid insoluble in water. Mainly used against broad-leaved and woody vegetation. One application defoliates hardwoods and kills some canopy trees; two applications produce a heavy kill of all woody vegetation; the resulting invasion by bamboo and grasses may arrest forest regeneration indefinitely. On mangrove forests Orange kills almost all trees in a single application; mangrove areas sprayed in 1961 have still shown no significant signs of regeneration. The chemical itself persists for only a few weeks, except in stagnant water or poorly aerated ground, where high concentrations could conceivably accumulate. 2,4,5-T or an associated impurity (dioxin) is thought to be a teratogen (causing serious birth deformities, like thalidomide); its use in the U.S. has been restricted since late 1969. Orange accounts for about 60 percent of the herbicide used in Vietnam; it was being sprayed at least until August 1970.

White: Composition, butyl esters of 2,4-D and picloram; a solution in water. Used much like Orange, but less volatile and therefore less subject to wind draft; it is preferred near populated areas. Picloram is one of the most potent herbicides known; it is remarkably persistent, like the insecticide DDT; its use on agricultural land in the U.S. is prohibited. Since White is water soluble, it can easily be washed by rainfall into adjacent areas.

Blue: Composition, organic arsenates including cacodylic acid; a solution in water. Its prime use is for crop destruction, especially rice. It is more effective against grasses than are Orange or White, and acts more rapidly (within a few days).

Herbicides are sprayed at a rate of about three gallons per acre, the stock solution of each agent being formulated to obtain the desired coverage. In the case of Orange, the rate of application is about 26 pounds per acre, almost ten times the rate recommended for use in the U.S. It is estimated that more than 100 million pounds of herbicides have by now been sprayed on Vietnam, covering a total of almost six million acres, . . .

The greatest impact has been on tropical hardwood forests. About 35 percent of South Vietnam's 14 million acres of dense forest have been sprayed one or more times, resulting in the destruction of enough merchantable timber (six billion board feet) to supply the country's domestic needs for about 30 years; this also represents a loss of about $500 million in taxes that would otherwise have accrued to the South Vietnamese Government. Of the three-quarter million acres of coastal mangrove forests, mostly in the Delta area, about one-half have been totally destroyed.

B. Bombing and Spraying: The Potential Consequences

Forests are first to go. Then the animals—some, like the elephant, are killed deliberately since they could be used to transport supplies; others just happen to be in the wrong place at the wrong time. Finally, the land itself is destroyed: farms, rice paddies, and village sites in many regions are bomb-pocked and barren.

In the brief discussion that follows, only the most obvious environmental effects of the air war will be mentioned, but even such a superficial enumeration conveys an idea of the pervasiveness of the damage. The very fact that data on the present extent of this damage are scant, combined with the virtual impossibility of predicting future consequences, is in itself one of the most ominous signs of danger.

The air war has been a severe shock to all the natural ecosystems of Indochina. Such damage would be of concern wherever it occurred since it affects an intricate web of relationships; but Indochina is especially sensitive because tropical ecosystems are thought to be less resilient than those of temperate regions. Tropical systems are characterized by many more species per unit area; each is finely adapted and food webs are complex and intricate. In a northern forest a major calamity has relatively short-term consequences, since most of the species are already adapted to surviving frosts and unseasonal floods. The rates of reproduction and recolonization are usually high. In tropical regions, where the climatic conditions are much more predictable and favorable, species tend to be less well adapted to rapid change.

Flora. The direct attack on the flora by defoliation and the use of herbicides has been described above. In addition to the very extensive damage done by this chemical warfare, fires—many undoubtedly caused by bombing and napalm—have consumed or defoliated large areas of forest. Revegetation of soils in severely defoliated forests may be retarded by rapid loss of plant nutrients following defoliation and by invasion of bamboo and other grasses. Tropical forests carry most of their nutrients in the vegetation itself, rather than in the soil; hence, following decomposition of the plants, most of the nutrients are lost directly, with the remainder being subject to leaching from the soils.

Mangrove forests have suffered particularly severe damage from defoliation—about half have been totally destroyed in South Vietnam—and so far there is no evidence of regeneration. These forests play an important part in the natural process of delta formation, and stabilize the coastline and river banks. They also provide essential cover and food during the life cycles of many fish and other animals.

Fauna. The weapons of air warfare affect animals directly by killing them, and indirectly by changing their environment, with the result that populations are changed and the diversity of species is reduced. Natural checks and balances to pests and disease vectors may be upset, particularly as predatory fauna are killed. The invasion of destroyed areas by other plant groups may result in larger populations of undesired animals favoring this new habitant—rats, for example, often thrive in bamboo, which is a predominant regrowth species in defoliated forest areas. The population of the tiger has apparently increased as its natural food supply has been augmented by battlefield casualties.

There are contradictory claims about the toxicity of herbicides to animals. Though some authorities claim there is little danger, evidence indicates that 2,4-D in moderate doses may be toxic to some fish, that plants treated with 2,4-D may accumulate toxic quantities of nitrates (which could affect domestic stock as well as wild fauna), and that dioxin, a contaminant of some 2,4,5-T solutions used, is toxic and concentrates in the food chain since it does not break down with time. Finally, domestic livestock are affected by herbicides, both directly and indirectly, as they eat plants that have been contaminated.

Agriculture. Agriculture, and land utilization in general, are affected not only by chemical warfare but also directly by bombing. One may estimate that at least 12,000,000 craters have been produced in the Indochina air war so far, covering an area of at least 200,000 acres and excavating about 1.5 billion cubic yards of soil. (Roughly two-thirds of the bomb tonnage was deployed within South Vietnam, whose total area is 42 million acres.) Some areas in Indochina have been likened to moonscapes. The long-term effects of this cratering are hard to assess, but the fact that craters do not naturally fill in is evidenced by craters from World War II which are still found in the jungles of New Guinea. A bomb crater destroys the surface organic layer and throws up subsoil; it creates severe local relief and erosion in the soil and may disrupt drainage patterns. Usually it fills with water and becomes very difficult to drain, making heavily bombed areas virtually unsuitable for cultivation.

Flooding. The control of water flow is a vital problem in many areas of Indochina. Defoliation and laterization lead to more rapid runoff of rain water; the destruction of many man-made control structures compounds the problem. The destructiveness of the floods in central South Vietnam in November 1970 was blamed in part on defoliation and bomb damage. People were driven by the floods out of refugee camps to which they had come, in the first place, because of crop destruction or bombing in their native highlands.

Malnutrition. It is generally recognized that crop destruction has had its chief impact on the civilian population rather than on enemy soldiers, who are in the best position to obtain food in times of scarcity. The Herbicides Assessment Commission has concluded that the food destroyed would have been enough to feed 600,000 persons for a year, and that nearly all of it would have been consumed by civilians. Although the amount destroyed is less than two percent of the national crop of South Vietnam in any one year, the most extensive crop destruction has been carried out in the central highlands, a food-scarce area with a population of about one million, mainly Montagnards. It is among these people that problems of malnutrition and starvation are most severe.

Birth abnormalities. According to a report released by the National Institutes of Health in the fall of 1969, 2,4,5-T (or an associated impurity, dioxin) was shown to produce significant increases in the incidence of fetus malformation in animals as early as 1965. Moreover, the Herbicide Assessment Commission team in Vietnam has found a suggestive correlation between years of peak defoliation in Tay Ninh province and an increase in stillbirths and birth deformities.

Malaria. Of the endemic diseases in Indochina, malaria is probably the most widespread; in the past it has been far more common in the upland regions than in the lowlands. Now, large numbers of bomb craters have filled with water. This stagnant water, present throughout Vietnam and parts of Laos and Cambodia, is an ideal breeding habitat for various species of mosquito, including those which are malaria vectors. . . .

Americans have begun to become aware of the vast complexity of their environment, and of the unpredictable consequences that go with disturbing it. In Indochina, the environment has not merely been disturbed—there has been a deliberate and unprecedented onslaught on it, with chemicals, with explosives, and with fire. The short listing just given, incomplete and inconclusive as it is, by its very open-endedness points up the ominous results which may have been, and which may continue to be, provoked in Indochina.

43
Henry A. Kissinger Appeals to Congress for Emergency Aid, 1975

Source: Secretary of State Henry A. Kissinger, April 15, 1975, testimony before Congress.

The long and agonizing conflict in Indochina has reached a tragic stage. The events of the past month have been discussed at great length before the Congress and require little additional elaboration. In Viet-Nam President Thieu ordered a strategic withdrawal from a number of areas he regarded as militarily untenable. However, the withdrawal took place in great haste, without adequate advance planning, and with insufficient coordination. It was further complicated by a massive flow of civilian refugees seeking to escape the advancing North Vietnamese Army. Disorganization engendered confusion; fear led to panic. The results, as we all know, were tragic losses—of territory, of population, of material, and of morale.

But to fully understand what has happened, it is necessary to have an appreciation of all that went before. The North Vietnamese offensive, and the South Vietnamese response, did not come about by chance—although chance is always an element in warfare. The origins of these events are complex, and I believe it would be useful to review them briefly.

Since January 1973, Hanoi has violated—continuously, systematically, and energetically—the most fundamental provisions of the Paris agreement. It steadily increased the numbers of its troops in the South. It improved and expanded its logistics systems in the South. It increased the armaments and ammunition of its forces in the South. And as you know, it blocked all efforts to account for personnel missing in action. These are facts, and they are indisputable. All of these actions were of course in total violation of the agreement. Parallel to these efforts, Hanoi attempted—with considerable success—to immobilize the various mechanisms established by the agreement to monitor and curtail violations of the cease-fire. Thus, it assiduously prepared the way for further military actions.

South Viet-Nam's record of adherence to the agreement has not been perfect. It is, however, qualitatively and quantitatively far better than Hanoi's. South Viet-Nam did not build up its armed forces. It undertook no major offensive actions—although it traded thrusts and probes with the Communists. It cooperated fully in establishing and supporting the cease-fire control mechanisms provided for in the agreement. And it sought, as did the United States, full implementation of those provisions of the agreement calling for an accounting of soldiers missing in action.

But perhaps more relevant to an understanding of recent events are the following factors.

While North Viet-Nam had available several reserve divisions which it could commit to battle at times and places of its choosing, the South had no strategic reserves. Its forces were stretched thin, defending lines of communication and population centers throughout the country.

While North Viet-Nam, by early this year, had accumulated in South Viet-Nam enough ammunition for two years of intensive combat, South Vietnamese commanders had to ration ammunition as their stocks declined and were not replenished.

While North Viet-Nam had enough fuel in the South to operate its tanks and armored vehicles for at least 18 months, South Viet-Nam faced stringent shortages.

In sum, while Hanoi was strengthening its army in the South, the combat effectiveness of South Viet-Nam's army gradually grew weaker. While Hanoi built up its reserve divisions and accumulated ammunition, fuel, and other military supplies, U.S. aid levels to Viet-Nam were cut—first by half in 1973 and then by another third in 1974. This coincided with a worldwide inflation and a fourfold increase in fuel prices. As a result almost all of our military aid had to be devoted to ammunition and fuel. Very little was available for spare parts, and none for new equipment.

These imbalances became painfully evident when the offensive broke full force, and they contributed to the tragedy which unfolded. Moreover, the steady diminution in the resources available to the Army of South Viet-Nam unquestionably affected the morale of its officers and men. South Vietnamese units in the northern and central provinces knew full well that they faced an enemy superior both in numbers and in firepower. They knew that reinforcements and resupply would not be forthcoming. When the fighting began they also knew, as they had begun to suspect, that the United States would not respond. I would suggest that all of these factors added significantly to the sense of helplessness, despair, and, eventually, panic which we witnessed in late March and early April.

I would add that it is both inaccurate and unfair to hold South Viet-Nam responsible for blocking progress toward a political solution to the conflict. Saigon's proposals in its conversations with PRG [Provisional Revolutionary Government] representatives in Paris were in general constructive and conciliatory. There was no progress toward a compromise political settlement because Hanoi intended that there should not be. Instead, North Viet-Nam's strategy was to lay the groundwork for an eventual military offensive, one which would either bring outright victory or at least allow Hanoi to dictate the terms of a political solution.

Neither the United States nor South Viet-Nam entered into the Paris agreement with the expectation that Hanoi would abide by it in every respect. We did believe, however, that the agreement was sufficiently equitable to both sides that its major provisions could be accepted and acted upon by Hanoi and that the contest could be shifted thereby from a military to a political track. However, our two governments also recognized that, since the agreement manifestly was not self-enforcing, Hanoi's adherence depended heavily on maintaining a military parity in South Viet-Nam. So long as North Viet-Nam confronted a strong South Vietnamese army and so long as the possibility existed of U.S. intervention to offset the strategic advantages of the North, Hanoi could be expected to forgo major military action. Both of those essential conditions were dissipated over the past two years. Hanoi attained a clear military superiority, and it became increasingly convinced that U.S. intervention could be ruled out. It therefore returned to a military course, with the results we have seen.

The present situation in Viet-Nam is ominous. North Viet-Nam's combat forces far outnumber those of the South, and they are better armed. Perhaps more important, they enjoy a psychological momentum which can be as decisive as armaments in battle. South Viet-Nam must reorganize and reequip its forces, and it must restore the morale of its army and its people. These tasks will be difficult, and they can be performed only by the South Vietnamese. However, a successful defense will also require resources—arms, fuel, ammunition, and medical supplies—and these can come only from the United States.

Large quantities of equipment and supplies, totaling perhaps $800 million, were lost in South Viet-Nam's precipitous retreat from the northern and central areas. Much of this should not have been lost, and we regret that it happened. But South Viet-Nam is now faced with a different strategic and tactical situation and different military requirements. Although the amount of military assistance the President has requested is of the same general magnitude as the value of the equipment lost, we are not attempting simply to replace those losses. The President's request, based on General Weyand's [Gen. Frederick C. Weyand, Chief of Staff, United States Army] assessment, represents our best judgment as to what is needed now, in this new situation, to defend what is left of South Viet-Nam. Weapons, ammunition, and supplies to reequip four divisions, to form a number of ranger groups into divisional units, and to upgrade some territorial forces into infantry regiments will require some $326 million. The balance of our request is for ammunition, fuel, spare parts, and medical supplies to sustain up to 60 days of intensive combat and to pay for the cost of transporting those items. These are minimum requirements, and they are needed urgently.

The human tragedy of Viet-Nam has never been more acute than it now is. Hundreds of thousands of South Vietnamese have sought to flee Communist control and are homeless refugees. They have our compassion, and they must also have our help. Despite commendable efforts by the South Vietnamese Government, the burden of caring for these innocent victims is beyond its capacity. The United States has already done much to assist these people, but many remain without adequate food, shelter, or medical care. The President has asked that additional efforts and additional resources be devoted to this humanitarian effort. I ask that the Congress respond generously and quickly.

The objectives of the United States in this immensely difficult situation remain as they were when the Paris agreement was signed—to end the military conflict and establish conditions which will allow a fair political solution to be achieved. We believe that despite the tragic experience to date, the Paris agreement remains a valid framework within which to proceed toward such a solution. However, today, as in 1973, battlefield conditions will affect political perceptions and the outcome of negotiations. We therefore believe that in order for a political settlement to be reached which preserves any degree of self-determination for the people of South Viet-Nam, the present military situation must be stabilized. It is for these reasons that the President has asked Congress to appropriate urgently additional funds for military assistance for Viet-Nam.

I am acutely aware of the emotions aroused in this country by our long and difficult involvement in Viet-Nam. I understand what the cost has been for this nation and why frustration and anger continue to dominate our national debate. Many will argue that we have done more than enough for the Government and the people of South Viet-Nam. I do not agree with that proposition, however, nor do I believe that to review endlessly the wisdom of our original involvement serves a useful purpose now. For despite the agony of this nation's experience in Indochina and the substantial reappraisal which has taken place concerning our proper role there, few would deny that we are still involved or that what we do—or fail to do—will still weigh heavily in the outcome. We cannot by our actions alone insure the survival of South Viet-Nam. But we can, alone, by our inaction assure its demise.

The United States has no legal obligation to the Government and the people of South Viet-Nam of which the Congress is not aware. But we do have a deep moral obligation—rooted in the history of our involvement and sustained by the continuing efforts of our friends. We cannot easily set it aside. In addition to the obvious consequences for the people of Viet-Nam, our failure to act in accordance with that obligation would inevitably influence other nations' perceptions of our constancy and our determination.

44
Joys and Sorrows

Truong Nhu Tang

Source: Excerpts from *A Vietcong Memoir,* copyright © 1985 by Truong Nhu Tang, Doan Van Toai, and David Chanoff. Reprinted by permission of Harcourt Brace Jovanovich, Inc. (Vintage Books edition, 1986), pp. 263–70.

On the fifteenth we woke to a clear, sunlit sky. Already at dawn crowds of people were pouring into Independence Palace Square to celebrate this most glorious of events, total victory after thirty years of grim and bloody sacrifice. The immense throng stretched out in all directions opposite the dais—over half a million we were told later, and that seemed a conservative estimate. Together with the rest of the PRG leadership, I climbed to my place on the reviewing stand and looked out on a sea of faces and banners. Our colleagues gathered around us, from the Front, the Alliance, the DRV, the Party, all beaming with happiness, some wiping away tears.

President Thang of the Northern government spoke for all of us, dedicating this day to Uncle Ho, whose spirit seemed all but palpable in the air around the dais. "From this time on," Thang declared, "the whole Vietnamese people will share a new happiness, in a new era." After Thang, Chairman Nguyen Huu Tho of the NLF spoke on behalf of the Front and the Provisional Revolutionary Government, recalling and celebrating the heroic struggle of the people. Pham Hung, representing the Workers' Party, then rose to comment on the earthshaking significance of our historic triumph and to appeal for national unity and reconstruction.

"Only the American imperialists," he said, "have been defeated. All Vietnamese are the victors. Anyone with Vietnamese blood should take pride in this common victory of the whole nation. You, the people of Saigon, are now the masters of your own city."

With this the parades began. First the mass organizations filed by, the youth, students, workers, Buddhists, Catholics, representatives of every group and stratum in the city. Above their smiles waved the flags of both the Northern republic and the South's proud new government. Portraits of Ho swung down the street, sprinkled among thousands of pennants and banderoles proclaiming "Nothing Is More Precious Than Independence and Liberty" . . . "Long Live Chairman Ho" . . . "Unity, Unity, Great Unity," and also "Glory to Marxism-Leninism" and "Glory to the Workers' Party of Vietnam."

Then the military units came in sight, troops from every North Vietnamese Army outfit, all of them wearing distinctive new olive-colored pith helmets. Tank squadrons, antiaircraft batteries and artillery rumbled by, as did sleek, murderous-looking Soviet missiles. All the while, air force overflights shook the dais, adding their din to the martial and patriotic music of the bands.

At last, when our patience had almost broken, the Vietcong units finally appeared. They came marching down the street, several straggling companies, looking unkempt and ragtag after the display that had preceded them. Above their heads flew a red flag with a single yellow star—the flag of the Democratic Republic of North Vietnam.

Seeing this, I experienced almost a physical shock. Turning to Van Tien Dung who was then standing next to me, I asked quietly, "Where are our divisions one, three, five, seven, and nine?"

Dung stared at me a moment, then replied with equal deliberateness: "The army has already been unified." As he pronounced these words, the corners of his mouth curled up in a slight smile.

"Since when?" I demanded. "There's been no decision about anything like that."

Without answering, Dung slowly turned his eyes back to the street, unable to suppress his sardonic expression, although he must have known it was conveying too much. A feeling of distaste for this whole affair began to come over me—not to mention premonitions I did not want to entertain.

In the days that followed, I became aware that our police and security were being handled exclusively by various DRV departments. Now that I thought about it, I realized that all the arrangements for the victory celebration had also been taken care of by the DRV. We all began to note the extent to which the Northern cadres were filling positions of responsibility on our staffs and handling business of every variety.

This was not a new development. But before this we had been involved in a common struggle, in which our organizations had faced severe manpower and expertise shortages. Now, with victory, it was somehow different.

A new tone had crept into the collaboration. All of the PRG cabinet began to feel uncomfortable, although we strove to put the best face on what was happening, attributing it to "organizational difficulties" (in the push to set up our new administrations and get them running) or our undeniable lack of experienced personnel. And indeed—as we kept reminding ourselves—we did desperately need all the managerial help we could find. Reasoning along these lines, we managed to bury our anxieties in the avalanche of work that engulfed us.

Meanwhile, the Military Management Committee that had been set up to maintain order was still functioning as the government pro tem. The real power in this group was Vo Van Kiet (Kiet at this time was a full member of the Party's Central Committee), who was in constant communication with the Politburo. All of the policies and directives concerned with the problems of victory and transition were in fact devised in the Politburo and administered through Kiet and his colleagues. The Provisional Revolutionary Government, "the sole genuine representative of the Southern people" (as the Party had so felicitously styled it over the years), was still playing a purely subordinate role—although to give these proceedings an air of legitimacy, all decisions were passed through the PRG staffs, to receive an imprimatur from the appropriate ministry. But in the heady and tumultuous days of May, no one gave much thought to this arrangement. Once the chaos of transition had been controlled and a semblance of calm restored, we would of course begin to use more normal avenues of government.

But as the weeks slid by, it became impossible to shut our eyes to the emerging arrogance and disdain of our Party staff cadres—almost as if they believed that they were the conquerors and we the vanquished. Try as we might to ignore the signs, each of us felt it. In the Justice Ministry, my administrators began claiming that they had to carry out orders from their superiors in the Northern government, rather than the directives they received from us. One of my cadres, an official of North Vietnam's High Tribunal, drew up plans to establish branches of the tribunal in each Southern province. Others, employees of the DRV's Supreme Council of Censors and State Juridical Committee, were anxious to confiscate some of the Justice Ministry's buildings for use by their own departments.

At first, I treated these and similar situations as opportunities to delineate the authority of my ministry. Still struggling to suppress the obvious, I reasoned that the entire cabinet could expect attempts to encroach on its jurisdiction and that this was essentially normal bureaucratic infighting. One of our first tasks, then, would be to establish a clear chain of command. I began this process by using the plans for province tribunals and the transfer of property as examples. Since my signature and seal were required for all magistrate appointments, as well as for property transfers, I decided to withhold approval. Such directives, I insisted, would have to originate with the ministry, and I would consider them on their merits. As long as the ministry was my responsibility, I was the one who should be making these and all other substantive decisions.

As the cadres' demands became more and more heated, I remained adamant, continuing to operate on the theory that authority would have to be grasped. Eventually, my obstinacy brought results—visitors from the North. I received word that the chiefs of the High Tribunal, the Censorate, and the Juridical Committee would meet with me to resolve the impasse that had developed. In an afternoon of discussion, my guests succeeded in conveying to me the fundamentality of the North's resolve to control the Provisional Government.

As we talked, the true outlines of power revealed themselves with painful clarity. Suddenly all the creeping fears that, until now, I had succeeded in holding down were released. When my visitors left, I felt all I had managed to retain was the respect due my office, for I had listened to their arguments and pleas as if these people were actually supplicants—the formal charade had been expertly maintained on both sides. But in the end I signed the directives.

By the time this diplomatic encounter was over, I had no illusions about what was happening, and I knew that neither I nor my colleagues would be in office long.

My fellow ministers quickly found their own illusions and rationalizations swept away just as cleanly. Like me, most of these veteran revolutionaries put up an initial fight, refusing to cooperate once they discovered they were involved in a farce. Many just left, keeping away from their offices while they mulled over what to do next. "Let the Northern cadres make the wind and the weather," growled Dr. Hoa as she stalked out of the Ministry of Health. A miasma of disgust hung over most of the NLF and PRG people who stayed.

There were several interesting exceptions to this, though. A few, Presidential

Minister Kiem, Professor Nguyen Van Hieu, and Culture Minister Luu Huu Phuoc kept their mouths shut, frightened by the thought of deviating from the Party's will. Meanwhile, NLF President Nguyen Huu Tho and PRG President Huynh Tan Phat took steps to secure their privileges by faithfully expounding the new line: forced reunification and the rapid socialization of the South.

As for me, for the time being I stayed, presiding over a department roiled with controversy. My embittered deputy minister, Le Van Tha, was intent on turning life into a bureaucratic torment for the Northern staff cadres, who, if they had been arrogant as subordinates, were insufferable now that the veil was lifted. Not content with the hard time Tha was giving them, they squabbled incessantly among themselves, chiefly about the best way to insure the demise of the ministry—the three DRV bureaus for which they worked each having its own distinct thoughts on the subject.

It was a time of unalloyed cynicism on the part of the Workers' Party and stunned revulsion for those of us who had been their brothers-in-arms for so long. About this period the Northern Party historian Nguyen Khac-Vien commented, "The Provisional Revolutionary Government was always simply a group emanating from the DRV. If we (the DRV) had pretended otherwise for such a long period, it was only because during the war we were not obliged to unveil our cards." Now, with total power in their hands, they began to show their cards in the most brutal fashion. They made it understood that the Vietnam of the future would be a single monolithic bloc, collectivist and totalitarian, in which all the traditions and culture of the South would be ground and molded by the political machine of the conquerors. These, meanwhile, proceeded to install themselves with no further regard for the niceties of appearance.

The PRG and the National Liberation Front, whose programs had embodied the desire of so many South Vietnamese to achieve a political solution to their troubles and reconciliation among a people devastated by three decades of civil war—this movement the Northern Party had considered all along as simply the last linkup it needed to achieve its own imperialistic revolution. After the 1975 victory, the Front and the PRG not only had no further role to play; they became a positive obstacle to the rapid consolidation of power.

This obstacle had to be removed. As Truong Chinh, spokesman for the Politburo, put it, "The strategic mission for our revolution in this new phase is to accelerate the unification of the country and lead the nation to a rapid, powerful advance toward socialism." Chinh's phrases were not simple rhetoric. They conveyed major policy decisions that were to change the fabric of the South's political, social, and economic life. No longer would South Vietnam be regarded as "a separate case" whose economy and government would have the opportunity to evolve independently, prior to negotiating a union with the DRV. All of the NLF and PRG emphasis on civil rights, land reform, and social welfare was "no longer operative." The program now was to strip away as fast as possible the apparent respect for pluralistic government, neutrality, and national concord and reconciliation in the South that the DRV had maintained with such breathtaking pretense for twenty-one years. We had entered, in Chinh's words, "a new phase."

In mid-July the organizations representing the old phase held one of their last general meetings. The leadership of the NLF, PRG, the Alliance of National, Democratic, and Peace Forces, and the mass organizations were called together to hear relevant portions of the new master plan. In a series of virtuoso speeches, Pham Hung (DRV Politburo member in charge of the South), Huynh Tan Phat, and Nguyen Huu Tho managed to address the subject of a unified Vietnam without once referring to the fate intended for the Front and the PRG, those erstwhile "sole authentic representatives."

While this amazing performance was going on, Presidential Minister Tran Buu Kiem (the former foreign affairs specialist) leaned over and whispered in my ear, "They are burying us without drums or taps. You'd think they would at least have the decency to say prayers for the dead."

"You're right," I whispered back. "We should insist on a formal funeral." During a break in the proceedings, I went up to Tho and said, "Listen, some of us feel we should get a funeral celebration out of this. What do you say?"

Tho stared at me quizzically, unsure that he had detected a note of mockery. After a moment he answered with stony seriousness, "Of course. We can easily arrange that."

Tho was as good as his word, though it turned out to be not quite so easy. The problem was that by this time all the Saigon government buildings and official residences had been appropriated by Party leaders from Hanoi, none of whom were anxious to sponsor such a possibly questionable affair. In the end, Tho hired the Rex Dance Hall for the Vietcong funeral celebration. This sleazy former pleasure land had been one of the magnetic poles of Saigon's demimonde. In its day it had seen deals of every description made by the most corrupt of the city's pre-1975 denizens. Drug transactions, debauchery, and the buying and selling of power had been its daily meat and drink. I am sure it never saw the likes of the gathering that met there for the last rites of South Vietnam's revolution.

About thirty of us were present, from the Front, the PRG ministries, and the Alliance. We ate without tasting, and we heard without listening as some revolutionary music was cranked out by a sad little band Tho had dredged up from somewhere. We even managed to choke out a few of the old combatants' songs. But there was no way to swallow the gall in our mouths or to shrug off the shroud that had settled on our souls. We knew finally that we had been well and truly sold.

Chapter VIII

Rationales and Retrospectives

The final chapter of this anthology discusses some of the reasons for the war and the lessons that have been learned from it. As in the other chapters, there is a divergence of views to present. The most commonly cited reason for U.S. involvement was belief in the domino theory. (See Document 6 in Chapter 2.) Enunciated by President Eisenhower in 1954, this rationale proved of lasting importance to America's involvement. As late as 1973, President Nixon continued to assert the importance of the American war in Vietnam in terms of its effect on the rest of the Third World, and even in 1985, he had not changed his position on the war's importance (see below).

The first document in this chapter, a speech delivered by President Lyndon Johnson on April 7, 1965, at Johns Hopkins University, presents a variant of the domino theory. In Johnson's view, "The rulers in Hanoi are urged on by Peking." According to the president, people all over the world were watching Vietnam, and an American retreat there would mean that "the battle would be renewed in one country and then another." Johnson's speech also contained an offer to Ho Chi Minh, which the president was sure "Old Ho" (as he called him in the presence of Bill Moyers) could not refuse: a billion dollar investment in the Mekong River which would rival the Tennessee Valley Authority, an investment that would be made only if Ho Chi Minh and the North Vietnamese would compromise. Johnson couched his message in language borrowed from Martin Luther King's "I Have a Dream" speech.

Eleven days later, Hans Morgenthau responded to President Johnson's speech with an article in the *New York Times* (Document 46). A distinguished professor and early critic of administration policy, Morgenthau believed the United States should withdraw from Vietnam for pragmatic, not moral, reasons. He pointed out some of the fallacies contained in the notions both of falling dominoes and of the invasion of South Vietnam by the North. According to the agreements reached in Geneva, Morgenthau reminded, Vietnam was one country, not two, and it was impossible for a country to invade itself. Although President Johnson maintained that the United States did not seek to impose its will, the President also committed the U.S. to defend "an independent South Vietnam," a commitment that violated the Geneva Agreement's stipulation that Vietnam was one nation.

Morgenthau also argued that U.S. military intervention is often counterproductive—leading to gains, not losses, by communism. Perhaps the most convincing single point he made was that the best way of containing Communist China would be by building a strong Vietnam in cooperation with the Soviet Union. With the hindsight possible today, his insight that communism is no monolithic system has an accuracy that one can only wish President Johnson and his circle of advisers had been able to appreciate.

Vo Nhan Tri presented an entirely different view (Document 47) of the American involvement in Vietnam. His thesis is that the United States was guided by the economic motive of capturing control of Vietnam's economy and resources. Published in 1972 in Hanoi, the article used documents from the United States, particularly from magazines like *Foreign Affairs* and statements from American corporate leaders, to make the case that American foreign investments and profits in Asia were even more important than they were in other parts of the world. He also analyzed American economic interests as based on exploiting the relatively low-paid labor market in Asia. Tri's perspective is obviously quite different from Johnson's or Morgenthau's.

The last three documents look back at the war. Document 48 is an excerpt from Richard Nixon's 1985 book, *No More Vietnams*. Nixon maintains that the United States was entirely in the right in prosecuting the war and even defends the domino theory. After our defeat in Vietnam, he claims that "the dominoes fell one by one: Laos, Cambodia, and Mozambique in 1975; Angola in 1976; Ethiopia in 1977; South Yemen in 1978; Nicaragua in 1979." With the end of the Cold War, this view has largely fallen by the historical wayside, but it reflects a sentiment that persists in one form or another.

Noam Chomsky, the renowned linguistics scholar and critic of American foreign policy, takes an entirely different point of view, one that claims the antiwar movement was moral and right. Chomsky believes that the same opinion makers who helped create the climate for intervention in Vietnam are today working to "obscure the fact that the U.S. did attack South Vietnam." In the aftermath of the war, Chomsky notes a hesitancy on the part of the American government to embark on massive military ventures abroad, a reluctance called the Vietnam Syndrome. With the quick victory over Iraq in 1991, however, the future of public constraints on American intervention abroad remains in doubt.

In the book's final document, Professor Ngo Vinh Long discusses the destruction of Vietnam, noting the starvation that existed in South Vietnam (historically a major exporter of rice) during the American involvement. Long's intimate knowledge of Vietnam (he was a map maker for the Diem government) allows him to make a convincing case that in 1954 support for the revolution led by Ho Chi Minh and the Vietminh existed "in almost every village and town in the whole country." Only American disregard for the desires of the people of Vietnam, he argues, made U.S. intervention necessary or possible.

45
A Pattern for Peace in Southeast Asia: the Johns Hopkins Speech

Lyndon B. Johnson

Source: Department of State Bulletin (April 26, 1965), pp. 606–10.

. . . Tonight Americans and Asians are dying for a world where each people may choose its own path to change.

This is the principle for which our ancestors fought in the valleys of Pennsylvania. It is the principle for which our sons fight in the jungles of Vietnam.

Vietnam is far from this quiet campus. We have no territory there, nor do we seek any. The war is dirty and brutal and difficult. And some 400 young men, born into an America bursting with opportunity and promise, have ended their lives on Vietnam's steaming soil.

Why must we take this painful road?

Why must this nation hazard its ease, its interest, and its power for the sake of a people so far away?

We fight because we must fight if we are to live in a world where every country can shape its own destiny. And only in such a world will our own freedom be finally secure.

This kind of a world will never be built by bombs or bullets. Yet the infirmities of man are such that force must often precede reason, and the waste of war, the works of peace.

We wish this were not so. But we must deal with the world as it is, if it is ever to be as we wish.

The world as it is in Asia is not a serene or peaceful place. The first reality is that North Vietnam has attacked the independent nation of South Vietnam. Its object is total conquest.

Of course, some of the people of South Vietnam are participating in this attack on their own government. But trained men and supplies, orders and arms, flow in a constant stream from North to South.

This support is the heartbeat of the war.

And it is a war of unparalleled brutality. Simple farmers are the targets of assassination and kidnapping. Women and children are strangled in the night because their men are loyal to their Government. Small and helpless villages are ravaged by sneak attacks. Large-scale raids are conducted on towns, and terror strikes in the heart of cities.

The confused nature of this conflict cannot mask the fact that it is the new face of an old enemy. It is an attack by one country upon another. And the object of that attack is a friend to which we are pledged.

Over this war, and all Asia, is another reality: the deepening shadow of Communist China. The rulers in Hanoi are urged on by Peking. This is a regime which has destroyed freedom in Tibet, attacked India, and been condemned by the United Nations for aggression in Korea. It is a nation which is helping the forces of violence in almost every continent. The contest in Vietnam is part of a wider pattern of aggressive purpose.

Why are these realities our concern? Why are we in South Vietnam? We are there because we have a promise to keep. Since 1954 every American President has offered support to the people of South Vietnam. We have helped to build, and we have helped to defend. Thus, over many years, we have made a national pledge to help South Vietnam defend its independence. And I intend to keep our promise.

To dishonor that pledge, to abandon this small and brave nation to its enemy, and to the terror that must follow, would be an unforgivable wrong.

We are also there to strengthen world order. Around the globe, from Berlin to Thailand, are people whose well-being rests, in part, on the belief that they can count on us if they are attacked. To leave Vietnam to its fate would shake the confidence of all these people in the value of American commitment, the value of America's word. The result would be increased unrest and instability, and even wider war.

We are also there because there are great stakes in the balance. Let no one think for a moment that retreat from Vietnam would bring an end to conflict. The battle would be renewed in one country and then another. The central lesson of our time is that the appetite of aggression is never satisfied. To withdraw from one battlefield means only to prepare for the next. We must say in Southeast Asia, as we did in Europe, in the words of the Bible: "Hitherto shalt thou come, but no further."

There are those who say that all our effort there will be futile, that China's power is such it is bound to dominate all Southeast Asia. But there is no end to that argument until all the nations of Asia are swallowed up.

There are those who wonder why we have a responsibility there. We have it for the same reason we have a responsibility for the defense of freedom in Europe. World War II was fought in both Europe and Asia, and when it ended we found ourselves with continued responsibility for the defense of freedom.

Our objective is the independence of South Vietnam, and its freedom from attack. We want nothing for ourselves, only that the people of South Vietnam be allowed to guide their own country in their own way.

We will do everything necessary to reach that objective. And we will do only what is absolutely necessary.

In recent months, attacks on South Vietnam were stepped up. Thus it became necessary to increase our response and to make attacks by air. This is not a change of purpose. It is a change in what we believe that purpose requires.

We do this in order to slow down aggression.

We do this to increase the confidence of the brave people of South Vietnam who have bravely borne this brutal battle for so many years and with so many casualties.

And we do this to convince the leaders of North Vietnam, and all who seek to share their conquest, of a very simple fact:

We will not be defeated.

We will not grow tired.

We will not withdraw, either openly or under the cloak of a meaningless agreement.

We know that air attacks alone will not accomplish all these purposes. But it is our best and prayerful judgment that they are a necessary part of the surest road to peace.

We hope that peace will come swiftly. But that is in the hands of others besides ourselves. And we must be prepared for a long, continued conflict. It will require patience as well as bravery, the will to endure as well as the will to resist.

I wish it were possible to convince others with words of what we now find it necessary to say with guns and planes: Armed hostility is futile. Our resources are equal to any challenge because we fight for values and we fight for principles, rather than territory or colonies. Our patience and determination are unending.

Once this is clear, then it should also be clear that the only path for reasonable men is the path of peaceful settlement.

Such peace demands an independent South Vietnam securely guaranteed and able to shape its own relationships to all others, free from outside interference, tied to no alliance, a military base for no other country.

These are the essentials of any final settlement.

We will never be second in the search for such a peaceful settlement in Vietnam.

There may be many ways to this kind of peace: in discussion or negotiation with the governments concerned; in large groups or in small ones; on the reaffirmation of old agreements or their strengthening with new ones.

We have stated this position over and over again fifty times and more, to friend and foe alike. And we remain ready with this purpose, for unconditional discussions.

And until that bright and necessary day of peace we will try to keep conflict from spreading. We have no desire to see thousands die in battle, Asians or Americans. We have no desire to devastate that which the people of North Vietnam have built with toil and sacrifice. We will use our power with restraint and with all the wisdom we can command. But we will use it.

This war, like most wars, is filled with terrible irony. For what do the people of North Vietnam want? They want what their neighbors also desire: food for their hunger, health for their bodies and a chance to learn, progress for their country, and an end to the bondage of material misery. And they would find all these things far more readily in peaceful association with others than in the endless course of battle.

These countries of Southeast Asia are homes for millions of impoverished people. Each day these people rise at dawn and struggle until the night to wrest existence from the soil. They are often wracked by disease, plagued by hunger, and death comes at the early age of 40.

Stability and peace do not come easily in such a land. Neither independence nor human dignity will ever be won by arms alone. It also requires the works of peace.

The American people have helped generously in times past in these works.

Now there must be a much more massive effort to improve the life of man in the conflict-torn corner of our world.

The first step is for the countries of Southeast Asia to associate themselves in a greatly expanded cooperative effort for development. We would hope that North Vietnam will take its place in the common effort just as soon as peaceful cooperation is possible.

The United Nations is already actively engaged in development in this area, and as far back as 1961 I conferred with our authorities in Vietnam in connection with their work there.

I would hope that the Secretary-General of the United Nations could use the prestige of his great office, and his deep knowledge of Asia, to initiate, as soon as possible, with the countries of the area, a plan for cooperation in increased development.

For our part I will ask the Congress to join in a billion-dollar American investment in this effort as soon as it is under way.

And I hope all other industrialized countries, including the Soviet Union, will join in this effort to replace despair with hope, and terror with progress.

The task is nothing less than to enrich the hopes and existence of more than a hundred million people. And there is much to be done.

The vast Mekong River can provide food and water and power on a scale to dwarf even our own TVA.

The wonders of modern medicine can be spread through villages where thousands die every year from lack of care. Schools can be established to train people in the skills that are needed to manage the process of development.

And these objectives, and more, are within the reach of a cooperative and determined effort.

I also intend to expand and speed up a program to make available our farm surplus to assist in feeding and clothing the needy in Asia. We should not allow people to go hungry and wear rags while our own warehouses overflow with an abundance of wheat and corn, rice and cotton.

I will very shortly name a special team of patriotic and distinguished Americans to inaugurate our participation in these programs. This team will be headed by Mr. Eugene Black, the very able former president of the World Bank.

In areas still ripped by conflict, of course, development will not be easy. Peace will be necessary for final success. But we cannot wait for peace to begin the job.

This will be a disorderly planet for a long time. In Asia, as elsewhere, the forces of the modern world are shaking old ways and uprooting ancient civilizations. There will be turbulence and struggle and even violence. Great social change, as we see in our own country, does not always come without conflict.

We must also expect that nations will on occasion be in dispute with us. It may be because we are rich, or powerful, or because we have made mistakes, or because they honestly fear our intentions. However, no nation need ever fear that we desire their land, or to impose our will, or to dictate their institutions.

But we will always oppose the effort of one nation to conquer another nation.

We will do this because our own security is at stake.

But there is more to it than that. For our generation has a dream. It is a very old dream. But we have the power and now we have the opportunity to make it come true.

For centuries, nations have struggled among each other. But we dream of a world where disputes are settled by law and reason. And we will try to make it so.

For most of history men have hated and killed one another in battle. But we dream of an end to war. And we will try to make it so.

For all existence most men have lived in poverty, threatened by hunger. But we dream of a world where all are fed and charged with hope. And we will help to make it so.

The ordinary men and women of North Vietnam and South Vietnam—of China and India—of Russia and America—are brave people. They are filled with the same proportions of hate and fear, of love and hope. Most of them want the same things for themselves and their families. Most of them do not want their sons ever to die in battle, or see the homes of others destroyed. . . .

Every night before I turn out the lights to sleep, I ask myself this question:

Have I done everything that I can do to unite this country? Have I done everything I can to help unite the world, to try to bring peace and hope to all the peoples of the world? Have I done enough?

Ask yourselves that question in your homes and in this hall tonight. Have we done all we could? Have we done enough?

We may well be living in the time foretold many years ago when it was said: "I call heaven and earth to record this day against you, that I have set before you life and death, blessing and cursing: therefore choose life, that both thou and thy seed may live."

This generation of the world must choose: destroy or build, kill or aid, hate or understand.

We can do all these things on a scale never dreamed of before.

We will choose life. And so doing we will prevail over the enemies within man, and over the natural enemies of all mankind.

46
Vietnam and the National Interest

Hans J. Morgenthau

Source: "We Are Deluding Ourselves in Vietnam," *New York Times Magazine* (April 18, 1965).

The address which President Johnson delivered on April 7 at Johns Hopkins University is important for two reasons. On the one hand, the President has shown for the first time a way out of the impasse in which we find ourselves in Vietnam. By agreeing to negotiations without preconditions he has opened the door to negotiations which those preconditions had made impossible from the outset.

By proposing a project for the economic development of Southeast Asia—with North Vietnam a beneficiary and the Soviet Union a supporter—he has implicitly recognized the variety of national interests in the Communist world and the need for varied American responses tailored to those interests. By asking "that the people of South Vietnam be allowed to guide their own country in their own way," he has left all possibilities open for the future evolution of relations between North and South Vietnam.

On the other hand, the President reiterated the intellectual assumptions and policy proposals which brought us to an impasse and which make it impossible to extricate ourselves. The President has linked our involvement in Vietnam with our war of independence and has proclaimed the freedom of all nations as the goal of our foreign policy. He has started from the assumption that there are two Vietnamese nations, one of which has attacked the other, and he sees that attack as an integral part of unlimited Chinese aggression. Consistent with this assumption, the President is willing to negotiate with China and North Vietnam but not with the Vietcong.

Yet we cannot have it both ways. We cannot at the same time embrace these false assumptions and pursue new sound policies. Thus we are faced with a real dilemma. This dilemma is by no means of the President's making.

We are militarily engaged in Vietnam by virtue of a basic principle of our foreign policy that was implicit in the Truman Doctrine of 1947 and was put into practice by John Foster Dulles from 1954 onward. This principle is the military containment of Communism. Containment had its origins in Europe; Dulles applied it to the Middle East and Asia through a series of bilateral and multilateral alliances. Yet what was an outstanding success in Europe turned out to be a dismal failure elsewhere. The reasons for that failure are twofold.

First, the threat that faced the nations of Western Europe in the aftermath of the Second World War was primarily military. It was the threat of the Red Army marching westward. Behind the line of military demarcation of 1945 which the policy of containment declared to be the western-most limit of the Soviet empire, there was an ancient civilization, only temporarily weak, and able to maintain itself against the threat of Communist subversion.

The situation is different in the Middle East and Asia. The threat there is not primarily military but political in nature. Weak governments and societies provide opportunities for Communist subversion. Military containment is irrelevant to that threat and may even be counter-productive. Thus the Baghdad Pact did not protect Egypt from Soviet influence and SEATO has had no bearing on Chinese influence in Indonesia and Pakistan.

Second, and more important, even if China were threatening her neighbors primarily by military means, it would be impossible to contain her by erecting a military wall at the periphery of her empire. For China is, even in her present underdeveloped state, the dominant power in Asia. She is this by virtue of the quality and quantity of her population, her geographic position, her civilization, her past power remembered, and her future power anticipated. Anybody who has traveled in Asia with his eyes and ears open must have been impressed by the enormous impact which the resurgence of China has made upon all manner of men, regardless of class and political conviction, from Japan to Pakistan.

The issue China poses is political and cultural predominance. The United States can no more contain Chinese influence in Asia by arming South Vietnam and Thailand than China could contain American influence in the Western

Hemisphere by arming, say, Nicaragua and Costa Rica.

If we are convinced that we cannot live with a China predominant on the mainland of Asia, then we must strike at the heart of Chinese power—that is, rather than try to contain the power of China, we must try to destroy that power itself. Thus there is logic on the side of that small group of Americans who are convinced that war between the United States and China is inevitable and that the earlier that war comes, the better will be the chances for the United States to win it.

Yet, while logic is on their side, practical judgment is against them. For while China is obviously no match for the United States in overall power, China is largely immune to the specific types of power in which the superiority of the United States consists—that is, nuclear, air, and naval power. Certainly, the United States has the power to destroy the nuclear installations and the major industrial and population centers of China, but this destruction would not defeat China; it would only set her development back. To be defeated, China has to be conquered.

Physical conquest would require the deployment of millions of American soldiers on the mainland of Asia. No American military leader has ever advocated a course of action so fraught with incalculable risks, so uncertain of outcome, requiring sacrifices so out of proportion to the interests at stake and the benefits to be expected. President Eisenhower declared on Feb. 10, 1954, that he "could conceive of no greater tragedy than for the United States to become involved in an all-out war in Indochina." General MacArthur, in the Congressional hearings concerning his dismissal and in personal conversation with President Kennedy, emphatically warned against sending American foot soldiers to the Asian mainland to fight China.

If we do not want to set ourselves goals which cannot be attained with the means we are willing to employ, we must learn to accommodate ourselves to the predominance of China on the Asian mainland. It is instructive to note that those Asian nations which have done so—such as Burma and Cambodia—live peacefully in the shadow of the Chinese giant.

This *modus vivendi,* composed of legal independence and various degrees of actual dependence, has indeed been for more than a millennium the persistent pattern of Chinese predominance on the mainland of Asia. The military conquest of Tibet is the sole exception to that pattern. The military operations at the Indian border do not diverge from it, since their purpose was the establishment of a frontier disputed by both sides.

On the other hand, those Asian nations which have allowed themselves to be transformed into outposts of American military power—such as Laos a few years ago, South Vietnam, and Thailand—have become the actual or prospective victims of Communist aggression and subversion. Thus it appears that peripheral military containment is counterproductive. Challenged at its periphery by

American military power at its weakest—that is, by the proxy of client-states—China or its proxies respond with locally superior military and political power.

In specific terms, accommodation means four things: (1) recognition of the political and cultural predominance of China on the mainland of Asia as a fact of life; (2) liquidation of the peripheral military containment of China; (3) strengthening of the uncommitted nations of Asia by nonmilitary means; (4) assessment of Communist governments in Asia in terms not of Communist doctrine but of their relation to the interests and power of the United States.

In light of these principles, the alternative to our present policies in Vietnam would be this: a face-saving agreement which would allow us to disengage ourselves militarily in stages spaced in time; restoration of the status quo of the Geneva Agreements of 1954, with special emphasis upon all-Vietnamese elections; cooperation with the Soviet Union in support of a Titoist all-Vietnamese Government, which would be likely to emerge from such elections.

This last point is crucial, for our present policies not only drive Hanoi into the waiting arms of Peking, but also make it very difficult for Moscow to pursue an independent policy. Our interests in Southeast Asia are identical with those of the Soviet Union: to prevent the expansion of the *military* power of China. But while our present policies invite that expansion, so do they make it impossible for the Soviet Union to join us in preventing it. If we were to reconcile ourselves to the establishment of a Titoist government in all of Vietnam, the Soviet Union could successfully compete with China in claiming credit for it and surreptitiously cooperate with us in maintaining it.

Testing the President's proposals by these standards, one realizes how far they go in meeting them. These proposals do not preclude a return to the Geneva Agreements and even assume the existence of a Titoist government in North Vietnam. Nor do they preclude the establishment of a Titoist government for all of Vietnam, provided the people of South Vietnam have freely agreed to it. They also envision the active participation of the Soviet Union in establishing and maintaining a new balance of power in Southeast Asia. On the other hand, the President has flatly rejected a withdrawal "under the cloak of a meaningless agreement." The controlling word is obviously "meaningless," and only the future can tell whether we shall consider any face-saving agreement as "meaningless" regardless of its political context.

However, we are under a psychological compulsion to continue our military presence in South Vietnam as part of the peripheral military containment of China. We have been emboldened in this course of action by the identification of the enemy as "Communist," seeing in every Communist party and regime an extension of hostile Russian or Chinese power. This identification was justified 20 or 15 years ago when Communism still had a monolithic character. Here, as elsewhere, our modes of thought and action have been rendered obsolete by new developments.

It is ironic that this simple juxtaposition of "Communism" and "free world" was erected by John Foster Dulles's crusading moralism into the guiding principle of American foreign policy at a time when the national Communism of Yugoslavia, the neutralism of the third world, and the incipient split between the Soviet Union and China were rendering that juxtaposition invalid.

Today, it is belaboring the obvious to say that we are faced not with one monolithic Communism whose uniform hostility must be countered with equally uniform hostility, but with a number of different Communisms whose hostilities, determined by different national interests, vary. In fact, the United States encounters today less hostility from Tito, who is a Communist, than from de Gaulle, who is not.

We can today distinguish four different types of Communism in view of the kind and degree of hostility to the United States they represent: a Communism identified with the Soviet Union—e.g., Poland; a Communism identified with China—e.g. Albania; a Communism that straddles the fence between the Soviet Union and China—e.g., Rumania; and independent Communism—e.g., Yugoslavia. Each of these Communisms must be dealt with in terms of the bearing its foreign policy has upon the interests of the United States in a concrete instance.

It would, of course, be absurd to suggest that the officials responsible for the conduct of American foreign policy are unaware of these distinctions and of the demands they make for discriminating subtlety. Yet it is an obvious fact of experience that these officials are incapable of living up to these demands when they deal with Vietnam.

Thus they maneuver themselves into a position which is antirevolutionary per se and which requires military opposition to revolution wherever it is found in Asia, regardless of how it affects the interests—and how susceptible it is to the power—of the United States. There is a historic precedent for this kind of policy: Metternich's military opposition to liberalism after the Napoleonic Wars, which collapsed in 1848. For better or for worse, we live again in an age of revolution. It is the task of statesmanship not to oppose what cannot be opposed with a chance of success, but to bend it to one's own interests. This is what the President is trying to do with his proposal for the economic development of Southeast Asia.

Why do we support the Saigon Government in the civil war against the Vietcong? Because the Saigon Government is "free" and the Vietcong are "Communist." By containing Vietnamese Communism, we assume that we are really containing the Communism of China.

Yet this assumption is at odds with the historic experience of a millennium and is unsupported by contemporary evidence. China is the hereditary enemy of Vietnam, and Ho Chi Minh will become the leader of a Chinese satellite only if the United States forces him to become one.

Furthermore, Ho Chi Minh, like Tito and unlike the Communist governments of the other states of Eastern Europe, came to power not by courtesy of another Communist nation's victorious army but at the head of a victorious army of his own. He is, then, a natural candidate to become an Asian Tito, and the question we must answer is: How adversely would a Titoist Ho Chi Minh, governing all of Vietnam, affect the interests of the United States? The answer can only be: not at all. One can even maintain the proposition that, far from affecting adversely the interests of the United States, it would be in the interest of the United States if the western periphery of China were ringed by a chain of independent states, though they would, of course, in their policies take due account of the predominance of their powerful neighbor.

The roots of the Vietnamese civil war go back to the very beginning of South Vietnam as an independent state. When President Ngo Dinh Diem took office in 1954, he presided not over a state but over one-half of a country arbitrarily and, in the intentions of all concerned, temporarily severed from the other half. He was generally regarded as a care-taker who would establish the rudiments of an administration until the country was united by nationwide elections to be held in 1956 in accordance with the Geneva accords.

Diem was confronted at home with a number of private armies which were politically, religiously, or criminally oriented. To the general surprise, he subdued one after another and created what looked like a viable government. Yet in the process of creating it, he also laid the foundations for the present civil war. He ruthlessly suppressed all opposition, established concentration camps, organized a brutal secret police, closed newspapers, and rigged elections. These policies inevitably led to a polarization of the politics of South Vietnam—on one side, Diem's family, surrounded by a Praetorian guard; on the other, the Vietnamese people, backed by the Communists, declaring themselves liberators from foreign domination and internal oppression.

Thus, the possibility of civil war was inherent in the very nature of the Diem regime. It became inevitable after Diem refused to agree to all-Vietnamese elections and, in the face of mounting popular alienation, accentuated the tyrannical aspects of his regime. The South Vietnamese who cherished freedom could not help but oppose him. Threatened by the secret police, they went either abroad or underground where the Communists were waiting for them.

Until the end of last February, the Government of the United States started from the assumption that the war in South Vietnam was a civil war, aided and abetted—but not created—from abroad, and spokesmen for the Government have made time and again the point that the key to winning the war was political and not military and was to be found in South Vietnam itself. It was supposed to lie in transforming the indifference or hostility of the great mass of the South Vietnamese people into positive loyalty to the Government.

To that end, a new theory of warfare called "counter-insurgency" was put into practice. Strategic hamlets were established, massive propaganda campaigns were embarked upon, social and economic measures were at least sporadically taken. But all was to no avail. The mass of the population remained indifferent, if not hostile, and large units of the army ran away or went over to the enemy.

The reasons for this failure are of general significance, for they stem from a deeply ingrained habit of the American mind. We like to think of social problems as technically self-sufficient and susceptible of simple, clear-cut solutions. We tend to think of foreign aid as a kind of self-sufficient, technical, economic enterprise subject to the laws of economics and divorced from politics, and of war as a similarly self-sufficient, technical enterprise, to be won as quickly, as cheaply, as thoroughly as possible and divorced from the foreign policy that preceded and is to follow it. Thus our military theoreticians and practitioners conceive of counter-insurgency as though it were just another branch of warfare like artillery or chemical warfare, to be taught in special schools and applied with technical proficiency wherever the occasion arises.

This view derives of course from a complete misconception of the nature of civil war. People fight and die in civil wars because they have a faith which appears to them worth fighting and dying for, and they can be opposed with a chance of success only by people who have at least as strong a faith.

Magsaysay could subdue the Huk rebellion in the Philippines because his charisma, proven in action, aroused a faith superior to that of his opponents. In South Vietnam there is nothing to oppose the faith of the Vietcong and, in consequence, the Saigon Government and we are losing the civil war.

A guerrilla war cannot be won without the active support of the indigenous population, short of the physical extermination of that population. Germany was at least consistent when, during the Second World War, faced with unmanageable guerrilla warfare throughout occupied Europe, she tried to master the situation through a deliberate policy of extermination. The French tried "counter-insurgency" in Algeria and failed; 400,000 French troops fought the guerrillas in Indochina for nine years and failed.

The United States has recognized that it is failing in South Vietnam. But it has drawn from this recognition of failure a most astounding conclusion.

The United States has decided to change the character of the war by unilateral declaration from a South Vietnamese civil war to a war of "foreign aggression." "Aggression from the North: The Record of North Vietnam's Campaign to Conquer South Vietnam" is the title of a White Paper published by the Department of State on the last day of February, 1965. While normally foreign and military policy is based upon intelligence—that is, the objective assessment of facts—the process is here reversed: a new policy has been decided upon, and intelligence must provide the facts to justify it.

The United States, stymied in South Vietnam and on the verge of defeat, decided to carry the war to North Vietnam not so much in order to retrieve the fortunes of war as to lay the groundwork for "negotiations from strength." In order to justify that new policy, it was necessary to prove that North Vietnam is the real enemy. It is the White Paper's purpose to present that proof.

Let it be said right away that the White Paper is a dismal failure. The discrepancy between its assertions and the factual evidence adduced to support them borders on the grotesque. It does nothing to disprove, and tends even to confirm, what until the end of February had been official American doctrine: that the main body of the Vietcong is composed of South Vietnamese and that 80 to 90 percent of their weapons are of American origin.

This document is most disturbing in that it provides a particularly glaring instance of the tendency to conduct foreign and military policy not on their own merits, but as exercises in public relations. The Government fashions an imaginary world that pleases it, and then comes to believe in the reality of that world and acts as though it were real.

It is for this reason that public officials are so resentful of the reporters assigned to Vietnam and have tried to shut them off from the sources of news and even to silence them. They resent the confrontation of their policies with the facts. Yet the facts are what they are, and they take terrible vengeance on those who disregard them.

However, the White Paper is but the latest instance of a delusionary tendency which has led American policy in Vietnam astray in other respects. We call the American troops in Vietnam "advisers" and have assigned them by and large to advisory functions, and we have limited the activities of the Marines who have now landed in Vietnam to guarding American installations. We have done this for reasons of public relations, in order to spare ourselves the odium of open belligerency.

There is an ominous similarity between this technique and that applied to the expedition in the Bay of Pigs. We wanted to overthrow Castro, but for reasons of public relations we did not want to do it ourselves. So it was not done at all, and our prestige was damaged far beyond what it would have suffered had we worked openly and single-mindedly for the goal we had set ourselves.

Our very presence in Vietnam is in a sense dictated by considerations of public relations; we are afraid lest our prestige would suffer were we to retreat from an untenable position.

One may ask whether we have gained prestige by being involved in a civil war on the mainland of Asia and by being unable to win it. Would we gain more by being unable to extricate ourselves from it, and by expanding it unilaterally into an international war? Is French prestige lower today than it was 11 years ago when France was fighting in Indochina, or five years ago when she was fighting in Algeria? Does not a great power gain prestige by mustering the wisdom and courage necessary to liquidate a losing enterprise? In other words, is it not the mark of greatness, in circumstances such as these, to be able to afford to be indifferent to one's prestige?

The peripheral military containment of China, the indiscriminate crusade against Communism, counter-insurgency as a technically self-sufficient new branch of warfare, the conception of foreign and military policy as a branch of public relations—they are all misconceptions that conjure up terrible dangers for those who base their policies on them.

One can only hope and pray that the vaunted pragmatism and common sense of the American mind—of which the President's new proposals may well be a manifestation—will act as a corrective upon those misconceptions before they lead us from the blind alley in which we find ourselves today to the rim of the abyss. Beyond the present crisis, however, one must hope that the confrontation between these misconceptions and reality will teach us a long overdue lesson—to rid ourselves of these misconceptions altogether.

47
The Economic Aims of U.S. Neo-Colonialism in Asia

Vo Nhan Tri

Source: Vietnamese Studies (Hanoi, 1977), pp. 147–216 (excerpts).

> *"There are two ways of conquering a foreign nation. One is to gain control of its people by force of arms; the other is to gain control of its economy by financial means."*
>
> —John Foster Dulles

"If the Atlantic Ocean keeps its privileged position in Western affection, the Pacific Ocean is the ultimate word of the march to the West. . . . In the prolongation of the Oregon trail, the Pacific and Far Eastern countries have always, through history, been destined to draw close to the United States." This was unequivocally written early this year in a review published by the US official services in France ("Information and Documents") which was devoted to the special theme "Opening on the Pacific."

This "justification" is proving to be all the more useful as Asia has been exercising an ever greater magnetic attraction over Yankee imperialism, especially since the end of World War Two.

This attraction is explained, among other things, by economic factors.

Remember in this respect that as early as the beginning of 1952, a statement made by the National Security Council on US policy in South-East Asia said that this region, above all Malaysia and Indonesia, "is the main source of natural rubber and tin in the world, and producer of oil and other important strategic products. The exports of rice by Burma and Thailand are of utmost importance for Malaysia, Ceylon and Hongkong and are of considerable importance for Japan and India, all these countries being key areas of free Asia."

In its October 1967 issue, *Foreign Affairs* quoted Richard Nixon, then candidate for the US presidency, as saying: "The US is a Pacific power . . . Both our interests and our ideals propel us westward across the Pacific . . . "

In fact, since 1967, the American firms most interested in US economic expansion to the Pacific—such as Kaiser, Union Oil, Bechtel, Bank of America, Castle and Cook, Utah Construction and Mining, Tenneco, etc.—have given a definite substance through the agency of the *Stanford Research Institute,* to the so-called "Pacific Rim Strategy." This strategy, conceived as an extension of their activities in that region of the world, is essentially aimed at maintaining South-East Asia and Japan in the capitalist orbit and integrating them in the "market economy" placed under the hegemony of the US. The core of that strategy is formed by the industrially-advanced countries, the US and Japan, and to a lesser extent Australia, Canada and New Zealand. These countries consider it essential for the future development of a new international division of labour to integrate the so-called under-developed countries lying on the fringes of the Pacific Ocean into the framework of their triangular or quadrilateral economic relations. In this perspective, the "under-developed" countries are, for the industrially-advanced nations, vast outlets and sources of raw materials whose importance is constantly growing. Confirming that strategy, Rudolph A. Peterson, Chairman of the *Bank of America* and Nixon's special adviser in international economic affairs, stressed that "there is no vaster or richer area for resource development or trade growth in the world today than this immense region and it is virtually our own front yard. Were we Californian businessmen to play a more dynamic role in helping trade development in the Pacific Rim, we would have huge new markets for our products and vast new potentials of profit for our firms."

In his message to the US Congress on February 9, 1972, on *"American Foreign Policy in the Seventies,"* Nixon said that "Our substantial interests in Asia assure that the US will continue to be a Pacific Power."—"By our actions as well as our words, we have demonstrated that America remains committed in Asia and determined to take part in the building of its future." (Read: to interfere in the domestic affairs of the Asian peoples—VNT). This theme also recurs in the US foreign policy report presented to Congress on March 7, 1972, by Secretary of State W. Rogers, in which he reaffirmed that the US is continuing to play the role of a Pacific power and to intervene in that region which, in his opinion, is of "vital importance" for the US.

The "substantial interests" referred to by Nixon become quite clear when one knows that by the beginning of the sixties at the latest, the American magnates were aware of the certain existence of huge oil reserves in South-East Asia. According to the *Wall Street Journal* (Sept. 22, 1970), "the potential here is as large if not larger than in the Middle East." And according to M. L. Laurence, director of the American firm Avery Laurence, South-East Asia could well become one of the five main oil-producing areas in the world in the seventies.

However, it is worth noticing that oil exists not only in the western part of the vast continental shelf, running from the Burmese coasts to the northern territorial waters of Australia, passing through Thailand, Cambodia, Malaya, South Viet Nam and Indonesia, but also in its eastern part, reaching up as far as South Korea, and passing by the Philippines and Taiwan. According to an ECAFE report, "the shallow sea-bed between Japan and Taiwan might contain one of the most prolific oil and gas reservoirs in the world, possibly comparing favorably with the Persian Gulf area." The oil in that region attracts the US (and Japan) all the more as it has a very low percentage of sulphur. The good quality of Pacific oil assumes growing importance since January 1971, when the US Treasury Department and the Council for the Quality of the Environment worked out a tax in order to discourage the discharge of sulphur into the atmosphere as a result of the burning of petroleum products. If we have laid so much emphasis on oil, it is because, as the *Boston Globe* affirmed on February 15, 1971, it "has transformed the area into a massive raw material and energy supplier for the capitalist industrialized world in a way that rubber and tin never did."

US Direct Investments in Asia

US long-term private investments—in Asia as in any other part of the world—can be considered under two main aspects: portfolio investments on the one hand, and on the other direct investments, which may be made either through the foundation of new companies or through partial (25%) or wholesale acquisition of foreign companies' shares. This latter method, which implies an "intention of control (of the foreign investor—VNT) over management" and gives higher interest rates, makes up the overwhelming majority of US long-term private investments abroad. What follows is therefore limited to examining their evolution.

During the post-war period, US direct investments recorded a tremendous leap forward: from 7.2 billion dollars in 1946 to 78.09 billion in 1970 (preliminary figures), or a more than tenfold increase.

In Asia alone (not including Japan and the Middle East) they rose from 200 million dollars in 1946 to 2,477 million in 1970, thus increasing by twelve and a half times.

We should add that these are simply the official figures which represent the *value in the books* of the direct investments. To assess their real value, i.e., the *value obtained through capitalization of incomes from these investments,* those figures should be doubled.

A close survey of the evolution of US direct Asian investments in the '60s shows that the latter's growth rate (exclusive of Japan and the Middle East) increased most rapidly during the latter half of the '60s, while in Europe we find the opposite situation. In fact from 1964 to 1969, US direct investments in Asia (exclusive of the Middle East and Japan) rose by 81.5%, against only 31.6% for the 1960–1964 period, while the respective growth rates for Europe are 77.7% and 81.3%.

This increase in US direct Asian investments will undoubtedly continue in the '70s.

The number of US companies having subsidiaries in Asia and Africa (excluding South Africa) rose from 83 in 1957 to 158 in 1967, or an increase of 90.36%. (We have unfortunately no figures concerning Asia alone in this respect.)

Among these companies, the foremost certainly are the oil companies, such as Standard Oil of New Jersey, Caltex, Gulf Oil, the big rubber companies such as Firestone, Goodrich, US Rubber, and Goodyear, and mining companies, etc.

In the structure of direct investments, US banks such as the Bank of America, Chase Manhattan Bank, and First National City Bank, play a vital role.

The overwhelming majority of US direct investments in developing Asian countries (excluding the Middle East and Japan) are usually directed toward the extractive industries, in the first place petroleum (1,066 million dollars) and mining (91 million dollars) in total 1,157 million dollars—and secondly toward the processing industries—only 692 million dollars—the remainder going to other industries and services.

The important petroleum and natural gas reserves in the immense crescent extending from South Korea through Indonesia to the Gulf of Siam have naturally drawn enormous US direct investments in this part of the world (1,066 million dollars out of the total of 2,477 million).

The continuously increasing energy needs of the United States make it all the more interested in the exploitation of the Far Eastern and South East Asian continental shelf—a fact which has a great influence on US strategy in the Pacific.

The *Oil and Gas Journal* (25–1–71) estimates that towards 1975, the USA will have to import some 450,000 barrels of petroleum from Asia per day.

Confronted with increasing pressure from Middle Eastern and North African petroleum exporting countries (members of OPEC) which have succeeded in wringing certain concessions from the International Petroleum Cartel (see the February 1971 Teheran agreement, and the Tripoli agreement in April of the same year), US petroleum companies now contemplate intensifying petroleum prospecting and exploitation at more advantageous terms in other regions of the world.

For both these reasons (rapid increase in US need for petroleum, concessions wrung from petroleum companies by Middle Eastern countries), South-East Asian and Far Eastern petroleum becomes more and more attractive for US companies, especially as its sulphur rate is known to be low, and its deposits are closer to the USA than those of the Middle East. Not only Washington, but also Tokyo, remarked a French journalist, "will increasingly need the crude oil which could be supplied in considerable quantities and at very interesting prices from South East Asia and the Far East."

US interest in petroleum in this part of the world was further confirmed by David Rockefeller, Chairman of the Chase Manhattan Bank, who declared in May 1970 that US petroleum companies were expected to invest 35 billion dollars over the next 12 years in Asia and the Western Pacific area, especially in South East Asia. This prompted the following remark by the journal *Petroleum Engineer:* "The Asian Pacific area seems to be the one where the next international boom will take place."

We should note that by 1970, the whole area of South East Asia with the exception of South Viet Nam, had already been divided among several international petroleum companies (most of them US) which were feverishly engaged in prospecting (see map) [not reproduced here—ed]. On this map—where only off-shore concessions are marked—the vast oil fields granted to US petroleum companies off the coasts of Thailand and Malaya, along the Indonesian archipelago and north of Borneo, can be clearly seen.

Concerning Indonesia the *Survey of Current Business* (10–1971) informs us that US "investments in the Far East also showed substantial gains (in 1970) mainly because of the development of new off-shore fields in Indonesia." It should be added that in 1970, the USA remained the only petroleum producer in Indonesia. It "assists" Indonesian national enterprises in all spheres, while dominating them in the field of production, since out of the 45 million tons extracted from Indonesian subsoil in the same year, five million only were extracted by Indonesian (Pertamina and Lemigas) and 40 million by the USA (Stanvac and Caltex).

Since 1970, US companies have extended their tentacles farther north, in the direction of South Viet Nam, which had its territorial waters divided into 18 blocks and promulgated Law 011–70 on petroleum prospecting and exploitation (December 1970) which granted much more favourable financial conditions to the US petroleum companies (with the country getting 35% and the company 65%) as compared with OPEC countries (where the revenues would be split 45/55).

By virtue of this law, each concession may cover an area of 20,000 square kilometres and each company may be granted as many as 5 prospecting perimeters. Companies are given guarantees that their property and rights will not be nationalized and that they will be allowed to refine the petroleum extracted. Income tax reductions on revenues are provided for and no tax is levied on exports. Moreover, profits may be freely repatriated.

US companies' interest in this is understandable the more so because, to quote an American oil geologist in Singapore, "South Viet Nam's potential production is larger than that of Indonesia and possibly comparable with leading producing areas in the Middle East."

US News and World Report (17–5–71) even remarks that "the current level of warfare is not expected to hamper off-shore exploration . . . Saigon's Navy backed up by American ships, is rated adequate to protect off-shore rigs from enemy harassment."

One of the reasons which prompted the USA to overthrow Sihanouk in Cambodia in March 1970 had its roots in petroleum. After that coup d'état, the Thailand–Cambodia–South Viet Nam petroleum axis came into being with a view to coordinating the distribution of off-shore concessions to US companies.

Recently, it is also reported that US companies have found petroleum deposits off the Tenasserim sea coast in Martaban Gulf, Burma.

In addition to such off-shore concessions, we should also consider the on-shore concessions. According to the *Petroleum Engineer* (November 1970), a big concession was granted to the US Gulf Oil Company around Bangkok. Now, *AFP* reports that under the Lower Menam's alluvial plain in the middle of which lies Bangkok, as well as in the Mekong delta, petroleum deposits may have been discovered, which first estimates put on the same rank as those of the Near East.

Gulf Oil has also signed a contract with the Lon Nol regime concerning on-shore petroleum exploitation through the whole of Cambodia.

Finally, therefore, when considering the question of petroleum we should bear in mind that the quadrilateral formed by Thailand, Malaya, Indonesia and the Philippines in South East Asia constitutes a vast petroleum-producing area, both *off-shore* and *on-shore,* larger than any other oil area in the world. And if the important petroleum deposits lying between Japan, Taiwan and South Korea are taken into account, it is not hard to foresee for the '70s a great boom of US direct investments in this domain in Asia.

Besides petroleum, US direct investors are also eager to plunder mining resources (tin, copper, zinc, nickel, bauxite, sulphur, etc.) in the area.

Another sector attractive to US direct investments is the processing industry in which they hold an appreciable share (692 million dollars out of the 2,477 million total of US investments in 1970).

However, it must be pointed out that the Philippines and India alone received a very substantial proportion of US direct investments in this sector (respectively 267 and 157 million dollars), an amount which is relatively comparable to that of advanced capitalist countries: the remaining Far Eastern countries (excluding Japan) are given only a relatively meagre proportion, the situation remaining nearly the same as before the Second World War.

The question we should now ask is: Why are US monopolies taking part in setting up in Asian and Latin American countries processing industries (metallurgy, electronic materials, chemicals, motorcars, chemical fertilizers, household utensils and precision instruments, food and light industry)?

US monopolies are the first to shift the production of electronic equipment to countries where labour is cheaper such as Hong Kong, Taiwan, South Korea. For instance, the US firm Scientific Corporation sends to Seoul all the parts for the assembly of integrated circuits which are then taken back to the USA for the production of I.B.M. machines.

It is known for instance that about one-third of the T.V. sets and 70% of the radio sets sold in the USA during the third quarter of 1969 are manufactured abroad, mostly in Japan, Taiwan, Hongkong, South Korea and Mexico.

The US automobile industry has followed the example of the electronics industry. It is known to have parts manufactured and assembly plants built in a number of Asian countries.

The tropical fruit and vegetables processing industry is also undergoing a great expansion. On account of its great demand on labour, US monopolies are intent on setting up more and more canning plants in developing countries. Thus, in the Philippines, there are US pineapple canning firms whose products are then sold on the US market.

The existence in Asian (and Latin American) countries of favourable climatic conditions for fruit and vegetable growing, low wages and a well-organized welling system (wide distribution network, established trade-marks, publicity) ensures fabulous profits to US monopolies.

By the end of 1970 several big US industrial corporations, using AID as their intermediary, expressed to the Indian government their desire to participate in creating a "free trade zone" in India, where joint enterprises would be set up specializing in the manufacture of articles for export to the USA and elsewhere.

Thus by setting up industrial enterprises turning out certain categories of equipment and parts in developing countries the US monopolies apparently meet those countries' desire to industrialize and to diversify their economy. In appearance the creation of such enterprises does in fact help to raise somewhat the level of employment, increase the export of finished products, improve the general indices of industrial development and contribute, though in a rather limited way, to fill up the gap of technical and economic backwardness. But the US monopolies are also making profits for themselves in the process. In face of ever fiercer competition on the world market, they can find new outlets in the developing countries, and avail themselves of local natural resources and, above all, cheap labour to cut down production costs. The US monopolies are eager to use their experience in intensifying labour and keeping down wages, and their knowledge of the natural resources to profit from favourable conditions for production existing in some developing countries.

In Latin American and Asian countries they usually set up those industries which require a large labour force. This policy of the US monopolies stands at the basis of the new international division of labour between two groups of countries in the world capitalist system: industrially-advanced and developing countries. This new division of labour, which is in fact a neo-colonialist division of labour, implies that industrial production with a large demand for manpower of a rudimentary technical level should be reserved for developing countries, and industrially advanced countries should specialize in industries requiring huge capital and sophisticated technology.

Such a division of labour certainly contributes to raising labour productivity, increasing output and *per capita* income in the world capitalist system as a whole. But there is no doubt that it keeps the developing countries in the background of technological and scientific progress. Within the framework of this division of labour they find themselves in a position of *inequality with and dependence on* US monopolies, and this position is very difficult to struggle against. The state of dependence is determined not only by orders from US firms or by the fact that it is these firms which supply the raw materials and semi-finished products or by the crazes of US fashion, but also by the very technology of production, which is entirely concentrated in the hands of the US monopolies. And it would be enough for these companies to cut off, for one reason or another, a single thread in the spindle of production, for an enterprise to be paralyzed.

Thus, the technological and economic links on which this specialization of industrial production is based are more solid than anything resulting from a mere exchange of goods, without considering the extra-economic restrictions. It is extremely difficult to break them by purely political action. This "new international division of labour," while it suits the US monopolies' taste, proves to be a new form of dependence from which the developing countries find it even more difficult to liberate themselves than from the old classical colonial rule.

* * *

Besides establishing their control over raw materials in Asian countries, US direct investments are also aimed at intensively exploiting local manpower through a combination of US modern techniques and low wages paid to Asian workers.

According to *Business Week* (7–5–1966) US corporations are flocking to Taiwan and especially to South Korea, because wages in Taiwan are only one-fourth those in Japan, and in South Korea, only one-eighth those in Japan; and according to the President of Mitsubishi Motor, wages in Japan are only one-fourth those in the USA, notwithstanding the Japanese workers' skill and obviously high technological qualifications.

Recently, an advertisement in the *New York Times* (18–4–1971) says that in South Korea there is "abundant cheap labour at costs half those in Hongkong and less than one-third those in Japan," and that "Government arbitration will prevent strikes and unreasonable union demands" in industries where foreign capital is invested.

"A young girl working on a transistor assembly line in Pusan (in South Korea) for example," says the *Business Week* already cited "gets about 35 cents a day." That is 3.5 cent an hour or one-fiftieth of the wages for similar work in the USA.

Anyhow, this young girl is still relatively better "favoured" than the Indonesian worker in Djakarta, who, working on a assembly line in a US electronic factory, is paid according to *Indonesia Today,* only 10 cents a day.

Dealing with the same subject, a booklet published by the United Electrical Workers reports that there is in South Korea, "a Motorola plant with production costs one-tenth those of a similar plant in Arizona with a labour force that works 6 days a week, 10 or 11 hours a day, for 11 to 17 cents an hour." (1971 minimum wages in the USA is 1.65 dollars an hour).

The above examples illustrate this phenomenon of over-exploitation of the local labour force which constitutes one of the purposes of US direct investment in Asia. Another aim is to secure or extend markets abroad, and this is particularly striking in these days of "multinational companies." A recent ECAFE report points out that "the application of the oligopoly theory to the behaviour of multinational companies has revealed a picture of international investments (mostly US—VNT) being made to gain, enlarge or defend positions in markets with attractive growth potentials, almost in disregard of short-term profit expectation."

Thanks to their direct investments, powerful US corporations can thus afford to enter into competition with rival companies of other imperialist countries and to exercise a more or less substantial control of markets till now hardly accessible.

US direct investments in processing industries in Asian countries are especially aimed at enlarging markets. If many assembly plants are set up by US monopolies in some Asian countries, it is merely because they are substitutes for exports hampered by the meager import capacities of those countries.

Moreover, according to press reports, US firms have been striving to establish themselves in the Indian market demanding as a condition for the setting up of joint enterprises the right for them to sell part of their production in India.

But the ultimate purpose of US direct investments in Asia as elsewhere is of course the pursuit of the greatest profit.

The profits gained by these investments include, besides those of direct investments proper, payments and royalties on direct investments transferred to North American mother companies.

Let us now examine the evolution of the *net profits* of US direct investments abroad as from 1957. (By net profits are meant the total net profits gained by US companies and their subsidiaries, both of them operating abroad, after local taxation but before paying US taxes.)

Between 1957 and 1968, the average net profit rate of US direct investments abroad presents the following picture, according to annual ECAFE economic reports:

Average Net Profit Rate of US Direct Investments Abroad from 1957 to 1968

All regions	10.11%
Including:	
Canada	7.19
Europe	8.82
Latin America	11.90
Africa (including RSA)	15.62
Oceania	8.98
Asia	34.27
Including:	
Middle East	59.36
Far East (excluding Japan)	14.12
Japan	12.29

Source: Economic Survey of Asia and the Far East 1970 UN. Bangkok, 1971, p. 19.

Note that this average profit rate is *undervalued* in those currencies which tended to depreciate in relation to the US dollar during that period, and that is precisely what happened to many developing countries.

Even so the above figures show clearly that during the period 1957–1968, the average net profit rate of US direct investments in Asia (Middle and Far East) is by far the highest (34.27% of the whole), in comparison with that in other parts of the world. It is over 3.8 times as high, for example, as that in Western Europe (8.82%). If the Far East alone is taken into consideration (exclusive of Japan), the figure is 1.6 times higher than that of Europe.

On the whole, the net profit rate of US direct investments is much higher (50 to 100%) in developing countries than in industrially advanced countries. This tendency is again confirmed in 1970: the net profit rate of US direct investments is 9.6% in the latter countries as against 18.3% (or nearly double) in the former, according to data recorded by the *Survey of Current Business*.

In other words, in 1970 for each dollar invested the US monopolies gained on an average twice as much profit in developing countries as in industrially advanced countries.

We have thus a new confirmation of the tendency pointed out by Marxist-Leninists: the lower the organic composition of capital and the higher the surplus-value rate the higher the profits, i.e., *mutatis mutandis* the more "under-developed" the recipient countries, the higher the profits. The profit rates mentioned above concern developing countries in general. For Asia alone (Middle and Far East, excluding Japan), the net profit rate of US direct investments reaches as much as 37%! And if the Far East alone is considered (excluding Japan), it is 14.61%, also in 1970. . . .

Besides drawing enormous profits from Asian countries, US monopolies also manage to exert great economic, political and ideological pressure on their governments. And this pressure, which is often in direct ratio to the relative magnitude of investments, leads in the end to the loss of sovereignty by the recipient countries.

And last but not least, US private direct investments are also considered an essential means to bring about the triumph of capitalist relations of production in recipient countries in Asia and elsewhere.

After this general survey of the main objectives of US direct investments, we shall now examine the problem of trade exchanges between the USA and Asian countries. . . .

[I]t should be emphasized that the characteristic feature of trade between the USA and most Asian countries (excluding Japan) is little different from that of trade between the USA and "Third World" countries in general. US sales to its trade partners include mainly manufactured goods and subsidiarily agricultural surpluses, whereas US purchases from them consist chiefly of raw materials, minerals, fuels (especially petroleum) and subsidiarily farm products (processed or not).

Thus, developing Asian countries are for the US monopolies, steady and stable suppliers of enormous quantities of natural resources on the one hand (which, as a result, generally makes them dependent on the US and puts them under its permanent control, this dependency and control being sanctioned and reinforced at the same time by the structure of the world capitalist market) and on the other hand, they constitute continuously expanding markets for US manufactured products (made in USA or locally). No wonder that the USA is doing its utmost, even waging neo-colonialist wars (the Indochina war) and instigating coups d'état (overthrow of Sukarno, Sihanouk, etc.) to preserve this state of things.

* * *

Let us now consider briefly the problem of unequal trade exchange between the USA and Asian countries. In a previous study, the various aspects of this important problem have been dealt with more generally. Here are only a few more facts. It is known that by exporting its manufactured goods to developing Asian countries and importing raw materials and agricultural products, etc., from them, the USA is selling commodities at prices higher and buying them at prices lower than what they are worth. This amounts to an exchange of less labour for more labour, or a transfer of value from developing Asian countries to the USA.

Thus, for Asian countries (excluding Japan) as a whole the considerable rise in the prices of manufactured commodities imported from industrially advanced countries—including the USA—on the one hand, and the substantial drop (or, in some cases, a rise which is, however, less than that of the imported manufactured goods) in the prices of raw materials and foodstuffs exported by them on the other hand, lead to a serious worsening of their terms of trade.

Unequal trade therefore brings to Asian countries a considerable loss of foreign exchange. When to this is added a no less considerable loss, resulting from repatriated profits of US direct investments (see above), it becomes clear that the US neo-colonialist plunder of these Asian countries far exceeds the "aid" granted by the USA, an "aid" which, as shown above, in fact opens the door to this plunder. Besides the three great economic levers mentioned above (bilateral and multilateral "aid"; export of private capital especially through direct investments; and unequal trade), US neo-colonialism also uses the dollar in its capacity as a reserve currency and means of international payment to serve its expansionist aims. (This role of the dollar has, however, been reduced since its recent devaluation). But, for lack of space, only the three great levers cited above have been dealt with in this article.

It must be stressed, in conclusion, that above all US neo-colonialism aims at *maintaining developing Asian countries in the orbit of the world capitalist system.* To this end, it is ready, when necessary, to make concessions likely to favour some economic growth in certain Asian countries, which nevertheless remain dependent on the US economy and the international capitalist division of labour. Aid either bilateral or multilateral, private direct investments and trade exchanges—all this aims in the end at directing Asian countries along the path of capitalist development, perpetuating their dependence upon the USA and maintaining, if not worsening, their economic and technical backwardness as a means to their further exploitation. But experience shows that—in Viet Nam as elsewhere—the peoples are growing more and more conscious of the traps of US neo-colonialism and are determined to struggle against any form of recolonization, even indirect.

May 1972

48
Richard M. Nixon Reads Vietnam's Lessons, 1985

Today, after Communist governments have killed over a half million Vietnamese and over 2 million Cambodians, the conclusive moral judgment has been rendered on our effort to save Cambodia and South Vietnam: We have never fought in a more moral cause. Assertions in the antiwar news media that life in Indochina would be better after our withdrawal served to highlight in a tragic way the abysmally poor level of their reporting throughout the war. But of all their blatantly inaccurate statements over the years, none was more hideously wrong than that one.

"If wise men give up the use of power," de Gaulle once said, "what madmen will seize it, what fanatics?"

When we abandoned the use of power in Indochina, we also abandoned its people to grim fate. When the American ambassador to Cambodia, John Gunther Dean, was about to be evacuated from Phnom Penh, he offered Lon Nol's closest colleague, Sirik Matak, asylum in the United States. The former Premier responded in a letter:

> Dear Excellency and Friend,
>
> I thank you very sincerely for your letter and for your offer to transport me toward freedom. I cannot, alas, leave in such a cowardly fashion. As for you, and in particular your great country, I never believed for a moment that you would have this sentiment of abandoning a people which has chosen liberty. You have refused us your protection, and we can do nothing about it.
>
> You leave and my wish is that you and your country will find happiness under this sky. But mark it well, that if I shall die here on the spot and in the country I love, it is too bad, because we are all born and must die one day. I have only committed this mistake of believing you.
>
> Sisowath Sirik Matak

It was a fittingly noble, if tragically sad, epitaph for his country, his people, and himself. He was among the first whom the Khmer Rouge executed.

After we abandoned the use of power, it was seized by the North Vietnamese and Khmer Rouge Communists. Our defeat was so great a tragedy because after the peace agreement of January 1973 it was so easily avoidable. Consolidating our gains would not have taken much to accomplish—a credible threat to enforce the peace agreement through retaliatory strikes against North Vietnam and a sufficient flow of aid to Cambodia and South Vietnam. But Congress legislated an end to our involvement. It also legislated the defeat of our friends in the same stroke.

A lesson that our adversaries should learn from our intervention in Vietnam is that the United States, under resolute and strong leadership, will go to great lengths and endure great sacrifices to defend its allies and interests. We fought in Vietnam because there were important strategic interests involved. But we also fought because our idealism was at stake. If not the United States, what nation would have helped defend South Vietnam? The fact is that no other country would have fought for over a decade in a war half a world away at great cost to itself in order to save the people of a small country from Communist enslavement.

One lesson we must learn from Vietnam is that if we do not exercise power for the good, there are plenty of men like Ho Chi Minh, Le Duan, Khieu Samphan, and Pol Pot who will gladly exercise it for evil purposes. Our armed intervention in the Vietnam War was not a brutal and immoral action. That we came to the defense of innocent people under attack by totalitarian thugs is no moral indictment. That we mishandled it at times in no way taints the cause. South Vietnam and Cambodia were worthy of our help—and the 3 million people who were killed in the war's aftermath deserved to be saved. Our abandonment of them in their moment of greatest need was not worthy of our country.

Another lesson we must learn is that in the real world peace is inseparable from power. Our country has had the good fortune of being separated from our enemies by two oceans. Others, like our friends in Indochina, did not enjoy that luxury. Their enemies lived just a few miles away up the Ho Chi Minh Trail. Our mistake was not that we did too much and imposed an inhumane war on peace-loving peoples. It was that in the end we did too little to prevent totalitarians from imposing their inhumane rule on freedom-loving peoples. Our cause must be peace. But we must recognize that greater evils exist than war.

Communist troops brought peace to South Vietnam and Cambodia—but it was the peace of the grave.

The Third World war began before World War II ended. Saigon's fall ten years ago was the Soviet Union's greatest victory in one of the key battles of the Third World war. No Soviet soldiers fought in Vietnam, but it was a victory for Moscow nonetheless because its ally and client, North Vietnam, won, and South Vietnam and the United States lost. After we failed to prevent Communist conquest in Vietnam, it became accepted dogma that we would fail everywhere. For six years after Vietnam, the new isolationists chanted "No more Vietnams" as the dominoes fell one by one: Laos, Cambodia, and Mozambique in 1975; Angola in 1976; Ethiopia in 1977; South Yemen in 1978; Nicaragua in 1979.

49
The Lessons of the Vietnam War—An Interview with Noam Chomsky

Source: Indochina Newsletter, no. 18 (Cambridge, Massachusetts), November–December 1982.

> American imperialism has suffered a stunning defeat in Indochina. But the same forces are engaged in another war against a much less resilient enemy, the American people. Here, the prospects for success are much greater. The battleground is ideological, not military. At stake are the lessons to be drawn from the American war in Indochina; the outcome will determine the course and character of new imperial ventures.
>
> — Noam Chomsky, 1975

[The following interview was conducted with Professor Chomsky in October, 1982]

Q: When the Indochina war ended in 1975 you wrote that our nation's "official" opinion makers would engage in distortion of the lessons to be drawn from the war so that the same basic foreign policy goals could be pursued after the war. You felt then that in order to keep the real meaning of the war from penetrating the general public they faced two major tasks: First, they would have to disguise the fact that the war "was basically an American attack on South Vietnam—a war of annihilation that spilled over to the rest of Indochina." And secondly, they would have to obscure the fact that the military effort in Vietnam "was restrained by a mass movement of protest and resistance here at home which engaged in effective direct action outside the bounds of propriety long before established spokesmen proclaimed themselves to be its leaders." Where do we stand now on these two issues—seven years later?

Chomsky: As far as the opinion makers are concerned, they have been doing exactly what it was obvious they would do. Every book that comes out, every article that comes out, talks about how—while it may have been a "mistake" or an "unwise effort"—the United States was defending South Vietnam from North Vietnamese aggression. And they portray those who opposed the war as apologists for North Vietnam. That's standard to say.

The purpose is obvious: to obscure the fact that the United States did attack South Vietnam and the major war was fought against South Vietnam. The real invasion of South Vietnam which was directed largely against the rural society began *directly* in 1962 after many years of working through mercenaries and client groups. And that fact simply does not exist in official American history. There is no such event in American history as the attack on South Vietnam. That's gone. Of course, it is a part of *real* history. But it's not a part of official history.

And most of us who were opposed to the war, especially in the early '60s—the war we were opposed to was the war on South Vietnam which destroyed South Vietnam's rural society. The South was devastated. But now anyone who opposed this atrocity is regarded as having defended North Vietnam. And that's part of the effort to present the war as if it were a war between South Vietnam and North Vietnam with the United States helping the South. Of course, it's fabrication. But it's official "truth" by now.

Q: This question of *who* the United States was fighting in Vietnam is pretty basic in terms of coming to any understanding of the war. But why would the U.S. attack South Vietnam, if the problem was not an attack from North Vietnam?

Chomsky: First of all, let's make absolutely certain that *was* the fact: that the U.S. directed the war against South Vietnam.

There was a political settlement in 1954. But in the late '50s the United States organized an internal repression in South Vietnam, not using its troops, but using the local apparatus it was constructing. This was a very significant and very effective campaign of violence and terrorism against the Vietminh—which was the communist-led nationalist force that fought the French. And the Vietminh at that time was adhering to the Geneva Accords, hoping that the political settlement would work out in South Vietnam.

And so, not only were they not conducting any terrorism, but in fact, they were not even responding to the violence against them. It reached the point where by 1959 the Vietminh leadership—the communist party leadership—was being decimated. Cadres were being murdered extensively. Finally in May of 1959 there was an authorization to use violence in self-defense, after years of murder, with thousands of people killed in this campaign organized by the United States. As soon as they began to use violence in self-defense, the whole Saigon government apparatus fell apart at once because it was an apparatus based on nothing but a monopoly of violence. And once it lost that monopoly of violence it was finished. And that's what led the United States to move in. There were no North Vietnamese around.

Then the National Liberation Front of South Vietnam was formed. And its founding program called for the neutralization of South Vietnam, Laos and Cambodia. And it's very striking that the National Liberation Front was the only group that ever called for the independence of South Vietnam. The so-called South Vietnamese government (GVN) did not, but rather, claimed to be the government of all Vietnam. The National Liberation Front was the only South Vietnamese group that ever talked about South Vietnamese independence. They called for the neutralization of South Vietnam, Laos and

Cambodia as a kind of neutral block, working toward some type of integration of the south with North Vietnam ultimately.

Now that proposal in 1962 caused panic in American ruling circles. From 1962 to 1964 the U.S. was dedicated to try to prevent the independence of South Vietnam, the reason was of course that Kennedy and Johnson knew that if any political solution was permitted in the south, the National Liberation Front would effectively come to power, so strong was its political support in comparison with the political support of the so-called South Vietnamese government.

And in fact Kennedy and later Johnson tried to block every attempt at neutralization, every attempt at political settlement. This is all documented. There's just no doubt about it. I mean, it's wiped out of history, but the documentation is just unquestionable—in the internal government sources and everywhere else.

And so there's just no question that the United States was trying desperately to prevent the independence of South Vietnam and to prevent a political settlement *inside* South Vietnam. And in fact it went to war precisely to prevent that. It finally bombed the North in 1965 with the purpose of trying to get the North to use its influence to call off the insurgency in the South. There were no North Vietnamese troops in South Vietnam then as far as anybody knew. And they anticipated of course when they began bombing the North from South Vietnamese bases that it would bring North Vietnamese troops into the South. And then it became possible to pretend it was aggression from the North. It was ludicrous, but that's what they claimed.

Well, why did they do it? Why was the United States so afraid of an independent South Vietnam? Well, I think the reason again is pretty clear from the internal government documents. Precisely what they were afraid of was that the "takeover" of South Vietnam by nationalist forces would not be brutal. They feared it would be conciliatory and that there would be successful social and economic development—and that the whole region might work!

This was clearly a nationalist movement—and in fact a radical nationalist movement which would separate Vietnam from the American orbit. It would not allow Vietnam to become another Philippines. It would trade with the United States but it would not be an American semi-colony.

And suppose it worked! Suppose the country could separate itself from the American-dominated global system and carry out a successful social and economic development. Then that is very dangerous because then it could be a model to other movements and groups in neighboring countries. And gradually there could be an erosion from within by indigenous forces of American domination of the region. So this was no small thing. It was assumed that the key to the problem was preventing any successful national movement from carrying out serious social and economic development inside Indochina. So the United States had to destroy it through a process which would become the war against South Vietnam. And, it should be pointed out that on a lower level we were doing the same things in Laos and Cambodia.

Q: So the irony is that the very reason given in the United States for fighting the war—the independence of South Vietnam—is exactly what had to be destroyed.

Chomsky: Exactly.

Q: Do you think this distortion of the war is successful?

Chomsky: It's hard to say. People who lived through the period know better. But younger people who are being indoctrinated into the contemporary system of falsification—they really have to do some research to find out what is the truth. In the general population, people forget or don't care that much. And gradually what you hear drilled into your head everyday comes to be believed. People don't understand what you're talking about anymore if you discuss the American war on South Vietnam.

Q: And the role of the anti-war movement?

Chomsky: The main effort has been to show that the opposition to the war was of two types: One was the serious responsible type that involved Eugene McCarthy and some senators—who turned the tide because we realized it wasn't worthwhile, or was too expensive or something. And then there were these sort of violent and irrational groups, teenagers and so on, whose behaviour had little to do with the war really, and whose activity was a form of lunacy. Now, anyone who lived through the period would have to laugh.

But my impression is that the effort to portray the peace movement this way is not working very well. For example, at the beginning of his administration, Reagan tried to set the basis for American military intervention in El Salvador—which is about what Kennedy did when he came into office in regard to Vietnam. Well, when Kennedy tried it in Vietnam, it just worked like a dream. Virtually nobody opposed American bombing of South Vietnam in 1962. It was not an issue. But when Reagan began to talk of involving American forces in El Salvador there was a huge popular uproar. And he had to choose a much more indirect way of supporting the collection of gangsters in power there. He had to back off.

And what that must indicate is a tremendous shift in public opinion over the past 20 years as a result of the participation in the *real* opposition to the war in Indochina—which has lasted and was resurrected when a similar circumstance began to arise.

Q: So you see the inability of the government to maneuver as it would like in El Salvador as directly related to the anti-war movement.

Chomsky: Oh yes. They even have a name for it: "Vietnam Syndrome." See, they make it sound like some kind of disease, a malady that has to be overcome. And the "malady" in this case is that the population is still unwilling to tolerate aggression and violence. And that's a change that took place as a result of the popular struggle against the war in Vietnam.

Q: So you feel it was the group officially defined as the "riff-raff, lunatic fringe" who really was the peace movement?

Chomsky: Oh, there's no question. You can see what happened. There were very extensive grass roots efforts beginning in the mid '60s, developing quite gradually against tremendous opposition. So that in Boston it was impossible to have an outdoor public meeting against the war until about the fall of 1966. Until then they would be broken up. And the media more or less applauded the violence and disruption that prevented people from speaking. But gradually that changed. In fact, it reached such a point that by 1967 it was impossible for the President to declare a national mobilization for war. He was restricted and forced to pretend he was conducting a small war. There were constraints. Because of public opinion which by then was considerably aroused by demonstrations and teach-ins and other types of resistance, Johnson had to fight the war with deficit spending, he had to fight a "guns and butter" war to show it was no big war.

And this policy just collapsed. And it collapsed totally with the Tet Offensive in 1968 which led major sectors of American power—corporate power and other centers of power—to realize we could not carry it off at this level. Either we go to war like in the Second World War, or we pull out. And that was a direct effect of the activities of the peace movement. After this decision was made, then politicians like Eugene McCarthy—whom you had never heard of before that time, came to announce themselves as the leaders of the peace movement.

But by then the basic decision to put a limit to direct American troop involvement had been made. You had to fight for a long time to get the U.S. out, but the basic decision had been made at the Tet Offensive. That's when the programs related to Vietnamization were put in place, and we began to fight a more capital intensive war with less direct participation of American ground troops.

Incidentally, another reason for this was that the American army began to deteriorate internally because, after all, the United States was fighting a very unusual type of war. It's very rare for a country to try to fight a colonial war with a conscript army. Usually wars like the Vietnam war are fought with mercenaries—like the French Foreign Legion. The U.S. tried to fight what amounts to a colonial war with a conscript army. And a colonial war is a very dirty kind of war. You're not fighting armed forces. You're fighting mostly unarmed people. And to fight that kind of war requires professional killers, which means mercenaries. The 50,000 Korean mercenaries we had in Vietnam were professional killers and just massacred people outright. And the American army did plenty of that too, but it couldn't take it after awhile. It's not the kind of job you can give to conscripts who are not trained to be murderers.

Q: And they had also heard of the anti-war movement's ideas against the war back home.

Chomsky: Exactly. It was a citizen's army, not separated from what's happening in American society in general. And the effect was that, very much to its credit, the American army began to crumble and deteriorate. And it became harder and harder to keep an army in the field.

Q: Are you aware of any other time in history when soldiers came home from the war and organized against their government as many Vietnam veterans did through the Vietnam Veterans Against the War organization?

Chomsky: It's rare. For example, it's happening now to a certain extent in Israel with reservists who are also fighting a war against a civilian population in Lebanon. And it's the same kind of phenomenon. If they just kept professional military men involved they could probably carry it off. But reservists are connected with the civilian population. That's why countries like France and England used mercenary forces to carry out these kinds of wars.

Let me make one final point about the peace movement which is often forgotten. When you look back at the internal documents that we have now you can see that when the big decision was made around the Tet Offensive in 1968—about whether or not to send a couple hundred thousand more troops—one of the factors was that the Joint Chiefs of Staff were concerned that they would not have enough troops for internal control of the domestic American population. They feared tremendous protest and disruption at home if they sent more troops to Vietnam. This means that they understood the level of internal resistance to be virtually at the level of civil war. And I think they were probably right about that. That's a good indication from inside as to how seriously they took the peace movement.

There are indications that the huge demonstrations of October and November of 1969 severely limited Nixon's ability to carry out some of the plans for escalating the war that he had. The domestic population was not under control. And any country has to have a passive population if it is going to carry out effectively an aggressive foreign policy. And it was clear by October and November of 1969 just by the scale of opposition that the population was not passive.

So those are all important events to remember. Again, they're sort of written out of history. But the record is there and the documentation is there, and it's clear that that's what happened.

Q: What is the current U.S. foreign policy toward Indochina?

Chomsky: Well, towards Indochina I think the main policy is what's called "bleeding Vietnam." Even conservative business groups outside the United

States are appalled at what the United States has been doing.

We fought the war to prevent Indochina from carrying out successful social and economic development. Well, I think the chances of that happening are very slight because of the devastation, because of the brutality of war. But the U.S. wants to make sure it will continue. And therefore we first of all of course refused any reparations. We refused aid. We try to block aid from other countries. We block aid from international institutions. I mean, sometimes it reaches a point of almost a fanatic effort to make them suffer.

For example, there was one point when the United States prevented the government of India from sending a hundred buffalo to Vietnam. (The buffalo stock in Vietnam had been decimated by American bombing.) We prevented them by threatening to cut off Food for Peace aid.

So in every conceivable way the United States has tried to increase the harsh conditions of life in Indochina. And right now one of the main ways we're doing it is by supporting the Khmer Rouge on the Thai-Cambodian border.

50
The War and the Vietnamese

Ngo Vinh Long

Source: Excerpt from *Vietnam Reconsidered: Lessons from a War* by Harrison E. Salisbury and Larry Ceplair (Harper Torchbacks, 1984), pp. 227–35.

During the last ten days or so, many former American policymakers, reporters, and other old Vietnam hands have taken to the air waves to draw the lessons of the war for the American people. By and large, most of these people have claimed that the war could have been won or that South Vietnam could have been maintained if the United States had been more decisive in its efforts at different stages of the war and if enough American arms had been made available to the Saigon regime.

On January 27, for example, Howard K. Smith and his son, Charles Smith, appeared for almost an hour on ABC's *The Last Word,* saying that the United States should have invaded North Vietnam and gone into the other Indochinese countries very early on to destroy the North Vietnamese bases and infiltration routes to the South. Charles Smith said that to try to maintain South Vietnam without invading North Vietnam or striking at troops in the other countries of Southeast Asia was like trying to defend France during the Second World War without going directly into Germany and the surrounding countries. Howard K. Smith stressed that the United States should have gone all out—short of nuclear weapons, of course. On the same evening, Henry Kissinger and Richard Nixon appeared on ABC's *Nightline* and blamed Congress for having made it impossible for the United States to enforce the Paris Peace Agreement and for having made the conquest of South Vietnam inevitable by cutting aid to the Saigon regime. They both added that the loss of South Vietnam weakened the conduct of American foreign policy. Howard K. Smith spelled this out a little more clearly when he said that the real tragedy of the Vietnam War was that it had made the United States afraid of intervening in other countries.

These remarkable statements, ten years after the United States was forced to withdraw all its troops from Vietnam, do not suggest that these intelligent men have not learned anything from the Vietnam experience. Rather, they seem to indicate that there are significant Americans willing to risk continued recrimination at home in order to get certain segments of the American public to overcome the so-called Vietnam syndrome—so that the American imperial ideology can be rebuilt. But this is something that I will not go into here.

What I want to do, rather, is to show very briefly how total American disregard for Vietnamese history and culture, as well as for the welfare and aspirations of the Vietnamese people, made it impossible for the United States to maintain a "free and independent South Vietnam." (The word "disregard" is used advisedly here because, from the vantage of his ivy tower at Harvard University, this writer had discussed very extensively, with quite a number of influential intellectuals and key policymakers, Vietnamese history, society, culture, nationalism, and other such irrelevant things, and found that these people were not all that ignorant. The point was, one of these influential intellectuals explained to this writer, "Every society, like every human being, has a breaking point.") To be sure, the United States could have destroyed Vietnam many times over with its military machine—and totally wrecked Vietnamese society and culture with its economic and cultural penetration. But as this writer pointed out to Henry Kissinger in a long letter in the spring of 1967 (later published in the June 2, 1967, issue of the *Harvard Crimson*), anything short of this would result in an eventual victory for the Vietnamese revolutionaries.

There were many reasons for this inevitable outcome. First, there was the historical factor. By 1930, the Indochinese Communist Party (ICP) had emerged as the undisputed leader in the struggle against French colonial rule and exploitation. Massive French pacification efforts and wholesale arrest of thousands of Communist cadres and sympathizers, as well as the terrible impact of the world depression, could dampen the revolutionary struggles for only three years, from

1932 to 1935. But beginning in 1936, when many of the cadres were released, thanks to the influence of the Popular Front in France, revolutionary struggles surged not only in the countryside but also in most towns and cities. At times, tens of thousands of peasants were brought into cities like Hanoi, Hue, and Saigon for massive demonstrations. Most interesting, by this time the population fully understood the importance of protecting their leaders and of listening to their analyses and instructions. As a result, we can now learn from existing French police reports and archival sources that there were very few political activities in the latter half of the 1930s that ever occurred without prior directives from the Indochinese Communist Party.

In fact, it can be said that the Communist party had already captured Vietnamese nationalism and gained deep-rooted support among the Vietnamese people by the latter part of the 1930s. The Second World War and the Japanese occupation of Vietnam further strengthened the political position and prestige of the ICP. By the time of the August Revolution of 1945, Ho Chi Minh and his ICP followers had captured the whole nation, not because of any political vacuum created by the Japanese, but because of the tremendous political and organizational efforts of the ICP in rallying the Vietnamese people against colonialism and imperialism for about a decade and a half. Joseph Buttinger, a noted Vietnam historian and an early mentor of Ngo Dinh Diem of South Vietnam, was correct when he concluded some time ago that the policy pursued by the United States in Vietnam was doomed to fail because:

It was bad enough not to take into consideration that the Vietnamese people had struggled for over two thousand years against being absorbed by China, and had for almost one hundred years fought against colonial rule in order to regain independence. Much worse still was not to know, or knowingly to disregard, the fact that as a result of French colonial policies in Indochina, the whole of Vietnam had become Communist by the end of World War II.

I say the whole of Vietnam, not only the North—something which, in spite of thirty years of French and American propaganda, remains an undeniable historical fact.

The deep-rooted popular support for the Vietnamese revolutionaries was again thoroughly tested during the 1946–54 period, when France, Great Britain, and the United States thought that they could destroy the Ho Chi Minh government with overwhelming military might. But the Vietnamese revolutionaries were only to emerge from this so-called First Indochina War victorious, not only at the famous battle of Dien Bien Phu, but also in almost every village and town in the whole country. The anti-Communist columnists Joseph and Stewart Alsop were forced to write, after a trip through southern Vietnam, that, "In the area I visited, the Communists have scored a whole series of political, organizational, military—and one has to say it—moral triumphs. . . . What impressed me most, alas, was the moral fervor they had inspired among the non-Communist cadres and the strong support they had obtained from the peasantry.''

Because of the obvious reason that the Vietnamese revolutionaries already had overwhelming support among the population, when the United States and Ngo Dinh Diem decided to install an ''independent South Vietnam,'' contrary to the stipulations of the Geneva Agreement, there was not much they could do except to carry out wholesale repression and ''pacification'' of the rural areas. Massive forced relocations of the rural population under programs such as the ''qui-khu/qui-ap," agrovilles, and ''strategic hamlets'' were carried out in the effort to control the population and to root out the ''Vietcong,'' or literally, ''Vietnamese Communists.'' Resentment ran high among the population. Demonstrations, petitions, and protests multiplied. Troops who came to demolish the people's houses and to destroy their gardens met with fierce resistance. Women, children, and old folks disputed every inch of land with the Saigon soldiers and policemen. Repressive measures backfired, and resulted in the downfall of the Diem regime. After that, the United States realized that there was nothing it could do to prevent a Communist victory except introduce American troops into the southern part of Vietnam, bomb the northern part, and in effect, start the ''Second Indochina War.''

The second factor making an ''independent South Vietnam'' all but impossible to achieve was the American conduct in that war. An area with fewer than eighteen million people, South Vietnam had a total of more than ten million refugees by 1972. Most of these people had been made refugees many times over through the American policy of ''emptying the countryside.'' In order to ''secure villages'' and to root out ''Vietcong infrastructures,'' bulldozers, bombers, and chemical defoliants were used. The villagers were forced into the ''New Life'' hamlets, the camps for refugees fleeing from Communism, and the towns and cities. To begin with, the tactics used in ''pacification'' ran counter to traditional Vietnamese customs and beliefs—the cultural and religious significance of the house, the land, the tomb. Then there were the horrible living conditions in the refugee camps, and the humiliation the refugees had to face there as well as in the ''New Life'' hamlets and the urban centers. The conditions of the refugees were so bad that Saigon newspapers felt compelled to run long articles on the misery. Even *Song*, a Saigon daily specifically created to justify the pacification program, had to say, on December 10, 1967, in a long article entitled ''Looking at the Face of the Two Quang Provinces in War, Hunger, Misery, and Corruption'':

This is a free area—free for depravity, corruption, irresponsibility, cowardice, obsequiousness, and loss of human dignity. What the devil is dignity when people sit there waiting to be thrown a few hundred piasters and allotted a few dozen kilos of rice a month? . . . I believe that even if a certain Communist had in his pocket a few dozen "open-arms" passes, after witnessing the humiliation of life in a refugee camp, he would be so shocked that he would run away without a single look back.

From February 1 to February 2, 1971, *Tin Sang,* a Saigon daily published by a group of Catholic deputies in the Lower House, ran a long report entitled "Hunger is Rampant in the Central Region," which documented the causes of the hunger and described the heart-rending condition of the population. The article described the hunger facing a "resettlement area," an area people were herded into after their villages had been destroyed:

At present in the settlement area of Gia Dang, where the population of the villages of Trieu Phong and Hai Mang districts is now living, starvation is widespread and is threatening the lives of the entire population living in this resettlement area. In the coastal areas of Thua Thien province it is the same: people have to eat banana roots and leaves after days of having no rice and greens. Let us witness these scenes: mothers have no more milk for their babies to suck at; fathers stare helplessly at their children lying about in hunger. Will the fathers die before the children or will the children die before them? Death appears before them. . . . In early January, 1972, dozens of people left the resettlement area to beg for food. Since January 15, every morning about a hundred persons from villages such as Co Luy, Da Nghi, Phuong Lan and Ba Du go up to the district town of Hai Long or the town of Quang Tin to beg. . . . Getting up on an empty stomach each morning, they walk across the hills and dunes to beg for food. Unable to lift their feet anymore, they lie down here to die. Each day brings new corpses.

The situation in the urban areas was a little brighter, but not by much. According to the February 25, 1974, issue of *Hoa Binh,* a Saigon daily, Deputy Premier Phan Quang Dan who was in charge of refugee resettlement, among other things, disclosed that from three to four million persons were unemployed in the urban areas. The premier gave the number of orphans as 800,000 or more.

Too much, and not too little, aid from the United States to the Thieu regime, especially after the signing of the Paris Agreement, brought about the fall of Saigon. Propaganda to the contrary, in the two years after the signing of the Paris Agreement, Congress actually voted more economic and military aid to Saigon than ever before. Immediately before and after the signing of the Paris Agreement, the Nixon administration sent nearly $1 billion worth of military aid to Saigon. The United States supplied the Thieu regime with so many arms that, as Maj. Gen. Peter Olenchuk testified before the Senate Armed Services Committee on May 8, 1973, "We shortchanged ourselves within our overall inventories. We also shortchanged the reserve units in terms of prime assets. In certain instances, we also diverted equipment that would have gone to Europe.''

In fiscal year 1974, Congress gave Saigon $1 billion more in military aid. Saigon expended as much ammunition as it could—$700 million worth. This left a stockpile of at least $300 million, a violation of the Paris Agreement, which had stipulated that equipment only be replaced on a one-to-one basis.

For fiscal year 1975, Congress again authorized $1 billion in military aid, but appropriated $700 million—about what was actually spent in 1974.

The military aid granted Thieu encouraged him to sabotage the Paris Agreement by attacking areas controlled by the Provisional Revolutionary Government (PRG). A study by the U.S. Defense Attaché office in Saigon revealed that ''the countryside ratio of the number of rounds fired by South Vietnamese forces (since the signing of the Paris Agreement) to that fired by the Communist forces was about 16 to 1. In military Regions II and III, where South Vietnamese commanders have consistently been the most aggressive, and where some U.S. officials said that random 'harassment and interdiction' fire against Communist-controlled areas was still common, the ratio was on the order of 50 to 1.''

Father Nguyen Quang Lam, an ultraconservative Catholic priest, wrote in the February 1975 issue of *Dai Dan Toc:*

Yesterday I wrote that whether there is an additional $300 million or $3,000 million in aid, South Vietnam will still not be able to avoid collapse. . . . In the afternoon a reader called me up and said that I should have put it more strongly. I must say that the more the aid, the quicker the collapse of South Vietnam. All I had to do was to take a look at our society.

Ever since the United States began to pour its troops and its dollars into South Vietnam, our society has been turned completely up-side-down. A prostitute is regarded with highest esteem because she can get lots of money from the American soldiers. Prostitutes are even ranked higher than priests and monks. . . . Come to think of it, the reader has a point there. The American dollars have really changed our way of thinking. People compete with each other to become prostitutes, that is to say, to get rich in the quickest and most exploitative manner.

Father Lam continued: ''No wonder whenever our soldiers see the enemy they run for their lives, even though they might have a basement full of ammunition which they could presumably fire till kingdom comes.''

It is clear that the American government's disregard for Vietnamese history and culture and its massive military, economic, and cultural penetration of Vietnam brought untold destruction to Vietnamese society and the consequent ''loss of South Vietnam.'' President Jimmy Carter was quoted by the Los Angeles *Times* on March 25, 1977, as saying: ''The destruction was mutual. We went to

Vietnam without any desire to capture territory or impose American will on other people. I don't feel that we ought to apologize or castigate ourselves or to assume the status of culpability.'' During my seven-month research trip to Vietnam in 1979 and 1980, many Vietnamese kept on reminding me of this remarkable statement. A professor at Hue University likened it to a rapist saying that his victims hurt him as much as he hurt them. Victims, he said, usually don't talk much about their suffering because they have to go on living. This writer hopes that, as Americans begin to assess the economic, political, psychological, and cultural impacts of the war on America, they will also begin to understand how much more that war hurt the Vietnamese. This is not to make Americans feel guilty so that they will castigate themselves or apologize to the Vietnamese. There is no need to do that. The damages have already been done. The hope here is that America will not inflict the same wounds elsewhere.

Index